The Macroeconomic Environment

The Macroeconomic Environment

SUBRATA GHATAK

Senior Lecturer in Economics, University of Leicester

NIGEL M. HEALEY

Lecturer in Economics, University of Leicester

PETER JACKSON

Professor of Economics, University of Leicester

WEIDENFELD AND NICOLSON
London

To our students, past and present

George Weidenfeld and Nicolson Ltd
91 Clapham High Street, London SW4 7TA

ISBN 0 297 82060 5 cased
ISBN 0 297 82061 3 paperback

Typeset by The Spartan Press Ltd.
Lymington, Hants.
Printed by Butler & Tanner Ltd,
Frome & London

Contents

Preface

PART I: INTRODUCTION TO THE
        MACROECONOMIC ENVIRONMENT

1 **Macroeconomic Perspectives**   3
2 **Measuring the Macro-Economy**   8
  2.1: Flow-of-Funds Accounts   10
  2.2: National Income Accounting   13
  2.3: GNP and the Quality of Life   21
  2.4: Nominal and Real Magnitudes   23
  2.5: Measuring Output   27
  2.6: Utilisation of Labour   28
  2.7: Potential Output and Economic Growth   31

PART II: MODELLING THE DOMESTIC MACRO-
         ECONOMY

3 **The Income-Expenditure Model**   37
  3.1: Preliminary Building Blocks   38
  3.2: The Determination of National Income   47
  3.3: The Multiplier   49
  3.4: The Nature of Economic Equilibrium   55
4 **A Complete Model of Income and Expenditure**
  Determination   61
  4.1: Income, Expenditure and Interest Rates   61
  4.2: The Money Market   65
  4.3: The *IS-LM* Model   69
5 **The Aggregate Demand and Supply Model**   76
  5.1: Aggregate Demand   76
  5.2: Aggregate Supply   79
  5.3: The Classical Theory of Aggregate Supply 80
  5.4: The Keynesian Theory of Aggregate Supply 83

v

5.5: The New Classical Theory of Aggregate Supply 92
5.6: Summary 98

PART III: DOMESTIC MACROECONOMIC PROBLEMS

6 **Business Cycles** **103**
  6.1: The Phases of the Business Cycle 104
  6.2: Multiplier-Accelerator Interaction 107
7 **Inflation** **111**
  7.1: Measuring Inflation 112
  7.2: The Monetarist Explanation of Inflation 113
  7.3: Alternative Theories of Inflation 115
  7.4: Inflation and Unemployment 118
  7.5: Counter-Inflation Policies 125
  7.6: The Impact of Inflation 127
  7.7: Inflation and Economic Growth 130
8 **Unemployment** **132**
  8.1: Theoretical Perspective on Unemployment 133
  8.2: The Costs of Unemployment 135

PART IV: MACROECONOMIC POLICY

9 **Basic Principles of Macroeconomic Policy** **139**
  9.1: Macroeconomic Policy Objectives 140
  9.2: Macroeconomic Policy Instruments 144
  9.3: Outside Lags, Intermediate Targets and Indicators 147
  9.4: Inside Lags and Macroeconomic Forecasting 151
  9.5: Constraints on Macroeconomic Policy 155
10 **Fiscal Policy** **158**
  10.1: Fiscal Policy in the *IS-LM* Model 159
  10.2: The Role of Automatic Stabilisers 164
  10.3: Measuring the Stance of Fiscal Policy 167
  10.4: Fiscal Policy and the National Debt 172
  10.5: Fiscal Policy and Crowding Out Revisited 177
11 **Monetary Policy** **184**
  11.1: Monetary Policy in the *IS-LM* Model 185
  11.2: The Money Supply Process 190
  11.3: The Basic Principles of Monetary Control 193
  11.4: The Practice of Monetary Control 196
  11.5: Problems of Monetary Policy 204

12 The Limitations of Macroeconomic Policy   **207**
   12.1: The Technical Limitations of Macroeconomic Policy   207
   12.2: Is Demand Management Futile?   208

PART V: THE INTERNATIONAL MACRO-ECONOMY

13 The Foreign Exchange Market and the Balance
    of Payments   **215**
   13.1: The Foreign Exchange Market Structure   215
   13.2: The Determination of Foreign Exchange Rates   217
   13.3: Covered Interest Arbitrage   221
   13.4: The Balance of Payments   223
   13.5: Balance of Payments Adjustment   227
14 Advanced Theories of Exchange Rate Determination   **232**
   14.1: Post-Keynesian Theories of Exchange Rate
       Determination   232
   14.2: The Monetary Approach to Exchange Rate
       Determination   237
   14.3: The Portfolio Balance Approach   241
   14.4: The Rational Expectations Hypothesis of Exchange
       Rate Determination   241
   14.5: Exchange Rate Dynamics and Overshooting   243
   14.6: The Importance of Exchange Rates for Business Firms   244

PART VI: STRATEGIC PLANNING AND THE
           MACROECONOMIC ENVIRONMENT

15 Cyclical Indicators of the Macro-Economy   **251**
   15.1: Types of Cyclical Indicators   254
   15.2: Definitions of Terminology   256
   15.3: Selection of Indicators   258
   15.4: Leading Indicators   260
   15.5: An Assessment of the Indicator Approach   261
16 Forecasting the Macro-Economy   **265**
   16.1: Why Forecasts Differ   267
   16.2: The Importance of Model Structure in Forecasting   268
   16.3: Forecasting Races   272
   16.4: Interpreting Forecasts   273
   16.5: The Lucas Critique   274
   Appendix: Multiple Regression Analysis   278

Index   283

Preface

When formulating their long-term strategies and also when designing tactical responses to changes in the market environment, managers need to pay attention to the wider macroeconomic trends. The term 'macroeconomics' appeared in the economics literature following World War II. This was due to John Maynard Keynes, who in 1936 published his influential book *The General Theory of Employment, Interest and Money*. In this book, Keynes set out the fundamental elements of macroeconomics, a study of the factors which affect total demand in an economy (consumption, investment and government expenditures) and, therefore, the level of employment. As the subject developed, other topics were incorporated into the study of macroeconomics: the determination of the price level and the rate of inflation; the influence of the money supply on economic magnitudes; the determination of exchange rates and the factors affecting aggregate supply.

Once the network of macroeconomic forces and the factors which influence them were better understood, it was a natural extension of the subject to consider how the *macroeconomy* could be shaped through policy interventions. Attention was in particular directed to the use of fiscal policy (changes in tax rates and public spending) and monetary policy (changes in interest rates and the money supply) to steer the economy closer to more desirable outcomes, measured in terms of target levels of unemployment and inflation rates.

This book covers these topics at a level which will inform managers who have little or no prior training in economics. It introduces them to a number of the technical debates in which professional economists engage, but without concentrating unnecessarily upon the technical infrastructure which students who specialise in economics must master. Thus, this book should be of particular interest to those students who are studying on management courses up to and including the MBA. By keeping the level of technique to a minimum, whilst confronting issues head on, we have written this book with the needs of those particular students continually in mind.

In the preparation of a text, authors incur a number of debts. To our colleagues in the profession generally, who have generated the knowledge without which no textbook could be written, we say thank you. We also thank Barbara Allen, Ann Crane, Joanne Gillespie and Pat Greatorex, who helped to turn our drafts into a book, and Rachelle Maxwell, who provided invaluable assistance in the final stages of preparation. Finally, to our readers, we would welcome your suggestions.

S. Ghatak
N. M. Healey
P. M. Jackson

Leicester 1991

Part I

INTRODUCTION TO THE MACROECONOMIC ENVIRONMENT

1

Macroeconomic Perspectives

Macroeconomics attempts to improve our understanding of recessions, booms, unemployment and inflation – all indicators of the performance of the economy. Since these issues are complex, our understanding of them is constantly developing. What we know about the behaviour of the economy today differs from that of 25 years ago. Since our knowledge advances through a series of challenges to existing understanding, what we shall find is that whilst there is a dominant perspective there is also a number of alternatives which conflict with it.

Macroeconomics is what most people think the study of economics is about. On the front page of newspapers we find headlines such as 'unemployment rises to 12%,' 'public spending reductions urged to balance the budget' and 'inflation hits double-digits'. At the macroeconomic level of the economy we are dealing with aggregates such as the total consumption or investment of the economy; total government spending; total export spending. These are the aggregates of millions of individual decisions. Each decision is based on its own *microeconomic* logic. The task facing the macroeconomist is to understand, by observing economic behaviour, how these aggregates behave on average. What are the general trends and what determines them? Alternative answers to these questions indicate the disputes that lie at the heart of macroeconomics.

Classical Economics

Classical economists (for example Adam Smith, David Ricardo and

3

Leon Walras) argued that market prices, equating demands and supplies, would, like an 'invisible hand', guide each input (labour, machines and land) into its most productive use. Those best at farming would be lured by good wages into farming, whilst those best at tailoring would make suits and those best at baking would make bread. Each person would *specialise* according to what they are best at, i.e. their **comparative advantage**. In a highly specialised economy, individuals exchange the products of their labour through trade. How does each trader know what to produce and how much to produce? These factors are determined by what their customers want. Thus, in the classical system, production, transactions and prices are all determined by demand and supply in the market-place. Moreover, these markets are assumed to help individuals to make efficient decisions and the resulting allocations of resources are efficient.

Keynesian Economics

A major problem for the classical economist's description of the capitalist system is that it fails to account for crises in the system, such as balance of payments problems, unemployment, recessions and inflation. Because the classical economists assumed that the economy would always come into equilibrium (balance) where demand equals supply, they ruled out, by assumption, displays of disequilibrium, such as unemployment and inflation.

The challenge of how to account for recessions was picked up by an Englishman, John Maynard Keynes, who in the 1930s wrote a very influential book, *The General Theory of Employment, Interest and Money*. This book not only changed our way of viewing how an economy behaves but also gave birth to a separate branch of economics which we now refer to as macroeconomics. Because Keynes challenged the traditional, and at that time dominant, framework of the classical economists, his perspective is referred to as Keynesian macroeconomics.

As our argument develops through this book we shall see that the classical economist's description of modern industrial economics is flawed. Prices do not adjust rapidly in response to inequalities between demand and supply. Prices are, instead, set by large industrial complexes which wield considerable market power. Markets are not perfect but instead contain important monopolistic and oligopolistic elements, which means that prices are inflexible. Instead of concentrating upon market equilibrium, as the classical economists did, Keynes insisted that we should focus on the turmoil of market disequilibrium.

For Keynes the short run, the present time within which we live, is usually in a state of disequilibrium; while a state of equilibrium for the economy is far off in the future, i.e. in the long run. In a now famous statement in *A Tract on Monetary Reform* Keynes wrote:

> 'In the long run we are all dead. Economists set themselves too easy a task if in tempestuous seasons they can only tell us that when the storm is long past the ocean again is flat.'

From the period beginning in 1945 Western governments decided to adopt the Keynesian perspective to guide their economic policies. There then followed the 'Keynesian era', which lasted until the 1970s. Keynes argued that markets do not work perfectly; they fail. Markets do not automatically come into equilibrium. In order to restore equilibrium, and to reduce unemployment, it is necessary for governments to intervene via fiscal and monetary policies.

Monetarism

Monetarist economists, led by intellectual leaders such as Milton Friedman, have challenged the modern Keynesian perspective. They maintain that markets are superior to government interventions and that markets work best when governments don't meddle in them. During the 1970s the teachings of monetarist economists displaced the Keynesian approach in the United Kingdom and the United States of America. One reason for this switch was the poor macroeconomic performance during the 1970s: inflation rose whilst output slumped and stagnated – a situation called 'stagflation'. Why, it was asked, is Keynesian economics unable to deliver low unemployment without high inflation?

Monetarists stress the importance of controlling the money supply as a way of achieving price stability and, with their support, numerous governments have experimented with monetary targeting. Monetarists also argue, like their classical predecessors, that rather than state intervention, policies to promote efficiency and market flexibility are the only way of reducing unemployment in the long term.

New Classical Economics

New Classical Economics grew out of monetarism during the 1970s. It focuses on the way in which economic agents form their expectations of the future. It argues that, since individuals are rational, they will make use of all available and relevant information in arriving at their expectations of the future course of output and inflation, rendering government policy both unnecessary and futile.

It is important that you realise that controversies abound within macroeconomics. However, these differences in perspective can be overemphasised. The majority of economists tend to share a similar perspective, and it tends to be economic advisers to political parties who exaggerate the differences in order to sell their particular brand of economics.

The task that we set ourselves is first to examine how macro-economic variables, such as output, unemployment and inflation, are measured. Then we proceed to present a simple macroeconomic model that can be used to explain fluctuations (cycles) in economic activity and the consequences of various economic events, such as government spending and taxation (fiscal policy) and changes in the money supply and interest rates (monetary policies).

Government Intervention

Political institutions play a large role in shaping economic perform-ance. We will, therefore, broaden our perspective on the determinants of government policies and their outcomes. Why does government intervene in the economy? What are the objectives of policy? How is the performance of the economy related to these public policy interventions?

To answer these questions we need a detailed model of how the economy operates. The performance of the wider economy can impact upon firms within the economy and influence their performance. If an economy is overheating and the price level is increasing (i.e. inflation), a government might respond by raising interest rates. Not only do we want to know why a government might make such a response, we also want to know how a firm's performance is affected. Inflation is accompanied by rising costs such as money wages, and debt charges (interest rates). These cut into profits, especially if consumer demand slows down also. Thus an overheating economy tends to end up in a downturn. If decision-makers can read the data they can respond in advance and maintain or improve the performance of their companies.

Econometric Models

The raw material for the analysis of policies and performance comes partially in the form of quantitative data. The purpose of analysing data is to identify patterns of past behaviour in order to gain insight into future behaviour. Do interest rates increase with an increase in fiscal deficits? Does inflation increase when money growth increases? To know if such relationships might exist we need a model of the economy and if we want to know by how much one variable changes if another changes then we need an econometric (statistical) model that puts numbers to these economic relationships. Econometric models enable us to make economic forecasts; they also impose consistency on forecasts by constraining them to conform to accounting rules and to be consistent with past observations. Forecasts are no better than the assumptions fed into them. To understand the significance of different assumptions the decision-maker needs to know something about the model of the economy within which the assumptions are embedded. The conceptual framework developed within this book will help to make these judgements as informed as possible.

Further Reading

Hoover, K. D. (1988) *The New Classical Macroeconomics*, Blackwell, Oxford.
Levacic, R. and Rebmann, A. (1982) *Macroeconomics: an Introduction to Keynesian and Neoclassical Controversies*, Macmillan, London.
Cross, R. (1982) *Economic Theory and Policy in the UK*, Blackwell, Oxford.
Tobin, J. (1977) 'How Dead is Keynes?', *Economic Inquiry*, October, pp. 459–68.

2

Measuring the Macro-Economy

A decision-maker often has to form a judgement about what is happening in the wider economic environment. Data are obtained from a variety of sources, e.g. from the financial press and media, from bankers' and stockbrokers' reports, from business analysts. In order to understand the messages contained in these data, in order to unpack the information contained within the many reports, and in order to know the relevance of the data for decision-making, it is necessary to understand the origins and significance of the underlying framework that has generated them.

Five basic questions should be asked of any data set:

(1) Which data should be used?
(2) Which time-period for the data should be used?
(3) Which form of the data should be used?
(4) How does one evaluate the data?
(5) What are the limitations of the data?

These questions will organise our thoughts as we work our way through this part of the book. Data are necessary for making decisions, but we need to know which data should be used and how useful they are. We begin by spending time examining the types of data, drawn from the general economic environment, that will be of interest to decision-makers.

The financial press, stockbrokers' reports and other professional documents make use of statements that contain terms such as GNP, inflation, price index, potential output, etc. What do these terms mean? How do economists set about measuring unemployment, inflation and the output of the economy? These questions and more will be answered in this chapter.

We have already listed a number of key questions that we should ask of any set of data. The quality of data is of great importance. Not only do good data help us to sort out competing theories by allowing us to reject those theories that are contradicted by the facts; good data also contribute to the quality of decisions that are made. More often than not, decisions require empirically based data. Good decisions require good data. This approach to decision-making stands in sharp contrast to the businessman who argues, 'my mind is made up; don't confuse me with the facts'.

In fact, data do not correspond perfectly to reality. Even if they did, data can become distorted by those who use them. Different people perceive reality differently. They extract from a situation different pieces of information depending upon their conceptual frame of reference, their beliefs and their value systems. Individuals coming to a situation from different cultural backgrounds will read the situation differently because their culture gives them different belief and value systems that will influence their perceptions. You should bear this point in mind when reading the units of this course.

Another reason why data do not correspond perfectly to reality is that data collection is expensive. Thus, given tight budget con-straints, decision-makers will fall short of having perfect data. Moreover, many economic variables cannot be measured adequ-ately, especially those that have a high subjective element, such as 'satisfaction', quality of life, etc. This means that decision-makers are left to apply judgement when taking decisions. However we would argue that informed judgement, especially when informed about the limitations of the data set, is more likely to result in better decisions than ill- informed judgement.

Most economies nowadays have two data sets that relate to the macroeconomic environment. First, there are the national income accounts: these measure the income, expenditure and production of the entire economy. Secondly, there are flow-of-funds accounts, which supplement the national product accounts with data on financial transactions. We will begin with the flow-of-funds accounts.

2.1 FLOW-OF-FUNDS ACCOUNTS

Flow-of-funds accounts summarise a nation's economic transactions – see Table 2.1. This is a very basic flow-of-funds table since it deals with the main sectors of the economy. In reality, more complex, disaggregated and more detailed tables exist. The table that we present here is for illustrative purposes and relates to a hypothetical economy.

The flow-of-funds accounts are set out as a matrix in which the principal economic agents appear across the top. An 'economic agent' can be thought of as a decision-maker in a particular role. Thus we distinguish between economic decision-makers as households, businesses or government. Down the side of the matrix are shown the types of transactions that those economic agents made. A negative entry in a cell of the matrix indicates that the agents in that sector of the economy were net sellers. Look at the labour row. That shows that the household sector was a net seller of its labour services and raised $1664.4 billion by doing so. On the other hand, the business sector was a net purchaser of $1600.9 billion of labour services from the household sector and the government sector was a net purchaser of $63.5 billion of labour services. For everyone who sells labour services in the economy there must be, by definition, someone who is buying. The rows of the matrix must, therefore, sum up to zero.

Table 2.1 A Hypothetical Set of Flow-of-Funds Accounts (billions of dollars)

	Households	*Business*	*Government*	*Sum*
Labour	−1666.4	1600.9	63.5	0
Interest, dividends, taxes	−607.3	699.6	−92.3	0
Goods & services	2158.6	−2370.3	211.7	0
Currency	9.3	2.0	−11.3	0
Securities	103.8	−67.8	−171.6	0
Sum	0	0	0	0

Look now at the household column of the matrix. Reading down that column we find, as before, that the households received payments of $1664.4 billion from the sale of their labour services and, in addition, they received $607.3 billion of income from interest, dividends and taxes (net), i.e. the household sector received income from interest and dividends and also paid taxes and interest on loans, but as a sector it was, in 'net' terms, better off by $607.3 billion. Taken together, the household sector's total net income was (1664.4 + 607.3) billion dollars, i.e. $2271.7 billion of disposable income (income available for spending). The business and government columns are read in the same way.

Self-Assessment Questions

Looking at Table 2.1, how much

(a) did the government sector spend on hiring labour?
(b) did the government sector obtain from interest, dividend and taxes?

What did the household sector do with its $2271.7 billion? Some of it was spent on goods and services, such as TVs, cars, food, housing and haircuts, etc. This amounted to $2158.6 billion. The remainder was saved in securities (i.e. shares in companies or in government securities) amounting to $103.8 billion, and $9.3 billion was saved in the form of cash. Since all income has to be accounted for, then total income equals spending on goods and services and saving. Thus the columns of the matrix will add up to zero.

The difference between the income that a sector receives and the expenditure it pays is its **financial saving**. An important feature of the data on saving is that the sum of saving across all sectors of an economy is zero.

Assets and Liabilities

The flow-of-funds accounts keep track of the financial assets and liabilities of each sector of the economy. An important relationship exists between a sector's financial savings and its assets and liabilities. Let us illustrate this by means of an example. Suppose that at the beginning of a year an individual has financial assets worth $30 000 (made up of $10 000 in saving deposits; $20 000 in corporate stocks) and $15 000 in financial liabilities ($10 000 owed on a mortgage and $5 000 owed to a bank), i.e. the individual's net worth is $15 000. (An individual's **financial net worth** is equal to the value of his or her financial assets minus the value of financial liabilities. Financial net worth can change in one of two ways; either by spending less than is earned (income), i.e. via saving; or if the value of one of the assets held changes.) Now suppose that during the year the individual's income is $25 000 and he spends $20 000. What happens to the unspent $5000? It can be used to increase the individual's assets by putting $5000 into a bank deposit or it could be used to reduce his financial liabilities by decreasing his mortgage by $5000. Finally, it could be put into his pocket, in which case his currency or cash holdings (an asset) would have increased by $5000.

The point is that no matter what the individual does, saving in any year must affect at least one of the individual's assets or liabilities. A flow variable (saving in this case) must result in a change in a stock variable (assets and/or liabilities in this case). At the end of the year, his net worth has risen by $5000 to $20 000.

Self-Assessment Questions

Looking at Table 2.1,

(a) what was the total value of the goods and services sold by the business sector?
(b) does this mean to say that the business sector was a net creditor?
(c) how much did the business sector borrow?
(d) was the government sector a net borrower or net lender?

Stocks and Flows

In macroeconomics we distinguish between stocks and flows. **Flow data** measure the volume of transactions over a period of time, say a week, a month or a year. **Stock data** measure the levels at a specific point in time. Flows are, therefore, changes in stocks. Thus, for example, if we were to look at the balance sheet of the British economy for 1990 we would find that the stock of government securities outstanding as at 31 March 1990 was £160 billion, but was £167 billion at 31 March 1989. The difference reflects net lending (debt repayment) by the British government in 1989/90.

Self-Assessment Questions

Which of the following are stocks and which are flows:

(a) car sales this year?
(b) the population of your country?
(c) the number of births in your country this year?
(d) the amount of money in your bank account?
(e) the government's budget deficit last year?
(f) the government's outstanding debt?

A lesson that we will learn and refer to time and again is that the decisions of the many individuals in an economy are interrelated. Output, employment, wages, prices and interest rates are determined by the simultaneous interaction of economic agents. A flow-of-funds table demonstrates these interrelations. One group's expenditure is another group's income, and vice versa; one person's purchase is another person's sale. There are always two sides to each transaction. When trying to understand the macroeconomic environment, we need to take these interrelationships into account.

2.2 NATIONAL INCOME ACCOUNTING

The first three rows of Table 2.1 showed the income and spending of each sector of the economy. The national income and product accounts focus upon income and spending and provide more detail on these items than the flow-of-funds accounts.

The Gross National Product

(GNP) is a measure of the market value of the total (aggregate) production of new goods and services (houses, automobiles, food, TVs, etc.) It is a flow concept since it measures the amount produced in the economy over a specified time-period – usually a year. A problem which faces the statisticians who measure GNP is that since so many goods are passed from hand to hand in a long chain of transactions, there is a danger of double or triple counting. When measuring GNP we are only interested in the **final value** of goods and services. Another way of thinking about this is to say that we are only interested in the **value added** at each stage of production. Value added is the difference between the value of goods as they leave one stage of production and their costs as they entered that stage.

Consider a simple example such as a loaf of bread. There are many stages in the production process, from the production of wheat by the farmer to the baking of bread by the baker and its sale to the customer by the grocer.

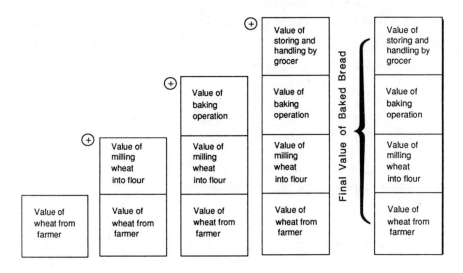

Figure 2.1

This is illustrated in Figure 2.1. Between one stage and another, value is added to the product. The final value of the bread is the sum of the value added at each stage. It would be a mistake of double counting to add up all of the prices at each stage.

Unrecorded Items

Not all transactions, however, get measured and they do not, therefore, all appear in official estimates of the GNP. This suggests that actual GNP is probably higher than that which is recorded. What are some of those items that are difficult to measure and record?

(1) Do-it-yourself and voluntary activities, e.g. if you repair your own car or house; this is a transaction that takes place within the household and is not recorded as GNP. The activities of housewives who do not sell their labour services on the open market are not recorded.

(2) Covert or illegal activities such as prostitution and the sale of illegal drugs. The reasons why these do not appear in the GNP statistics should be obvious!

(3) Those who receive income but do not declare it to the tax authorities. Again, for obvious reasons, these transactions are not recorded in the GNP. This unreported part of the economy, along with that in (2) above, is called the 'underground economy'.

(4) Those activities which are not sold on the open market, such as the output of the government sector. Value is added by most government activities but we don't know how much value is added because there is no market price available. For the GNP calculation, government activities are valued at cost (i.e. civil servants' salaries, etc.). This is clearly not their true value but it is the best that can be done.

Other National Income

Gross National Product is only one national income aggregate. There are others which we shall now define. GNP excludes output produced within an economy by foreign-owned factors of production, i.e. GNP is the output produced by domestically owned factors of production. This is in contrast to 'Gross Domestic Product' (GDP) which is the total value of all goods and services produced in the country by the factors of production located in the country, regardless of who owns them.

The capital stock of a nation is consumed (depreciates) during the production process. Depreciation is valued as the amount of money that would be necessary to be spent each year to maintain the capital stock in its current state. If we deduct depreciation from GNP we get 'Net National Product' (NNP), i.e. net of depreciation.

If we then deduct indirect taxes (i.e. sales taxes, excise taxes, etc.) and subsidies from net national product, this gives us **national income**.

The relationships in the macro-economy can be visualised by means of a flow-of-income diagram: see Figure 2.2. Firms (and other organisations) in the economy hire factors of production (labour, capital and land) in the factor markets. The payments made to the factors of production are their incomes (wages, profit, interest and rent). This is the income of the households. Individuals then spend their incomes on goods and services in markets. This expenditure flows back to the firm as revenue. The flow of income moves round the

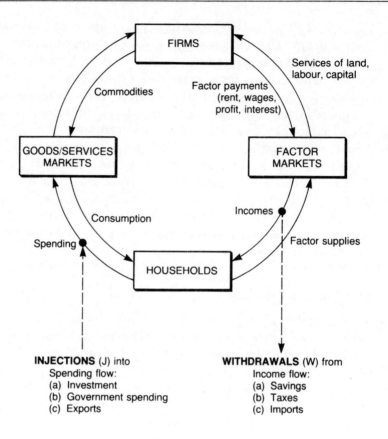

Figure 2.2

economy in a circle: expenditure becomes income and income becomes expenditure, and so on.

Withdrawals and Injections

Over time, there are withdrawals (W) from the income flow. If individuals save, then income is taken out of the circular flow. If an individual's income is $100 and he saves $25, then only $75 is passed on as expenditure. Other withdrawals are taxes and imports. The latter represent a loss of income from the domestic economy to some overseas economy.

Alongside withdrawals there are also injections (J) into the flow of income. These are in the form of investment, government spending and exports. Savings are withdrawn and used to finance investment, either directly through the purchase of capital goods or indirectly via financial institutions such as banks. The original withdrawal (savings) ends up as an injection elsewhere in the system. Taxes end up as government spending. Exports are financed from spending made by other countries. This expenditure enters into the circular flow as an injection of income.

For equilibrium we require all withdrawals to equal all injections, i.e. $W = J$. If injections are greater than withdrawals then the level of national income (total incomes) will rise, and vice versa.

Income and Expenditure

We have seen that as incomes are spent they generate expenditure and that the value of these expenditures must, by definition, be equal to the value of the goods and services that an economy produces. Thus, national income (Y) equals total expenditure (E). National income can, therefore, be measured and expressed either as the sum of all incomes in the economy or the sum of all expenditures (and these are equivalent to the value of output). There are three alternative and equivalent means of measuring national income: (a) the income approach; (b) the expenditure approach; (c) the output approach. They are equivalent because one person's expenditure is another person's income and that expenditure is on output.

Expenditure (E) in an economy can be broken down into various categories: private consumption (C); private investment (I); government expenditure (G); exports (X); imports (M).

$$E = C + I + G + (X - M)$$

The reason that imports are subtracted is that some expenditures contained in C, I and G will have been imported. This means that $(C + I + G - M)$ represents expenditure on domestic goods only. Including foreign expenditures on domestic goods (i.e. exports) gives total expenditure on domestic goods.

Total expenditure is another way of thinking about total (aggregate) demand, whilst we also know that the total expenditure is equivalent to total output (i.e. supply). In equilibrium, aggregate demand equals aggregate supply. This is a concept that will be developed later.

17

Self-Assessment Questions

Obtain a copy of the national income and production accounts for your country for a recent year. From these accounts can you find:

(a) the values of GNP and national income?
(b) the percentage of total expenditure allocated to private consumption?
(c) the percentage of total expenditure allocated to investment?
(d) the percentage of total expenditure allocated to government spending?
(e) the percentage of total expenditure allocated to exports?

Consumption

It might appear that economic statisticians have a clear idea of the distinction between consumption and investment. This is true in some cases, but not in others. Consumption refers to expenditure on those goods which are consumed shortly after production, e.g. bread, soft fruit. But there are other goods which can be consumed over several periods of time after the date of purchase, e.g. an automobile, refrigerator, TV, even shoes. Whilst these could be thought of as investment expenditure, it is more useful to think of them as being 'consumer durables'. Private consumption expenditure is divided into:

(1) durable goods – household appliances, automobiles, etc.
(2) non-durable goods – food, clothing, gasoline, tobacco.

Investment

Investment expenditure refers to that carried out by the private sector. Investment by the government is included in government spending. Private investment spending can be divided into: (1) residential and (2) non-residential.

Residential investment spending is allocated to housing, i.e. the building of new houses. Non-residential investment spending is divided into 'fixed investment' in plant and machinery and 'inventory investment'. Fixed investment is mainly used by the business sector to produce more goods and services. Inventory investment includes raw materials, goods that are still being processed, and finished goods that have not yet been sold.

A large proportion of a firm's inventories (stock) are planned (i.e. they are intentional). It is rational to hold on to stocks of finished and unfinished goods, plus raw materials, in order to be able to meet sudden and unexpected increases in consumer demand. If there is a downturn in demand, however, then some of the stocks held will be unintentional (unplanned). There is nothing in the national income accounts to tell us whether or not inventories are intentional or unintentional.

Economists very often use data on changes in the value of inventories from one quarter (three-month period) to another as an indicator of the performance of the economy. If inventories are rising then this often indicates that sales are weak and that production will probably be slowed down in the near future. That is, it signals that the economy will probably enter into a recession. If, however, inventories are falling rapidly, then the economy is probably moving into a boom phase and inflation might follow.

Government Expenditure

Care has to be taken when considering what is and what is not included in government spending. An examination of the accounts of any government will show that expenditures are grouped into the following broad categories:

(1) Purchases of goods and services;
(2) Transfer of payments to persons;
(3) Grants-in-aid to state and/or local governments;
(4) Interest on the government debt;
(5) Subsidies paid to government enterprises.

(Transfer payments to persons include social security payments.)

Which of the items listed above are included in government spending (G) when calculating national income? The answer is that only government spending on the purchase of goods and services is included, i.e. expenditure on the salaries paid to public-sector employees, on paper clips, warships and bombs, etc. Transfer payments are not included in G because, as the term suggests, it is a transfer of purchasing power from one sector of the population to another via the intermediary of the government sector. These transfer payments are financed out of taxation which is also a transfer. Grants-in-aid are a transfer from the federal (or central) level of

19

government to lower levels of government. Interest on the government debt is a transfer as, too, are subsidies paid to government enterprises.

Total government spending (G) is subdivided into current expenditure on goods and services, and capital spending. The latter refers to government investment spending, e.g. on activities such as highways, dams and irrigation projects, hospital building, land reclamation, etc.

Summary of National Income Accounts

The main points discussed above can be brought together.
1. GNP *minus* depreciation *equals* NNP.
2. NNP *minus* indirect taxes *minus* subsidies *equals* national income.
3. Personal disposable income *equals* national income *minus* corporate profits *minus* social security taxes *plus* interest income *plus* transfer payments *minus* personal taxes.
4. Personal savings *equals* personal disposable income *minus* personal sector expenditure.
5. $Y = C + I + G + (X - M)$
   Total supply *equals* total demand.
6. Consumer expenditure can be divided into:
   (a) Expenditure on durable goods:
   (b) Expenditure on non-durable goods.
7. Investment spending can be divided into:
   (a) Residential;
   (b) Non-residential.
   Non-residential investment spending can be divided into:
   (a) Expenditures on plant and machinery;
   (b) Expenditures on inventories.
8. Only government spending on goods and services (current and capital) is counted as G in the national income accounts. Transfer payment spending is not included.
9. The difference between gross investment spending and net investment spending is depreciation (i.e. capital consumption). In other words, $I_n = I_g -$ depreciation, where I_n is the value of net investment over the period and I_g is the value of gross investment over the period.

2.3 GNP AND THE QUALITY OF LIFE

GNP is often measured in per capita terms. Per capita GNP is simply GNP divided by the population of the country. If GNP is growing at the same rate as the population then per capita GNP will remain constant. Per capita GNP is sometimes used as an indicator of the prosperity of a country. In Table 2.2, Switzerland is at the top of this league table and Portugal and Turkey are at the bottom. From these figures it would appear that the quality of life in those countries at the top is better than in those at the bottom. It would be foolish to deny that this is probably true. People living in those countries at the top of the per capita GNP table do have a better chance of access to superior quality housing, automobiles, hospital, medical and educational services, and so on. It is better to be at the top than near the bottom, and a country's economic policy is directed at improving its perform-ance and thereby pushing it up the league table.

Table 2.2 Per capita GNP: country comparisons, 1988

Country	*US dollars*
Switzerland	27 500
Japan	21 020
Norway	19 990
United States	19 840
Sweden	19 300
Finland	18 590
Germany	18 480
Denmark	18 450
Canada	16 960
France	16 090
Austria	15 520
Netherlands	14 520
Belgium	14 490
Italy	13 330
United Kingdom	12 810
Australia	12 340
Spain	7 740
Greece	4 800
Portugal	3 650
Turkey	1 280

Source: The World Bank, *World Development Report 1990*

However, while the GNP per capita indicator attempts to gauge economic activity by measuring the production of new goods and services, there is much more to a nation's well-being and to the quality of life than those data counted by GNP statisticians. GNP data ignore unpaid leisure activities. So a question to ask is how much leisure time do people in a country have and what do they do with this time? By taking a single country and looking at what has been happening to its GNP per capita statistic over a number of years, we might conclude that the quality of life has been improving. But has it? If the rise in GNP per capita has come about by individuals reducing the amount of time that they spend in leisure, can we say that the production of new goods and services has improved the quality of living in that country?

Environmental Costs

GNP statistics do not measure pollution and the environmental costs that often accompany growth of GNP per capita. Poisonous fumes, disruptive noises, dangerous working conditions, ugly environments, deforestation, and distasteful water are some of the byproducts of industrialisation and economic growth. These environmental costs (the costs of economic growth) reduce the welfare of those living in the country. Economic growth is, therefore, achieved at the expense of a deterioration of the environment. For some it might, in the short run, be considered a reasonable price to pay; they have jobs and a higher income as a result of the increase in economic growth, and the environment is someone else's problem! This, however, is too often a short-sighted approach. Environmental decay tends to be cumulative; the stock of non-renewable resources eventually runs out so that short-term gains in incomes are paid for through higher environmental costs in the future.

Distribution of Income

Finally, GNP per capita figures tell us nothing about the distribution of income (GNP) within a country. The way in which it is calculated assumes that everyone has an equal amount of income. But how does the distribution of income change over time as GNP grows?

Is the extra GNP concentrated in a small group of the population – do the rich get richer whilst the poor get poorer? This is another dimension that has to be considered when asking the question, what does GNP per capita tell us about the quality of life? Quality of life for whom?

2.4 NOMINAL AND REAL MAGNITUDES

One crucial distinction made in economics is between real and nominal magnitudes. Economic data on GNP record the volume of transactions measured in some currency, say dollars, for example. This is the market value of all final goods and services produced in a country within a given period of time. It is equivalent to taking the quantity of every good and service produced in the economy and multiplying it by its *current* market price.

$$\text{Expenditure on good } (i) = P_i Q_i$$

If there are four goods produced in the economy, then

$$\text{GNP} = P_1 Q_1 + P_2 Q_2 + P_3 Q_3 + P_4 Q_4$$

This means that GNP will increase over time if one or all of the quantities rise (whilst the prices remain constant); or if one or all of the prices rise (whilst the quantities remain constant); or if prices and quantities rise at the same time. The problem that we face is – if GNP increases from one year to another then how much of this is due to price changes and how much to quantity changes?

Nominal GNP is GNP measured at the prices of the *current* time-period. Real GNP is determined by taking the same quantities of every good and service produced and multiplying each by a base-year (constant) price. Whilst nominal GNP can change, either because prices or quantities change from one year to the next, real GNP can only change if quantities change because prices have been kept constant (by definition).

Why do we make the distinction? The reason is that it is real GNP, or more generally real data, that affect individual behaviour. Individuals work more hours in order to get more income that will enable them to purchase more real output of goods and services. If you are asked to work an extra hour for two dollars, your decision to do so (or not) will depend upon how much extra real goods that two dollars will purchase. Are the extra purchases worth the effort?

If an individual thinks only about nominal income rather than real income (or any nominal data rather than real income) then economists say that they are suffering from **money illusion**. Someone who feels better off if their income rises by 5% whilst prices rise by 10% is suffering from money illusion because real incomes, in this case, have fallen.

In summary then, the nominal magnitude of any economic variable is measured at the prices of the current time-period, whilst the real magnitude of that variable is measured at constant prices. We distinguish between the real and nominal magnitudes of a variety of economic variables; for example, nominal and real incomes, nominal and real interest rates, nominal and real investment, nominal and real money supply, etc.

The general relationship between nominal GNP and real GNP can be expressed in the following form:

Nominal GNP = Price Deflator × Real GNP, therefore

$$\text{Real GNP} = \frac{\text{Nominal GNP}}{\text{Price Deflator}}$$

Price Indices

The price deflator is calculated as a price index (P), which shows the cost of a bundle of goods and services in one year relative to the cost in a given base year:

$$P = \frac{\text{cost of bundle in this year}}{\text{cost of bundle in base year}}$$

How is a price index calculated? Consider the following example. The representative bundle contains 10 loaves of bread, 6 kilos of meat and 2 litres of milk. The price of bread doubled between 1980 and 1990; the price of meat rose by 50% and the price of milk rose by 30%. The cost of the bundle of commodities, shown in Table 2.3, was $15 in 1980 and $25 in 1990.

Using 1980 as the base year, the price index in 1990 is:

$$P = \frac{\text{cost in 1990}}{\text{cost in 1980}} = \frac{25}{15} = 1.67$$

This calculation shows that the cost of this (fixed) bundle of commodities rose by 67% between 1980 and 1990.

Very often price indices are scaled by choosing a particular base year and setting it equal to 100. Care has to be taken, if a number of different price indices are being used, that each is on the same base year.

Table 2.3

	Quantity	1980		1990	
		Price	Cost of Bundle	Price	Cost of Bundle
Loaf of bread	10	0.60	6.00	1.20	12.00
Kilos of meat	6	1.00	6.00	1.50	9.00
Litres of milk	2	1.50	3.00	2.00	4.00
			15.00		25.00

Suppose we examine a time series of data for an economy and that we find that the price deflator for GNP was 49.3 in 1980 and that the base year is 1990 = 100. This means that the price level in 1980 was 49.3% of the price level in 1990. If real GNP in 1980 was $183.5 billion then we can calculate nominal GNP as follows.

Price deflator × Real GNP = Nominal GNP

.493 × 183.5 = 90.4

In practice, the calculation of price indices for an economy is a complex activity because there are a large number of goods and services and the prices for each category have to be accounted for. In the United States of America, for example, the **consumer price index**, which is an index of the prices of a basket of consumer goods, is calculated by 250 agents each month, visiting about 20 000 stores in more than 50 cities and collecting price data on about 400 specified goods and services purchased by typical urban households. This bundle of typically consumed goods is based on a detailed survey of consumer purchasing patterns which was last carried out in the early 1970s.

Indices are calculated by similar means for a variety of other prices such as the producer price index. This index surveys the prices paid by businesses for about 2700 commodities ranging from raw materials, to partly processed commodities, to finished goods.

Price indices need to be used with care. There are a number of problems associated with interpreting the information provided by price indices. Purchases of goods and services respond to price changes. Therefore, as time passes, the typical basket of goods and services which is used in calculating the price index can become out of date. If individuals substitute cheaper goods and services for more expensive ones then a price index based upon the original basket of goods and services will tend to overstate the cost of living. On the other hand, if a more recent basket of goods is used, then the index will understate the cost of living because it may ignore the effects of the price rises on living standards.

Types of Indices

Two price indices are available, depending upon the base that is chosen. **Laspeyres indices** use the quantities purchased in the base period. **Paasche indices** vary the bundle of goods and services year to year and reflect changing spending habits. Since the Paasche weights vary from year to year, changes in the index reflect quantity as well as price changes.

A Paasche index can rise or fall even when prices are constant. Lying somewhere in between the Paasche and Laspeyres indices is the **chain index**, in which each period's computations use the market basket from the immediately preceding period. In an annual chain index, for example, a calculation of the average change in the prices in 1991 would be based on 1990 spending habits, while the 1992 calculation would be based on 1991 spending patterns. (More details of the construction, use and limitations of index numbers can be found in any book on economic statistics.)

Another difficulty with price index numbers is that the quality of many goods and services changes over time. When the price of an item rises by 10% and its quality has improved by 10% also, then there has been no inflation in price; it is equivalent to (but not the same as) purchasing 10% more of a commodity – you simply paid 10% more in order to get 10% more.

The problem facing the statistician is how to measure quality and quality changes because quality is such a subjective characteristic of a commodity or service. However, the point to be made is that price changes which reflect quality changes can overstate the extent of price inflation.

2.5 MEASURING OUTPUT

In the previous section we have seen that by using suitably constructed price indices we are able to break down a change in a nominal magnitude into price changes and quantity changes. Having calculated, for example, real GNP by deflating nominal GNP by the GNP deflator, we would have a series over time for real GNP, i.e. the real output of the economy. If this series is rising over time then it is an indication that the economy is producing more output (bearing in mind the limitations of price indices, especially quality adjustments). Figure 2.3 illustrates the differences between nominal and real GNP. Over the 20-year period from 1970 to 1990 nominal GNP had increased by 200% (from 100 to 300) whereas real GNP had increased by 100% (from 100 to 200). Thus, half of the increase in nominal GNP was due to price rises and the other half was due to increases in quantity (production).

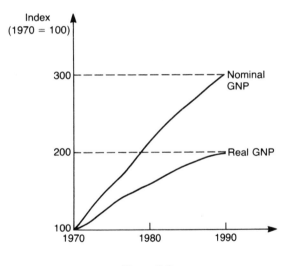

Figure 2.3

What determines the amount of output that an economy produces? Primarily it depends upon the quantity of resources (factor inputs) utilised and the productivity of these resources. A combination of fertile land, high-tech capital equipment, and skilled labour, co-ordinated efficiently by a skilled management team, will produce a large quantity of top quality output. An economy's output will be low if it lacks vital raw materials, fertile land and/or skilled labour. Even if it has all of the necessary inputs, output may still be low if these inputs are combined inefficiently by untrained managers. It is clear, therefore, that the level and quality of a nation's output depend upon (amongst other things) the quality of its managers.

Capacity Utilisation Index

Each business firm has a productive capacity, i.e. the maximum output that could be produced if all inputs (land, labour and capital) were fully employed and were combined efficiently. If we were to add this up for every firm in the whole economy, this would give us the economy's **productive capacity**: the maximum output that a fully employed efficiently operating economy could produce. It is also called the **productive potential**.

Not all firms operate at the frontier of their productive capacity. An amount of slack is built in which enables firms to accommodate sudden short-run increases in consumer demand. It is impossible to adjust to an increase in demand in the short run by adding to physical plant because it takes many years to construct new factories, etc. Also, it is not sound business practice to respond by building new factories if that demand is short-lived. Fluctuations in demand are, therefore, met from a margin of spare capacity.

During booms, capacity is used up, and as demand for output grows, a nation's capacity is used at 95% or close to 100% of its capacity. In a recession, when demand falls, the capacity used falls to 80% or even 60%.

A capacity utilisation index is constructed which measures how fully *capital* is being utilised. An examination of the capacity utilisation index shows a record of the booms and recessions of an economy over time.

2.6 UTILISATION OF LABOUR

The utilisation of labour also varies over the business cycle. A measure of labour utilisation is the rate of unemployment. The measuring of unemployment is, however, a tricky business. We need to distinguish between those who are out of work and who are actively seeking employment and those who are out of work but are not actively seeking employment. Those who are actively seeking are unemployed but those who are not actively seeking are not counted as unemployed. Whilst this distinction might seem reasonable, how do we treat those workers who have become 'discouraged', that is, when they first become unemployed they actively seek employment but as time passes and they find no work they become discouraged and simply give up searching for work. This is a problem which is faced by many of the long-term unemployed. Are they to be counted as unemployed?

Unemployment is calculated differently in different countries. There are two ways of going about it:

(1) The government, through the Department of Labour, will carry out a sample survey of a large number of households to estimate what proportion of the working-age population is neither working nor looking for work. Subtracting those from the working-age population leaves the available civilian labour force, i.e. those who are able and willing to work. The labour force 'participation rate' is the ratio of the labour force to the working-age population.

   Those who have paid jobs are regarded as being employed. The remaining people in the labour force who do not have jobs are labelled as unemployed. The unemployment rate is the ratio of the number unemployed to the civilian labour force and is expressed as a percentage.
(2) The number of unemployed are counted as those who are in receipt of unemployment insurance benefit. The participation rate and unemployment rate are calculated as above.

Another measure of labour utilization is the **employment ratio**. This is the proportion of the working-age population that is actually employed, to that not employed. The unemployment rate differs from the employment ratio, as a measure of labour utilisation, in that it considers only the presently available labour force rather than the total working-age population.

The unemployment rate can only give a rough and ready indication of the performance of an economy because there are a number of problems involved in its construction:

(a) There is the problem of the discouraged worker, outlined earlier.
(b) Some individuals may indicate that they are available for work

29

and are actively seeking work but have unrealistically high expectations of the kind of job that will suit them.

(c) Wasteful unemployment does not appear in the unemployment statistics, e.g. a Ph.D. graduate waiting on tables in a restaurant is counted as being employed.

The Rise and Fall of Employment

Unemployment is a stock – it is the number of people at a particular moment in time who are regarded, by the definitions already given, as being without work. This stock, however, depends upon complex flows into and out of the labour market. Unemployment will rise if those entering the labour market are increasing in number at a faster rate than those leaving it.

Thus, the demographic structure of the population will influence the rate of unemployment. Suppose there had been a 'baby boom' (i.e. the birth rate suddenly increased) 16 years ago. These babies will now have been through school and those who do not go on to college and university will seek employment. There is, therefore, suddenly a big increase in the number of people joining the labour force. Unless the number leaving increases in proportion, which is unlikely because retirement behaviour will not have changed, then unemployment will increase. To contain this kind of increase in employment a large number of 'new' jobs would need to be created in the economy.

During a recession, when unemployment increases month after month, there might suddenly be a fall in the unemployment rate. Does this mean that the performance of the economy has improved? Not necessarily – it could be that discouraged workers have stopped looking for jobs and have withdrawn. Equally, during a boom, as unemployment falls, it might in one month start to rise. Does this mean that the boom is over? Again, not necessarily so. Because of the boom a number of workers might be encouraged to look for work. They therefore enter the labour force as 'new' workers and are classed as being unemployed until they find work.

Finally, unemployment might be an indicator of an efficiently operating economy. What does this puzzling statement mean? As workers move from one job to another they register as temporarily unemployed for a few weeks. Unemployment in this case simply reflects an efficiently functioning labour market. Thus, we must ask questions about the *duration of employment*. What proportion of those who are counted as unemployed have been unemployed for three months; six months; over 12 months? During a recession the duration of unemployment increases. It is the duration of unemployment that is the useful indicator of the health of the economy.

Self-Assessment Questions

(a) Plot on a graph the capacity utilisation index for your own economy over the past ten years.
(b) Plot on the same graph the unemployment rate.
(c) Can you identify the maximum and minimum points on the graph?
(d) How is unemployment measured in your country?
(e) What can you find out about the duration of unemployment in your country?

2.7 POTENTIAL OUTPUT AND ECONOMIC GROWTH

The notion of potential output was introduced briefly earlier. This concept was first introduced by the American economist Arthur Okun in the early 1960s. Potential output is what the economy could produce if capital and labour were fully utilised (with a margin of slack to accommodate short-term increases in demand).

Measuring potential output has a number of problems. We are trying to find the limit of the economy, but how do we know by looking at past data whether or not the economy has ever been at full employment? One way is to examine the peaks of the economy. If real GNP is plotted over time, as in Figure 2.4, then, joining a line from peak to peak gives a measure of the trend in productive potential. The rate of increase in real GNP from one peak to another gives an indication of the rate of growth of productive potential. What is the logic behind this approach? As GNP rises, the resources in the economy become more fully employed. Slack is used up and capacity is utilised. Once the full-employment position of the economy is reached, the boom moves down into a recession. Thus, the peak of the boom should be in a position of full employment. Joining up the peaks over time shows the path that the economy would move along if it was at full capacity.

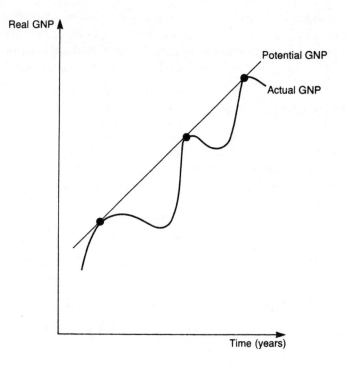

Figure 2.4

An alternative approach is to calculate the long-run determinants of output growth:

$$\text{Output} = \frac{\text{Output}}{\text{Hour}} \times \frac{\text{Hours}}{\text{Worker}} \times \frac{\text{Workers}}{\text{Population}} \times \text{Population}$$

What this says is that output is the product of output per hour, hours per worker, the employment ratio, and total population. The percentage change in output is equal to the sum of the percentage changes in these four elements. Data from several years are used in the calculation to obtain a trend.

Comparison of the two approaches produces broadly similar results.

Productivity and the Business Cycle

Capital utilisation changes over the business cycle, as has been noted already. It increases in booms and declines in slumps. During a slump, industries do not auction off all of their capacity. They ride it out, waiting for the next upturn. If the recession is prolonged they might be forced to sell off marginal plant and equipment, that is if buyers can be found. Likewise, they do not, in a recession, lay off their highly skilled workers because such employees are very hard to find and train.

When sales decline in a recession, labour and capital utilisation decline also, whilst fixed costs (for the reasons given above) remain. It follows, therefore, that measured productivity slumps. The reverse is true in a boom. Thus, the question which is asked is how much of any change in productivity is due to the business cycle over the short run and how much of the change is a long-run trend? Later we shall examine the factors which cause productivity to change in the long run.

The Growth Rate

The growth rate (i.e. percentage growth rate or compound growth rate) of a variable over one period of time (for example, real GNP (Q) for the one-year period 1991–92) is given by:

$$\frac{\text{Change in real GNP}}{\text{Real GNP}} = \frac{Q_{1992} - Q_{1991}}{Q_{1991}} = i$$

If $Q_{1992} = \$183.5$ billion and $Q_{1991} = \$203.6$ billion, then:

$$i = \frac{183.5 - 203.6}{203.6} = -0.098 \text{ (i.e. } -9.8\%)$$

This shows a negative growth rate between 1991 and 1992.

Suppose we want to calculate the compound growth rate between two dates several years apart, how do we do that? We can use the following formula:

$$\text{Future Value} = (\text{Present Value}) \times e^{in}$$

where e (the 'exponential' function) $= 2.718$, i is the annual compound rate of growth and n is the number of years between the two dates over which the growth rate is to be calculated.

Thus, we want to solve for i in the above equation. The equation can be simplified and approximated to the following:

$$\text{Future Value} = (\text{Present Value}) \times (1 + i)^n$$

If $Q_{1991} = 203.6$ billion dollars and $Q_{1986} = 165.5$ billion dollars, then:

$$\text{Future Value} = \text{Present Value} \times (1 + i)^5$$

$$Q_{1991} = Q_{1986} \times (1 + i)^5$$

$$203.6 = 165.5 \times (1 + i)^5$$

Then, by entering the future value, present value and number of time-periods into a calculator, the value of the annual compound growth rate is found to be 4.23 per cent.

A useful *approximation* to the growth rate of *nominal* GNP is the sum of the growth rates of the price level and of real GNP. In symbols:

$$GNP = P \times Q$$

$$\frac{\text{Change in GNP}}{\text{GNP}} + \frac{\text{Change in Price}}{\text{Price}} + \frac{\text{Change in Quantity}}{\text{Quantity}}$$

This relationship holds for any variable (C) that can be expressed as a product of other variables (A and B or more):

$$\text{If } C = A \times B$$

$$\text{then } \frac{\text{Change in } C}{C} + \frac{\text{Change in } A}{A} + \frac{\text{Change in } B}{B} \quad \text{(approximately)}$$

Self-Assessment Questions

Using the National Income and produce accounts of your own country, calculate the following:

(a) the annual compound growth rate of GNP for the past 10 years.
(b) the annual inflation in the GNP deflator over the past 10 years.

Further Reading

Backus, D., Brainard, W., Smith, G. and Tobin, J. (1980) 'A Flow of Funds Model of U.S. Financial Markets', *Journal of Money, Credit and Banking*, pp. 259/83.

Gordan, R. J. (1981) 'The CPI: Measuring Inflation and Causing It', *The Public Interest*, Spring, pp. 112–34.

American readers should consult the annual editions of the *Economic Report of the President*, U.S. Government Printing Office, Washington, D.C.

British readers should look at annual editions of the *Financial Statement and Budget Report*, Her Majesty's Stationary Office, London.

Part II

MODELLING THE DOMESTIC MACRO-ECONOMY

3

The Income–Expenditure Model

In Part II, we are going to build up a model of economic activity which illustrates how incomes and expenditures are determined in an economy. This will then be used to demonstrate how other economic magnitudes, such as output and employment, are determined. We will also show that many parts of the economy are interdependent. As one economic magnitude changes, for example output, then another does also, for example employment. A simple model will be used to begin with. This will illustrate the basic principles of macroeconomic reasoning. The simple model will then be made more complex so that some of the features of a real economy can be represented.

In all macroeconomic models, whether or not they are complex, a simple rule is used to guide our thinking – everyone's spending depends upon their income and one person's spending is another person's income. This not only captures the idea of interdependence, it is also a powerful force shaping economic activity. If a large number of people in the economy spend less, then the incomes of those who produce the goods and services will fall. Indeed, if spending falls by a sufficiently large amount then many people will become unemployed because profit-maximising businessmen will simply not wish to keep on such a large labour force to produce a smaller volume of output. But the story does not stop there. Those whose incomes have now fallen (or who are unemployed) will now spend less, which means that the process of falling demand will continue. This simple idea that one person's spending is another person's income has generated for us an account of how recessions start and how they continue. If spending and income get out of balance then the consequences are undesirable for everyone.

Self-Assessment Questions

Using this simple idea, think about what happens at the global level of the international economy. If a large international economy such as the USA was to cut back on its spending on imports from other countries,

(a) what is likely to be the consequence for income and employment in other countries?
(b) what type of country would be worst affected?
(c) what might happen to world trade?

3.1 PRELIMINARY BUILDING BLOCKS

Before proceeding to construct a model of income determination, it is necessary to define a number of the elements that will be used in the subsequent analysis.

In the circular flow of income diagram that was established earlier, all inflows and outflows to and from the economy were in balance. The suppliers of goods and services paid wages and these were used to purchase goods and services. This led some economists to believe that supply created its own demand. If this view of the economy was true then the economy would always be in equilibrium. But simple observation shows that real economies are characterised by periods of disequilibrium, i.e. unemployment, accelerating inflation and balance of payments deficits. Moreover, disequilibrium can exist for many years, as in the case of a severe recession. The observation of disequilibrium caused the British economist John Maynard Keynes to propose an alternative view of how the economy works. His analysis culminated in the famous book, *The General Theory of Employment, Interest and Money*, published in 1936. It created a revolution in economic thinking: 'The Keynesian Revolution'.

The Keynesian View

What was Keynes's message? Markets left to their own devices will fail to bring the economy back into equilibrium. Prices are slow to adjust and while they are slowly adjusting it is quantities that adjust instead, i.e. in the labour market individuals are made unemployed. When a recession hits an economy, individuals' incomes are cut back. They spend less and firms are left with excess stocks of unsold goods. Moreover, individuals run down their stock of savings (wealth) in order to maintain their levels of living standards. This saving could have been used to finance business investment rather than consumption. But businessmen will not want to invest – in a recession they have excess capacity, cannot sell all that they are currently producing and have depressed expectations about the future. Clearly supply does not create its own demand.

To restore expansion in the economy, individuals need to spend more. If they spend more then producers will produce more to meet the increase in demand. This expansion in demand can come from consumers' spending, from the investment spending by businessmen purchasing new capital goods, or from government spending. In an open economy the extra demand can come from an expansion in foreign spending on the country's exports.

The principal conclusion of the Keynesian view of the world is that the level of national income, national output and hence employment is largely determined by the level of aggregate demand in the economy. Demand determines how much is supplied.

The Keynesian Model

A number of assumptions are made when constructing the basic Keynesian model. These assumptions will be relaxed as the analysis proceeds. They are made in order to keep the model as simple as possible so that we might understand some of the economic processes at work. Whilst it is simple, however, it is not a complete fiction.

(1) Assume wages and prices are fixed. This implies that the model applies to the short run, i.e. a period of time so short that wages and prices don't vary. In the short run producers will respond to changes in demand by varying quantities rather than prices. It follows from this that the economy is at less than full employment. If the economy was at full employment (i.e. labour and capital fully employed) then producers would have no extra capacity to vary output.

(2) The money market is not included in the model at this stage. This means that we need to wait until later to consider how interest rates are determined and how they might affect the model.

(3) Consumption (C) and saving (S) are both dependent upon national income (Y). The consumption function and savings function are assumed to be linear, i.e. straight lines: see Figure 3.1.

(4) There is no government sector, i.e. there is no government spending, nor are taxes imposed on households and firms.

(5) There is no depreciation of capital. All investment is investment in new capital goods.

(6) The economy is 'closed', in the sense that it does not trade with the outside world.

The consumption function is shown in Figure 3.1. This shows how much the households in the economy *plan* to spend at each

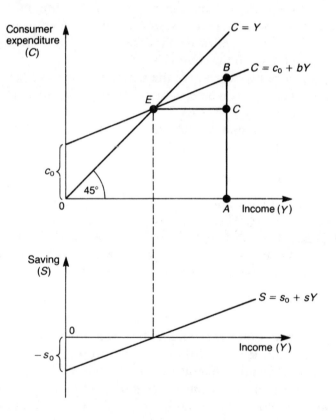

Figure 3.1

level of income (Y). At a zero level of income, consumption spending is positive and is given by the intercept c_0. This level of consumer spending is independent of the level of income – it is said to be autonomous or exogenous consumer spending (i.e. not determined by income). Autonomous consumer spending depends instead on a variety of factors such as the level of an individual's wealth (i.e. savings); expectations about the future such as expectations about future income; the rate of interest (i.e. the cost of credit); the availability of credit if credit is rationed by the banks.

The linear relationship between consumption expenditure and income can be written as:

$$C = c_0 + bY$$

where C = total consumer expenditure; c_0 is autonomous consumer spending (the intercept in Figure 3.1); b is the slope of the consumption function and Y is income.

The Consumption Function

The slope of the consumption function has a special significance. Let us see what it refers to. The gradient of the consumption function in Figure 3.1 is defined as

$$\text{gradient} = \frac{BC}{EC} = b$$

As we move from E to C, income changes; it increases. At the same time as income increases, consumption spending increases, from C to B. Thus, we can write the gradient b as:

$$b = \frac{\text{change in consumption}}{\text{change in income}}$$

The gradient (slope) of the consumption functions shows by how much consumer spending increases for each dollar increase in income. This is given a particular name, the **marginal propensity to consume** (mpc).

$$\text{mpc} = b = \frac{\triangle C}{\triangle Y}$$

The **average propensity to consume** (apc) is simply:

$$\text{apc} = \frac{C}{Y} = \frac{AB}{OA}$$

The basic consumption function outlined above related consumption to income and an autonomous element. It is now necessary to examine the consumption function more closely. For example, which income is it that affects consumption expenditures and what are the autonomous elements?

Early attempts to estimate consumption functions used current-period income. A moment's reflection suggests that whilst current incomes might explain short-run consumption, it will not be a useful explanation of long-run consumption expenditures. In that case the appropriate income variable is the individual's permanent or lifetime income. When making decisions about how much to spend on consumer durable goods (automobiles, fridges, furniture, etc.), individuals take their expected future incomes into account. If they expect higher levels of income in the future because they know that their career path will progress in a particular way they will tend to spend more in the current period. Consumption will be higher than could be justified by current-period income and saving will be lower. Indeed, on the expectation that future income will be higher than current income, individuals in the current period will probably dissave – i.e. run deficits and borrow in the knowledge that they will pay back their borrowings in the future. Thus consumption is more likely to be sensitive to expected lifetime income.

What about the factors that enter the autonomous element which influences consumption? First, there are expectations. These have already been introduced along with lifetime income. Different individuals with different attitudes to risks will form different expectations. Those who are 'risk-averse' will form conservative expectations about their future income and will, therefore, tend to depress current consumption levels and will save more. Expectations about inflation will also affect consumption. If consumers expect prices will rise in the future they will tend to spend now, whilst goods and services are cheap, rather than tomorrow.

Wealth levels will affect consumption. In the middle of their lifecycle individuals save and accumulate wealth which they use to maintain their consumption levels and lifestyle later when they have retired and their current-period income has fallen. Wealth does not only affect consumption levels in retirement. It will also influence the level of consumption of anyone who owns a stock of wealth. Wealth can be liquidated to finance consumption plans. Inflation will influence wealth decisions and, therefore, consumption. Rising prices will reduce the real value of a stock of wealth. If individuals have a target level of real wealth then they will tend to save more during and immediately after an inflation in order to build up their real wealth.

Finally, interest rates will have an impact on consumption. Not only will an increase in interest rates provide an increase in nominal income for those who have savings and financial wealth which can be used to finance additional consumption, but a rise in interest rates will also depress consumption because funds borrowed to finance consumption become more expensive.

Self-Assessment Questions

Using the savings function in Figure 3.1, can you label it and work out:

(a) the marginal propensity to save?
(b) the average propensity to save?

Returning to the consumption function of Figure 3.1, the 45° line shows points of equality between consumer spending and income. If all income is spent, then by definition there is no saving. Thus, at the point E, where the consumption function crosses the 45° line, there is zero saving. This is shown in the bottom part of Figure 3.1 where the saving function crosses the horizontal axis.

Self-Assessment Questions

Obtain information on the annual value for consumer spending and saving for your country over the past 20 years. Plot them against national income. From your set of points, draw in the savings and consumption functions. What is:

(a) the marginal propensity to consume in your country?
(b) the average propensity to consume?

Investment

In our Keynesian model we shall assume investment is autonomous, i.e. independent of income changes. Investment is shown as a horizontal line in Figure 3.2. So what affects the level of investment? First, businessmen keep an eye on the level of current sales relative to plant capacity. If plant capacity is placing a persistent constraint upon the ability of businesses to produce output to clear their order books then there will be a strong incentive to add to the existing capital stock (plant and machinery) through increases in investment.

Expectations also play an important role in influencing investment. If businesses expect sales to continue to rise then they will expect plant capacity to become inadequate and will invest in advance of the capacity constraint becoming binding. Expectations of profit levels are also significant. Profits provide an internal source of finance which can be used to finance investment. Strongly held expectations of rising sales and rising profits will provide a strong incentive for businessmen to invest.

Finally, interest rates (and expectations of future interest rates) affect investment. Rising interest rates increase the cost of capital. They create a higher hurdle which any investment project has to clear. The rate of return required on a project rises as interest rates rise. Thus, rising interest rates will depress investment whilst falling interest rates will stimulate investment.

Government Spending

In our basic Keynesian model, we shall assume that, like investment (*I*), government spending (*G*) is autonomous and depends on political decisions. Because *G* is independent of income, it is, like *I*, shown as a horizontal line in Figure 3.2.

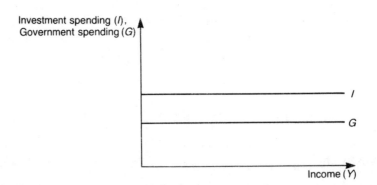

Figure 3.2

Now that we have introduced the role of government into the economy, we have to consider how this government spending is to be financed. For simplicity, let us assume that the government levies a lump-sum tax (T) on households. This lump-sum tax drives a wedge between the income (Y) that households earn and the amount of 'disposable' income (Y_d) they actually receive (where $Y_d = Y - T$). Because households' decisions to consume (and save) depend on Y_d, the introduction of taxes alters the relationship in which we are interested, namely that between C and Y.

With a lump-sum tax (T):

$$C = c_0 + bY_d$$
$$= c_0 + b(Y - T)$$
$$= (c_0 - bT) + bY$$

In other words, a lump-sum tax, T, simply shifts the consumption function vertically downwards by an amount bT, effectively changing the size of the autonomous component in consumer spending. (You should work out for yourself the impact of a lump-sum tax on the savings function.)

In what follows, the consumption functions used in the diagrams below are drawn on the assumption that households pay a lump-sum tax. We shall later consider how more realistic assumptions about taxation, e.g. taxes which are a proportion of income rather than a fixed lump-sum, affect our model, but the assumption of lump-sum taxes is a useful starting point. (You should ask yourself how the consumption function would be affected by an increase or cut in the lump-sum tax.)

Aggregate Demand

Given these elements let us now begin to put them together. First, we define total spending (E) or, as it is also known, aggregate demand:

$$E = C + I + G$$

i.e. it is the sum of consumer spending, investment spending and government spending.

These expenditures generate incomes in the economy – national income is Y. This income is either used for spending on consumer goods (C), or is saved (S) or paid in taxes (T). Sometimes S, and T are referred to as withdrawals from the circular flow of income, whilst I and G are referred to as injections into the circular flow of income.

For equilibrium it is necessary that:

(a) The total value of spending (E) is equal to the total value of the supply of goods that are produced.

(b) Stated in a different way: the level of output and incomes in the economy will not change if the sum of the values of the injections (J) into the economy equal the sum of the values of the withdrawals (W):

$$I + G = S + T$$

This equilibrium can be thought about by using a physical analogy. Imagine a bath tub filled with water. The level of water (national income) will remain at the same height (equilibrium) if the volume of water coming in from the taps each second (injections) equals the volume of water leaving by the drain each second (withdrawals).

Our economic equilibrium is shown in Figure 3.3 at the point E. At E aggregate demand equals aggregate supply. This point corresponds to $W = J$. The equilibrium level of national income is Y_e.

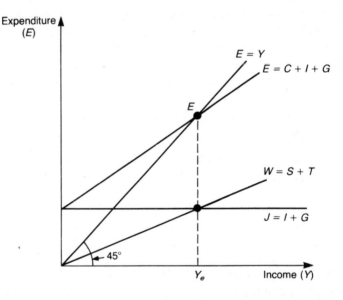

Figure 3.3

3.2 THE DETERMINATION OF NATIONAL INCOME

Having established the basic income and expenditure model let us now set it down more formally so that we can use it to obtain additional insights into how an economy operates at the macro level. We already know that aggregate demand, or, in other words, the total of expenditure in the economy, provides incomes (in the form of wages/salaries, profit, interest and rents). We also know that when the economy is in balance aggregate demand (expenditure) equals aggregate supply and that these equal national income.

Let total expenditures be represented by E and total income by Y. It has already been established that some expenditures are autonomous (such as investment, government spending and exports). Let autonomous expenditures be represented by e_0. Other expenditures (consumption and imports) are related to income. Given these definitions we can now write down the general equation for expenditures:

$$E = e_0 + e_y Y \qquad (3.1)$$

where e_y is the marginal propensity to spend (in the case of consumption spending this would be the mpc – see above).

Again we have assumed a linear expenditure relationship, not because we necessarily believe that the world behaves like this but because it is easier to use linear relationships for analysis. Economists spend a good deal of their time using advanced statistical methods (called econometrics) to find out the true nature of economic relationships of this kind – are they linear; if they are not linear then what shape are they? The precise nature of the relationship is important for forecasting purposes. In Figure 3.4 a linear relationship is shown alongside the true relationship. If we start at A and extrapolate to B then we would end up making an error of BC if we used the linear relationship for forecasting, rather than the true relationship.

What we want to do now is to look more closely at the equilibrium conditions. We know that for an equilibrium incomes must equal expenditures; hence we can write

$$Y = E \qquad (3.2)$$

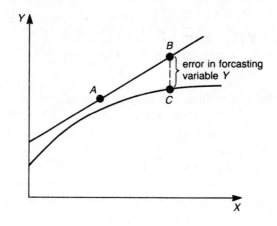

Figure 3.4

If we now substitute equation (3.2) into equation (3.1) we obtain

$$Y = e_0 + e_y Y \qquad (3.3)$$

Therefore:

$$Y - e_y Y = e_0$$
$$Y(1 - e_y) = e_0$$

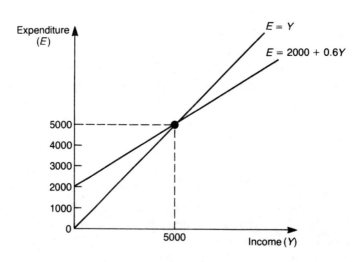

Figure 3.5

48

$$Y = \frac{e_0}{(1 - e_y)} \qquad (3.4)$$

Suppose the general expenditure equation is $E = 2000 + 0.6Y$. This is shown graphically in Figure 3.5. It can be written in the form of equation (3.4). That is

$$Y = \frac{2000}{1 - 0.6}$$

Thus $Y = \$5000$. That is to say the equilibrium level of income and aggregate demand is $5000.

3.3 THE MULTIPLIER

We have now put together a very simple income and expenditure model. Simple it might be, but it enables us to illustrate a very powerful process that takes place in the economic environment if we change spending. This is called the multiplier process and its discovery in the 1930s was very important in changing our view of how the economy works.

Consider what happens if autonomous expenditure, such as investment, increases. In particular what will happen to income as a result of this change? We will demonstrate this as follows:

$$E = (e_0 + \triangle e_0) + e_y Y$$

where $\triangle e_0$ is the increase in autonomous spending.

An increase in spending causes an increase in income (one person's spending is another's income), an increase in income causes an increase in spending, which causes an increase in income, and so on and so on. The question that we want to answer is what is the total increase in income and expenditure once this process has worked its way through the economy? This question can be answered as follows:

$$\text{We know that} \quad Y = \frac{e_0}{1 - e_y}$$

After the increase in spending which causes income to increase, the new level of income is:

$$(Y + \Delta Y) = \frac{e_0 + \Delta e_0}{1 - e_y}$$

where Y is the original level of income. The change in income can be written as:

$$(Y + \Delta Y) - Y = \left(\frac{e_0 + \Delta e_0}{1 - e_y} \right) - \frac{e_0}{(1 - e_y)}$$

$$\Delta Y = \frac{\Delta e_0}{1 - e_y}$$

Thus, by dividing both sides by Δe_0 we obtain:

$$\frac{\Delta Y}{\Delta e_0} = \frac{1}{1 - e_y}$$

This is an important expression and is an example of an important concept in economics, namely the **multiplier**.

In the equation above, $\dfrac{1}{1 - e_y}$ is a multiplier.

If we rewrite the equation as

$$\Delta Y = \frac{1}{(1 - e_y)} \cdot \Delta e_0$$

then this informs us that the change in income is equal to the change in autonomous expenditure times a multiplier $1/(1 - e_y)$.

Let us now examine this operation. Look at what happens to the value of the multiplier as the value of the marginal propensity to spend (ey) varies.

Marginal Propensity to Spend (e_y)	Multiplier
0.0	1.0
0.1	1.1
0.3	1.4
0.5	2.0
0.7	3.3
0.9	10.0

Why does the multiplier increase in value as the value of the marginal propensity to spend increases? The reason is that as e_y increases in value then more of each dollar of income is passed on as expenditure, which then becomes someone else's income, and so on. In other words, the higher the value of e_y the smaller are withdrawals from the circular flow of income.

An Example

What will happen to incomes if autonomous spending, e_0, increases by $1000 and if the marginal propensity to spend is 0.5?

$$\Delta Y = \frac{1}{(1 - e_y)} \cdot \Delta e_0$$

i.e.
$$\Delta Y = \frac{1}{(1 - 0.5)} \cdot 1000$$

i.e.
$$\Delta Y = 2000$$

Income will, therefore, increase by $2000. The multiplier in this example is 2. Any change in autonomous spending will increase by a multiple of 2 in this example.

This is an important result. It demonstrates, as the British economist John Maynard Keynes first pointed out in the 1930s, that if autonomous business investment spending in an economy rises, then incomes will expand by a multiple of this investment spending through the income and expenditure linkages already discussed.

Self-Assessment Questions

Suppose business investment was suddenly to fall in the economy. Using the multiplier analysis above, what is likely to happen to:

(a) incomes?
(b) the level of employment in the economy?
(c) How might the government intervene to counteract the fall in investment?
(d) If government spending (which is autonomous spending) is increased by $1000 and the marginal propensity to spend is 0.7, what will happen to incomes in the economy?

Economic Limits

One question that we must ask is does the multiple expansion of income following an increase in expenditures have a limit? Does the economy just keep on expanding? The multiplier process concentrates upon demand, i.e. demand for output expands. But what about supply? The process assumes that there is sufficient capacity in the economy to supply additional output for the increase in demand. Excess capacity means that unemployed labour will be hired to produce the extra output, or labour which is employed will work overtime, and that the part of the capital stock which is not in use will be made operational. Once full capacity is reached (i.e. full employment) and there are no additional labour or capital resources available, then an increase in spending will not result in an increase in output or incomes but will, instead, spill over into price rises.

This last point will be elaborated upon later. In the meantime it is ruled out by assumption – we are dealing with the short-run period up to full employment but not beyond it, and under these conditions we assume that quantities adjust rather than prices.

Once-for-all versus Sustained Changes in Spending

It is important to distinguish between a once-and-for-all-time increase in autonomous spending and a sustained increase. In the case of a once-only increase in e_0 then the effect of this rise in spending will die out. Total income and spending will rise but only momentarily. In each successive time-period, income and spending decline and eventually reach the original level (see Figure 3.6). The reason for this is that only a fraction of income is passed on as extra spending from one

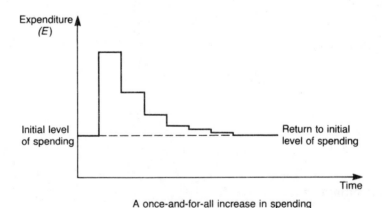

A once-and-for-all increase in spending

Figure 3.6

time-period to the next. It also shows that the increase in income and spending does not suddenly take place within a single time-period. There are time lags between receiving income and spending it. Thus, the impact of a change in autonomous spending is spread over a number of time-periods.

What would happen if the increase in autonomous spending is maintained from one time-period to another? In this case, income and expenditures do not return to their original levels. Instead a new equilibrium level of income and expenditure is reached (see Figure 3.7). This is quite easy to appreciate. Suppose the marginal propensity to spend is 0.5 and the rise in autonomous spending is $1000 in each time-period. Then the process is as shown in Table 3.1.

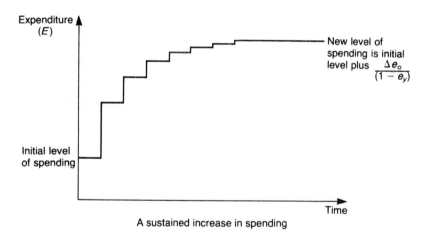

Figure 3.7

Table 3.1

	Period 1	Period 2	Period 3	Period 4
Initial Injection	1000	500	250	125
Second Injection		1000	500	250
Third Injection			1000	500
Fourth Injection				1000

The initial injection of $1000 is then passed on as $500 of extra income in period 2, which is spent and passed on as $250 of extra income in period 3, and so on. This is the multiplier process. In period 2, there is a further injection of $1000 of autonomous spending and a similar multiplier process follows this injection. If this process is pushed forward through several time-periods, then income and spending move to a new level, as Figure 3.7 demonstrates.

The Multiplier Process

The preceding discussion has set out the broad principles of the multiplier process. We will now be more specific and illustrate the multiplier through examples.

Investment depends upon a number of different factors: businessmen's expectations of future sales and profits or the cost of capital. If these change, for whatever reason, there will be an impact upon the equilibrium level of income. In this example autonomous spending (e_0) is investment, i.e. it does not depend upon income. Suppose autonomous investment spending increases by $2 million, what happens?

In the first period (the first round of the multiplier), national income will increase by the full $2 million. These extra incomes are, however, spent by those who receive them. If the marginal propensity to spend is 0.6 then the original increase of $2 million of income will generate, in the second period (the second round of the multiplier), 0.6 times $2 million, i.e. $1.2 million additional income. This, in the third period, will generate 1.2 times 0.6, i.e. $0.72 million of extra income. The first five rounds of the multiplier are shown in Table 3.2.

Table 3.2

	Change in expenditure	*Change in income*
Period 1		
(round 1)	$2 million	$2 million
Period 2	$1.2 million	$1.2 million
Period 3	$0.72 million	$0.72 million
Period 4	$0.432 million	$0.432 million

After five periods following a once-and-for-all increase in autonomous investment spending of $2 million, incomes and expenditures have increased by $4.611 million. For each subsequent time-period the increase is smaller than in the previous period. Eventually the increase for a time-period in the future will be zero and the *level* of income and expenditures will return to their original level, as in Figure 3.6.

In this example, we have only looked at the first five rounds of the multiplier. What will be the total income and expenditure generated by the increase of $2 million in autonomous investment spending once all rounds of the multiplier process are taken into account? To answer this we return to the formula

$$\frac{\triangle Y}{\triangle e_0} = \frac{1}{1 - e_y}$$

Then in this example

$$\triangle Y = 2. \ \frac{1}{1 - 0.6}$$

$$\triangle Y = 5$$

and the value of the multiplier is 2.5.

Let us now gather together what we have learned so far. A macroeconomic equilibrium requires a balance of forces in the economy. In particular we require that aggregate demand (expenditures) equals aggregate supply (output). This has also been expressed in terms of the total of withdrawals from the circular flow of income being equal to the total of injections. It was also shown that this equilibrium could be disturbed and the economy could move to a new equilibrium if autonomous spending was increased and if this increase was maintained from one time-period to the next. The amount by which income and spending change following the increase in autonomous spending depends upon the size of the multiplier and this, in turn, depends on the value of the marginal propensity to spend (the size of withdrawals).

3.4 THE NATURE OF ECONOMIC EQUILIBRIUM

It is now necessary to be more precise about the notion of equilibrium that is being used. The concept of an equilbrium in economics refers to a situation in which there is no tendency to change any of the economic variables in our model of the economy. All forces are in balance. This can be thought of as a static equilibrium. Economic agents (households and business firms) make plans. They plan how much to consume and save. Businessmen plan how much to produce and to invest.

An economic equilibrium occurs when these plans are fulfilled. That is, when actual consumption equals planned consumption; when actual savings equal planned savings; when actual investment equals planned investment, and so on. If plans did not match up against the outcome then households and firms would either revise their plan or would act upon the economic environment to make outcome equal the plan. In other words, if plans are not realised then there cannot be an equilibrium because individuals will set up forces for change.

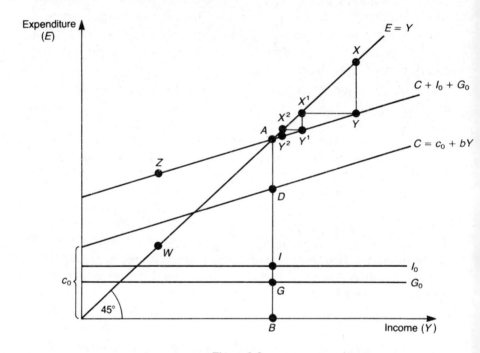

Figure 3.8

This notion of equilibrium, shown in Figure 3.8, is now familiar. Total planned spending is given by the line $(C + I_0 + G_0)$. The 45° line shows planned spending equal to planned production (output).

Take some point such as X. At this point planned production by firms is greater than planned spending by households. Firms' plans will not be realised. What will happen is that firms will accumulate unplanned inventories (i.e. stocks of unsold output). But the process doesn't stop here. Firms do not want to accumulate stocks because there is an opportunity cost of doing so. In the next time-period firms will adjust their production plans by cutting back on what they plan to produce. They will cut production back to the level of actual sales in the previous period (i.e. Y). They will set the new production plan X^1 equal to Y. As they cut back on production they will lay off some of their labour and cut back on hours worked. This means that incomes in the economy will fall, so that consumption plans are revised down to Y^1. Again, planned production X^1 exceeds planned consumption.

This process continues until plans are revised to such a level that they are in balance, i.e. at point A. At point A the economy is in a static equilibrium, i.e. planned expenditures equal planned output. There is now nothing to cause the economy to change from this point. Only a change in autonomous spending will bring about a shift in the equilibrium.

Self-Assessment Question

Take two points such as Z and W in Figure 3.8. Planned expenditure (Z) is greater than planned output (W). Carry out a similar reasoning as that which was used for X and Y and explain how the economy will move to the equilibrium A.

A Desirable Equilibrium?

At equilibrium, therefore, businessmen are producing as much as people want to buy and their inventory levels are in equilibrium (planned inventories equal actual inventories). But this macro-economic equilibrium is not the same as a market (or micro) equilibrium. Businessmen might prefer it if people were prepared to buy more output – they would then invest in extra capacity and realise expanded profit opportunities.

An equilibrium such as A need not be desirable. As the economy moved from X to A, labour was made unemployed. Keynes referred to a point such as A as an under-employment equilibrium. Those who are unemployed will not regard A as a desirable equilibrium – they would prefer an equilibrium that gives better job opportunities. Also, businessmen would prefer an equilibrium at which they could sell more and realise profit opportunities.

In Figure 3.9 the full-employment level of income, expenditure and output is shown at the point F. The point A is below it. The question is, how can the economy get closer to F? The answer is clear. We need to shift the level of planned spending. If we were to shift the line $C + I_0 + G_0$ upwards so that the new line passed through F then planned spending would equal planned production at a level of full employment. That is, we would have a full-employment equilibrium. But how could we do this? Consider the following means:

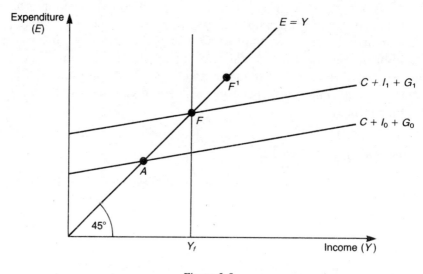

Figure 3.9

(1) Cut taxes. This will increase personal disposable incomes and therefore consumption will be higher at each level of income;
(2) Increase government spending;
(3) Make credit cheaper by reducing interest rates. This will stimulate autonomous consumption and investment.

How to move towards full employment is a question that is asked in relation to the design of economic policy and is discussed in much greater detail later when we consider monetary and fiscal policies. In the meantime you should realise that an economy can and often does get stuck at an under-employment equilibrium which requires government action to get it unstuck. Also, the full-employment equilibrium is not static. Increases in the size of the population, innovations in product design, increases in the size and capacity of the capital stock all cause the full-employment equilibrium to shift to the right, i.e. from F to F^1 in Figure 3.9. Policies therefore need to be designed to chase a moving full-employment equilibrium.

Summary

We have used a simple model to explain the determination of income and expenditure and employment in an economy. We have shown that one person's spending is another's income and that when expenditures change in an economy this sets up a multiplier process such that the change in income is greater than the change in the original expenditure. To sustain this income, the change in expenditure needs to be sustained also: a once-only change in expenditure will cause income to change for a short while but the economy will eventually return to its original level of income. The size of the multiplier depends upon the value of the marginal propensity to spend.

Equilibrium in the economy exists when everyone's plans are being realised. If the economy is out of equilibrium then individuals change their plans – producers change production and investment plans; consumers change consumption expenditure and savings plans. As the economy adjusts to the equilibrium level of output, employment changes.

If an economy is stuck in a less-than-full-employment equilibrium, then, by changing planned expenditures, government policies can move the economy closer to full employment. Because the policies operate on planned expenditures (i.e. demand), these policies are called 'demand management'.

Further Reading

Ando, A. and Modigliani, F. (1963) 'The Life-Cycle Hypothesis of Saving: Aggregate Implications and Taste', *American Economic Review*.

Anderson, G. T. (1981) 'A New Approach to the Empirical Investigation of Investment Expenditures', *Economic Journal*, Vol. 91, March.

Bhalla, S. S. (1980) 'The Measurement of Permanent Income and its Application to Savings Behaviour', *Journal of Political Economy*, Vol. 88, Number 4, August.

Deaton, A. (1977) 'Involuntary Saving Through Unanticipated Inflation', *American Economic Review*, December.

Nickell, S. J. (1978) *The Investment Decisions of Firms*, Cambridge University Press, Cambridge.

4

A Complete Model of Income and Expenditure Determination

The income and expenditure model set out above is constrained by the restrictive assumptions which were made. These assumptions enabled us to introduce and to illustrate a number of important concepts that are used throughout any discussion about the macroeconomic environment in which organisations operate. We shall now relax some of these assumptions in order to make the model a better (but by no means complete) representation of reality. In doing so, however, we also introduce a greater degree of complexity into the analysis.

4.1 INCOME, EXPENDITURE AND INTEREST RATES

In the simple model we ignored financial markets and interest rates. We know from our own experiences that interest rates influence spending decisions. High interest rates will, for example, discourage consumer spending. In terms of the consumption function it is the autonomous element which is depressed by high interest rates. High interest rates will also affect business investment because of the higher costs of borrowing. Even those firms who have cash balances from retained profits and who, therefore, do not need to borrow to finance their investment in new plant and machinery will, at high interest rates, find it more profitable to invest in bonds or other financial assets rather than in physical plant. Thus, at high rates of interest we would expect consumer and investment expenditures to be depressed.

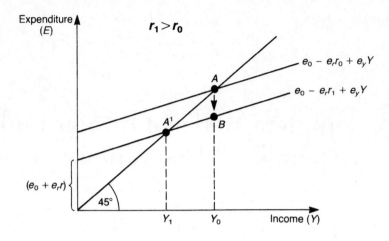

Figure 4.1

Interest rates can easily be introduced into the expenditure model as follows:

$$E = e_0 - e_r r + e_y Y \qquad (4.1)$$

In equation (4.1) e_r measures the impact of interest rates on spending. It has a negative impact. This is illustrated in Figure 4.1. The graph in Figure 4.1 shows the relationship between expenditure and levels of income. If the rate of interest varies, this will cause a parallel shift of the expenditure function. A rise in the rate of interest from r_0 to r_1 will shift the expenditure function down because, at each level of income, expenditure will now be lower at the higher rate of interest. This is represented by a shift from some point, such as A, to a point B.

As the rate of interest changes so also does the equilibrium level of income. The equilibrium has shifted from A to A^1, i.e. the equilibrium level of income has changed from Y_0 to Y_1.

Changing Interest Rates

Imagine what would happen if interest rates were continuously changing. For each level of interest rates there would be a corresponding value for the equilibrium level of income. This would give a series of interest-rate and equilibrium income combinations (r_0, Y_0), (r_1, Y_1), (r_2, Y_2) ... (r_n, Y_n). If these combinations are plotted on a graph then we would obtain Figure 4.2. As r rises in value, the value of Y

falls. You can check this out for yourself by putting numerical values into the graph in Figure 4.1 and then reading off interest-rate and income combinations that will produce Figure 4.2.

The line labelled *IS* in Figure 4.2 shows combinations of levels of income and interest rates at which spending equals income. In other words, as we move along the *IS* line, withdrawals are equal to injections – planned spending equals actual spending. All points along *IS* represent an equilibrium for the economy. Two of the injections and withdrawals that we are already familiar with are investment and savings – hence the label of *IS* that is given to this equilibrium line.

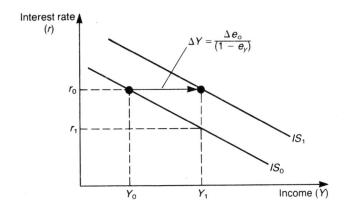

Figure 4.2

It is important that you understand the significance of the *IS* line. If you are not sure what it means then go back to Figure 4.1 and work out that, as interest rates change, so too will the equilibrium for the economy. (A more formal derivation of the *IS* schedule is presented in Chapter 10.)

A movement along the *IS* line is caused by a change in interest rates. If interest rates change from r_0 to r_1 then autonomous expenditures that are sensitive to interest rates (i.e. that are interest-elastic) will change. In Figure 4.1 a *fall* in interest rates would cause the expenditure function to shift upwards. This shift in the expenditure function will produce a new equilibrium level of national income. At the new equilibrium we find an equilibrium combination of national income and interest rates, such as (r_1, Y_1) shown in Figure 4.2. All points along *IS* are equilibria.

Changing Autonomous Spending

Now consider what happens if there is a change in autonomous spending ($\triangle e_0$) such as a change in government spending or investment spending which is not related to the rate of interest. This will cause the *IS* curve to change. Why? Go back to the expenditure equation,

$$E = e_0 - e_r r + e_y Y$$

The *IS* curve was drawn by varying r whilst e_0 remained constant. If, after having derived the *IS* line, we now vary e_0 then we will produce a new *IS* curve for each value of e_0.

By how much will the *IS* line shift as a result of varying e_0? It will be recalled that if autonomous spending changes there will be a multiplier impact upon income. Thus, if we keep interest rates constant at r_0 in Figure 4.2 and increase autonomous expenditures ($+ \triangle e_0$) then the *IS* line will shift out to the right by the amount of the multiplier times the change in autonomous spending. This is:

$$Y = \frac{\triangle e_0}{(1 - e_y)}$$

where $1/(1 - e_y)$ is the multiplier.

The answer to the question, by how much will the *IS* line move following a change in autonomous spending, can now be answered. It will move by the amount:

$$\frac{\triangle e_0}{(1 - e_y)}$$

What causes the *IS* line to shift? The answer is a change in autonomous spending. What would be an example of a change in autonomous spending? Consider the following:

(1) a change in lump-sum taxes: this will change autonomous consumption spending.
(2) a change in investment spending brought about by a change in decision-makers' expectations of the future.
(3) a change in government spending.

Self-Assessment Question

Show what will happen to the *IS* line if government spending decreases. Will the size of the shift in the *IS* line be greater or smaller for a low value of the marginal propensity to spend compared to a higher value of the marginal propensity to spend?

4.2 THE MONEY MARKET

Another feature of reality that has been left out of the simple model is the existence of money and financial markets. Why are these of importance? Interest rates, which have been used to determine expenditures, are determined in financial markets. Given the importance of interest rates for spending decisions, we need to know how interest rates are determined and hence our interest in financial markets.

We begin the analysis by considering the demand for money. Money performs a number of important functions in an economy. Primarily it is a medium of exchange which is used in the payment mechanism when goods and services are transacted. Thus money is demanded for transaction purposes. This is referred to as the transactions demand for money. As incomes in the economy rise, more transactions are carried out because a greater volume of sales takes place at higher incomes. Thus the transactions demand for money is sensitive to the level of income. But money is also a store of value. Between transactions, purchasing power can be stored in cash balances. Individuals will, therefore, hold money balances not only to make immediate transactions but also to store value for future transactions. The size of the money balances that individuals hold is sensitive to the rate of interest. There is an opportunity cost of holding on to idle money balances. These idle balances could be invested in financial assets such as bonds. Thus, if an individual has a simple portfolio made up of money and bonds, as the rate of interest rises the opportunity cost of holding money balances increases, with the result that wise individuals will wish to move out of money into bonds. The demand for money will fall as the rate of interest rises.

It is now possible to write this story down more formally:

$$L = l_0 + l_y Y - l_r r \tag{4.2}$$

where L = demand for money; Y = income; l_y shows the effect of a change in income upon the demand for money, i.e. it is the value of the income elasticity of demand for money balances; r = rate of interest; l_r is the interest elasticity of demand for money.

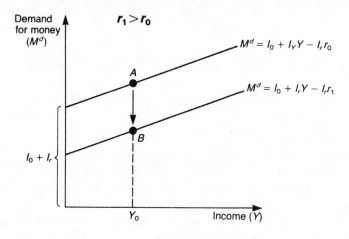

Figure 4.3

Equation (4.2) is illustrated in Figure 4.3. The relationship between income and the demand for money is shown by the graph. As incomes increase, the demand for money increases also, all other things remaining equal. A change in the rate of interest will bring about a shift in the demand for money function. Thus, for example, an increase in interest rates from r_0 to r_1 will, for a given level of income Y_0, shift the demand for money from A to B.

The Money Supply

Now consider the money supply. The money supply is assumed to be under the control of either the government or the central bank, or both. Thus, the supply of money balances is exogenous and this is shown as M^s in Figure 4.4. A word of caution is in order. There is a long debate in economics about whether or not the money supply is truly exogenous. We shall ignore this in order to keep the story simple. But in so doing we are assuming that the central bank has perfect control over the money supply. In reality it does not and the factors that affect the money supply are complex.

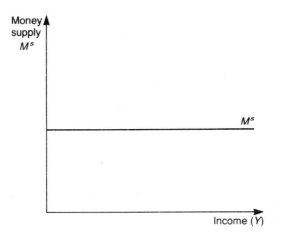

Figure 4.4

Now put Figures 4.3 and 4.4 together. Rather than writing out the complete equation for the demand for money $(L = l_0 + l_y Y - l_r r)$, let us simply refer to it as M^d.

Figure 4.5 shows a fixed money supply M^s and a demand for money function M^d_0. They intersect at the level of national income Y_0. M^d_0 has been drawn assuming some rate of interest r_0 is fixed. If we now change the rate of interest to r_1 (i.e. raise the rate of interest), the

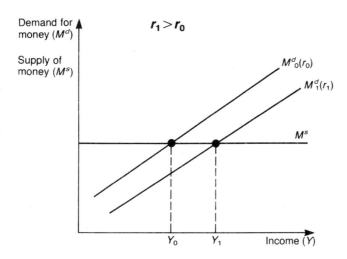

Figure 4.5

67

demand for money will shift from $M^d{}_0$ to $M^d{}_1$. The demand for money now equals the supply of money at a higher level of income. Imagine that we vary the rate of interest several times and redraw the demand for money each time. This will generate a series of combinations of interest rates and levels of income for which the demand for money equals the supply: (r_0, Y_0), (r_1, Y_1), (r_2, Y_2), (r_3, Y_3) . . . (r_n, Y_n).

These combinations can now be drawn on another graph, such as the *LM* line in Figure 4.6. The *LM* line shows the combinations of interest rates and levels of income for which the money market is in equilibrium, i.e. $M^d = M^s$. (L represents the demand for money and M represents the supply of money.) As we move along the *LM* line, the planned demand for money is equal to the planned supply of money.

The *LM* line shows that, as income increases, then the transactions demand for money increases. Given that the money supply is fixed, then the price of money (the rate of interest) must rise in order to bring about demand equal to supply in the money market. The *LM* curve is therefore drawn assuming that the supply of money is fixed. (A more formal derivation of the *LM* schedule is presented in Chapter 10.)

What happens if the money supply changes? This causes a shift in the *LM* line. If the money supply increases then the *LM* line will shift to the right, i.e. from LM_0 to LM_1 (see Figure 4.6).

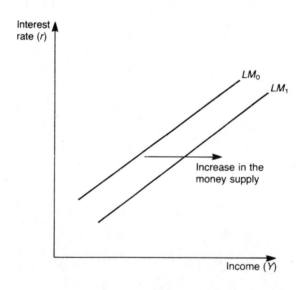

Figure 4.6

4.3 THE *IS–LM* MODEL

The *IS* line shows combinations of interest rates and income levels for which planned spending equals actual spending. Thus, the *IS* line shows a set of equilibria for the economy. The *LM* line shows the combinations of interest rates and income levels for which the money market is in equilibrium. Now we put the two together in Figure 4.7. The point at which the two lines intersect gives the level of national income Y_0, and the level at which the expenditure side of the economy is in equilibrium (*IS*), and at which the money market is also in equilibrium (*LM*): Y_0 is, therefore, the equilibrium level of national income and r_0 is the equilibrium rate of interest.

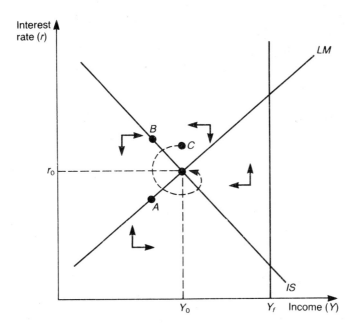

Figure 4.7

A Stable Economy?

Is this equilibrium for the economy stable? This is an important question for decision-makers who are making their own plans. Is the macroeconomic environment a stable one? Are there forces in the economy that will drive the economy closer to its equilibrium or is there a tendency for the economy to be unstable and for it to move further away from equilibrium? Return to Figure 4.7. Consider a point to the left of the *IS* line, such as *A*. The level of income is below the equilibrium level of income (Y_0). Aggregate demand is greater than output – inventories will be run down. Seeing their inventories falling, businessmen will produce more during the next period. This is the economic force driving up national income. Conversely, for all points to the right of the *IS* line there are forces causing national income to fall.

Take a point, such as *B*, which lies above the *LM* curve. At this point the rate of interest is too high to bring about equilibrium in the money market, i.e. the demand for money is less than the supply of money. Forces will bring down the rate of interest and, as it falls, the demand for money will increase. The opposite is true for points below the *LM* curve.

The directions of the pressures being exerted on incomes and interest rates in the four quadrants of Figure 4.7 are shown by arrows. Take a disequilibrium point such as *C*; economic forces will push it towards the equilibrium. Over time the disequilibrium point *C* will move to the equilibrium, although this might take a long time to achieve. The speed of adjustment towards equilibrium depends upon how quickly individuals' plans can adjust. If consumers or businessmen are locked into plans and are not prepared to adjust them, then it will take the economy a considerable amount of time to reach equilibrium. Or if decision-makers refuse to adjust their plans but wait for others to change theirs then, once again, adjustment will be slow.

Employment

Nothing is being said about the desirability of the equilibrium Y_0. It might be that an equilibrium such as Y_0 is a long way from the full-employment level of income Y_f. If the economy is stable then it can get stuck into a less than full-employment equilibrium. That is to say, left to itself, there are no forces in the economy that will move it to full employment.

One can move towards a full-employment equilibrium by shifting *either* the *IS* or the *LM* curve: see Figure 4.8. A shift in the *IS* curve would move the economy from point *A* to point B. At *B*, full employment Y_0 is achieved. A shift in the *LM* curve from LM_0 to LM_1

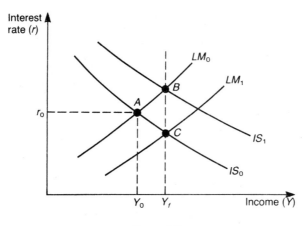

Figure 4.8

will move the economy from point *A* to point *C*, which also coincides with full employment Y_f.

In the first case the shift from *A* to *B* is accompanied by a rise in interest rates, whereas a move from *A* to *C* is associated with a fall in interest rates. Thus we have a choice of route to full employment – one will have high interest rates and the other will have low interest rates.

Let us set down the factors that will bring about shifts in the *IS* and *LM* lines.

Increase in investment	*IS* shifts right
Decrease in investment	*IS* shifts left
Increase in consumption	*IS* shifts right
Increase in savings	*IS* shifts left
Increase in government spending	*IS* shifts right
Increase in taxation	*IS* shifts left
Increase in money supply	*LM* shifts right
Decrease in money supply	*LM* shifts left
Increase in price level	*LM* shifts left
Decrease in price level	*LM* shifts right
Increase in demand for money	*LM* shifts left
Decrease in demand for money	*LM* shifts right

Price Levels

Since we have not explicitly discussed price-level changes, some explanation is necessary to account for shifts in the *LM* line following a change in the price level. In the *LM* analysis it is the demand for, and supply of, real money balances (M/P) that are being analysed. Thus, a rise in the price level will reduce M/P, which is equivalent to saying that the supply of real money balances has fallen.

Self-Assessment Questions

Draw an *IS* and *LM* system. Now work out what will happen to the level of income if:

(a) an increase in government spending is financed by an increase in the money supply.
(b) there is a decrease in investment spending.
(c) savings increase.

The listing above, showing what happens to the *IS* and *LM* lines following a particular change in the economic environment, can be thought of as a ready reckoner. Decision-makers are able to work out how interest rates and incomes might change. Emphasis is placed on 'might'. In economics we can only make probabalistic statements. That is to say we can make statements of the kind 'if *X* happens and everything else remains constant then there is a chance that *Y* will occur'. Now, we know that other things do not remain constant and so we need to balance up all of these different influences and work out what the net effect will be. In reality this is not possible as a paper and pencil exercise of drawing *IS* and *LM* lines and shifting them on the page. If both the *IS* and *LM* lines are moving at the same time, where the economy ends up in terms of national income and the interest rate will depend upon whether the *LM* line moves further than the *IS* line. We can only know the size of these movements if we have detailed knowledge about how the economy behaves. It is the task of the professional economist to generate information about the behaviour of the economy and to assign values to the *IS* and *LM* functions.

However, without being a professional economist it is possible to obtain an intuitive idea of how the economy might respond to changes such as investment spending. The simple model set out above gives decision-makers the ability to form a view about what might happen to their decision variables (e.g. interest rate). This is the purpose of presenting this model to you.

The Multiplier in the *IS–LM* Model

You will recall that the change in income following a change in autonomous spending is a multiple of that change. In Figure 4.9 the shift from E_0 to E_2 (i.e. the change in income) is equal to $\triangle e_0 (1 - e_y)$. This is brought about by a shift in the *IS* curve (from IS_0 to IS_1). However, this multiple change in income assumes that interest rates remain constant at r_0. With a rising *LM* curve (LM_0), as the *IS* curve moves out then interest rates will rise. Why do interest rates rise? The LM_0 curve is drawn for a fixed money supply. As incomes rise following the injection of additional spending ($\triangle e_0$), then the demand for money rises. A rising demand for money with a fixed money supply can only be accommodated if the price of money (i.e. the interest rate) rises.

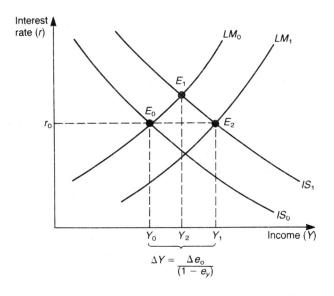

Figure 4.9

Because the money supply is fixed and the *LM* curve is upward-sloping, the economy will come to equilibrium at E_1, not E_2. As the interest rate rises, interest-sensitive expenditures, such as investment, are cut back. Thus the initial expansion in incomes generated by the injection of new spending is reduced by the impact of rising interest rates on expenditures elsewhere in the economy. The multiplier is now smaller since incomes rise from Y_0 to Y_2. To obtain the full impact of the multiplier would require the money supply to increase (i.e. for LM_0 to move to LM_1).

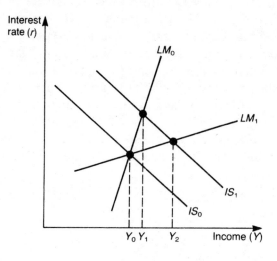

Figure 4.10

The impact of rising interest rates on the multiplier will depend upon the slope of the LM curve (see Figure 4.10). For LM_0 the expansion on income following a shift from IS_0 to IS_1 is $(Y_1 - Y_0)$, whereas for LM_1 it is greater $(Y_2 - Y_0)$. The nature of the slope of the LM curve is hotly disputed amongst economists:

(a) those who follow Milton Friedman argue that the demand for money is not sensitive (elastic) to the rate of interest. They argue that the demand for money depends only upon income levels. Money is only held for transactions purposes and not as a store of wealth. In this case the LM curve will be vertical.

(b) Keynesian economists dispute the claim that the demand for money is insensitive to the rate of interest. They therefore believe that the LM curve is upward-sloping.

Who is correct? We could only answer this with reference to empirical evidence, but that which exists is inconclusive and so the debate goes on.

Self-Assessment Question

Draw an IS and LM system in which the LM curve is vertical. Show that the expenditure multiplier in this system is zero. If the actual level of income in this system is below the full-employment level, what is the only way that the economy will get closer to full employment?

Further Reading

Gapinski, J. H. (1982) *Macroeconomic Theory: Statics, Dynamics and Policy* McGraw-Hill, New York.
Levacic, R. and Rebmann, A. (1982) *Macroeconomics*, London: Macmillan.

5

The Aggregate Demand and Supply Model

5.1 AGGREGATE DEMAND

The *IS* and *LM* curves describe the demand side of an economy, since lying behind the *IS* curves are all expenditures which are made effective through the supply of money balances for transactions purposes. The interaction of *IS* and *LM* determine the interest rate and level of output that are consistent with incomes being equal to expenditures and with the demand for money being equal to the supply of money. But the *LM* curve also depends upon the price level, because it is the demand for *real* money balances to fund real expenditures that is of interest ot us. If the price level changes (and these changes need not concern us now) then there will be a change in the value of real money balances (M/P).

This means that we draw the *LM* curve for different values of the price level: see Figure 5.1. Thus, if the nominal value of money balances is 1000 units and the price level is 25, then the value of real money balances is $1000/25 = 400$ units. Keeping the nominal value of money balances constant at 1000 units, now raise the price level to 50. The value of real money balances falls to 200 units. Thus, a change in the price level is equivalent to a change in the real money supply. That is to say, a change in the price level will cause the *LM* curve to shift.

Now turn to the *IS* curve in Figure 5.1. Recall that all points that lie along the *IS* curve are equilibria where expenditures equal incomes. The point of intersection between *IS* and *LM* gives us a value for the

76

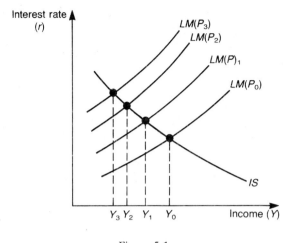

Figure 5.1

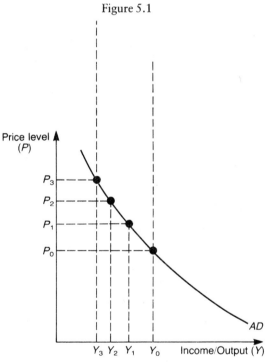

Figure 5.2

equilibrium level of output for the economy. As the price level changes in Figure 5.1, the *LM* curves sweep across the *IS* curve. Thus, for each level of prices, say P_0, there is a corresponding value for equilibrium output, say Y_0, where $IS = LM$. By varying the price level we can read off different values for Y at the points of intersection between IS and LM. In Figure 5.1 we have the combinations (P_0, Y_0), (P_1, Y_1), (P_2, Y_2), (P_3, Y_3). These combinations of price level (P) and equilibrium output (Y) are now plotted in Figure 5.2.

This curve, which is traced out, is called the aggregate demand curve for the economy (AD). Notice that it is drawn for a fixed IS curve in Figure 5.1. If the IS curve were to shift, the aggregate demand curve would shift too. Also, if the LM curve shifts for any reason other than that the price level has changed, then the aggregate demand curve will change. We demonstrate this in Figure 5.3.

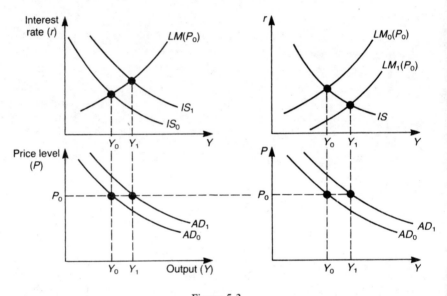

Figure 5.3

Anything that shifts the IS and LM curve, other than a change in the price level, will shift the AD curve.

Self-Assessment Questions

Show what will happen to the aggregate demand curve if (all other things remaining equal):

(a) government spending increases.
(b) taxation falls.

(c) savings increase.
(d) the central bank increases the real money stock.

5.2 AGGREGATE SUPPLY

Having answered the question of what determines aggregate demand in the economy, let us now turn to the supply side and ask what determines aggregate supply in an economy. Three principal factors determine aggregate supply. They are:

(1) The supply of labour – the number of people available for work and their productivity. The larger the supply of labour is, the more output can be produced. The more productive the labour force is, the greater the volume of output that can be supplied with a given stock of labour.

(2) The supply of capital – i.e. the amount of equipment, plant, machinery and land. The greater the capacity of the capital stock, the greater the volume of output that can be produced. Also, the more technically sophisticated (i.e. productive) the capital used, then the greater is the volume of output that can be produced.

(3) Technologies – new technology expands the capabilities of both the stock of labour and the stock of capital, to produce more output.

Actual and Potential Aggregate Supply

We need to distinguish between *actual* aggregate supply and *potential* aggregate supply. The potential supply of the economy (also called **potential output**) is that level of output that could be supplied if labour and capital were working at full capacity. It is an upper limit on the economy, given the existing stock of labour and capital and the existing state of technology. If the economy is operating at the potential level of output, then all of those who wish to work and who are eligible for work will be in employment. Thus, we can define the potential level of output of the economy as the full-employment level of output.

Increasing Labour

What does the supply of labour depend upon? If the real wage

79

increases then more people can be persuaded to supply more hours of work to the economy. At a higher real wage they will be prepared to trade in (give up) some of their leisure time in order to increase their real incomes (income = real wage *times* the number of hours worked). Of course it is not income that they are trading off against leisure. It is instead the real value of the goods and services which that income will purchase that is being set off against the value of leisure time.

Another factor that will bring about an increase in the supply of labour is, of course, population growth. Technological change, which improves labour productivity, and the training of labour in new skills will also produce changes in the supply of labour. A doubling of one person's productivity is equivalent to doubling the size of the labour force whilst keeping productivity constant.

For example, let us say that one person produces 100 units of output per week; after a productivity improvement the same person now produces 200 units of output per week. But if we keep productivity constant and double the labour force, we also get 200 units of output per week.

Productivity improvements, technological change, population growth and increases in the capital stock all take time to bring about. Thus, these tend to be the *long-run* determinants of aggregate supply and are treated later when we consider the growth and development of the economy. In the meantime, the *short-run* aggregate supply of the economy depends upon the changes in the supply of hours of work that are made available by the existing labour force and this, in turn, depends upon the real wage.

Economists have two alternative theories of aggregate supply to choose from. The differences between each theory are of importance because they highlight different perspectives about how the economy behaves. Those differences will also determine how a government will choose to respond to a disturbance in the economy, that is to say, the differences between the theories of aggregate supply will have important influences upon the design of economic policy.

5.3 THE CLASSICAL THEORY OF AGGREGATE SUPPLY

Let us begin with one of the oldest theories of aggregate supply – the classical theory. In recent years a group of economists have made this

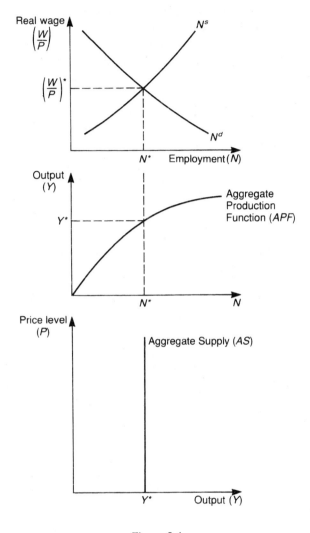

Figure 5.4

theory popular once again. The classical view is that all markets in an economy are in equilibrium. If there is a shock to the economic system, which causes a disequilibrium in a market so that demand is not equal to supply, then powerful economic forces come into effect very quickly and restore that equilibrium. In particular, prices adjust rapidly, bringing demand and supply into equality. The view which underlies the classical theory is, therefore, one which believes that the economy is made up of efficiently operating markets that are very flexible and with rapidly adjusting prices. Indeed, the modern classical theory is often referred to as being a 'flexprice' model.

If all markets are in equilibrium (according to the classical flexprice model) then it means that the labour market must be in equilibrium also. Any disequilibrium will immediately be corrected because the price of labour (i.e. the real wage) will adjust. If the labour market is always in equilibrium then this means that everyone who wants to work is working. The economy must, therefore, always be at full employment. There can be no unemployment. If anyone isn't working, it is because they have chosen not to. That is to say, they are voluntarily unemployed. (If you are thinking that these are extreme views you are probably correct.)

The classical view of aggregate supply is shown in Figure 5.4. The top part of the figure shows the labour market: N^d is the demand for labour. If we assume that profit-maximising firms hire labour, then as the real wage falls firms will find it to their advantage to take on more workers and produce more output. Hence the demand for labour line (N^d) slopes down from left to right. A profit-maximising firm will hire labour up to the point at which the value of the extra unit of output sold is equal to the real wage paid to the extra unit of labour that produced the output.

Real Wages

The supply of labour also depends upon the real wage. As was pointed out earlier, workers will supply more hours of work and give up their leisure time if the real wage rises. Hence the labour supply line (N^s) slopes upwards from left to right. As the real wage rises, individuals can afford to purchase more goods and services. They are really deciding to consume more of these goods and services and to take less leisure time when they make the decision to supply more hours of work.

At the point of intersection between N^d and N^s the labour market is in equilibrium. The equilibrium real wage is W/P^* and the equilibrium level of employment is N^*.

The Production Function

The middle section of Figure 5.4 shows the aggregate production function (APF) for the whole economy. This shows the relationship between total output (Y) and the level of employment (N) in the short run (i.e. keeping the stock of capital and technology constant). As N increases, Y increases also. The production function is not a straight line but is curved, as shown in the Figure. This demonstrates diminishing returns to the fixed factor, capital. The level of output that corresponds to full-employment equilibrium in the labour market (N^*) is Y^*.

Now suppose that the price level rises. The classical economists argue that the nominal wage rate (W) will adjust after a change in the price level in order to keep the real wage constant at the equilibrium level now (W/P)*. If the world does behave in this way (i.e. flexible nominal wages always adjusting rapidly to keep the labour market in equilibrium) then the economy will always be at its full-employment level of output, Y^*.

The **full-employment level of output** is often called the potential output of the economy or the 'natural' or equilibrium level of output. At the full-employment level of output, any unemployment which might exist is voluntary and is referred to as the 'natural' rate of unemployment. Because the level of output for the economy is always at full employment, it will not vary as the price level changes. The economy is always producing its full-employment level of output. Therefore the aggregate supply curve is vertical, as is shown in the bottom part of Figure 5.4.

5.4 THE KEYNESIAN THEORY OF AGGREGATE SUPPLY

Keynes, and Keynesian economists thereafter, disputed this approach to analysing economic behaviour. It is clear that all unemployment is not voluntary. There are many who wish to work but cannot find work. How do we account for this?

The approach which Keynesians adopt is to point out that we don't live in a perfectly efficient 'flexprice' world. Different prices adjust at different speeds. Some adjust very rapidly whilst others are slow to change. Interest rates and exchange rates tend to change quickly but wage rates do not. Thus, for example, if the money wage rate is W_0 and the price level is P_0 and if the real wage (W_0/P_0) is the full-employment real wage then the labour market is in equilibrium as is shown in Figure 5.5.

Assume now that the price level falls from P_0 to P_1. This means that the real wage will rise to (W_0/P_1). In this case, compared to the classical case, the money wage (W_0) does not adjust but remains fixed at W_0. We say that money wages are 'sticky'. At the new real wage (W_0/P_1) the demand for labour falls back to N_1: at a higher real wage, business firms will not wish to hire as many workers. But the higher real wage brings forth an increase in the supply of labour to N_2. At the new real wage (W_0/P_1), N_2 workers are willing to work. Unemployment is equal to the difference between the supply of labour N_2 and the demand for labour N_1, i.e. $N_2 - N_1$.

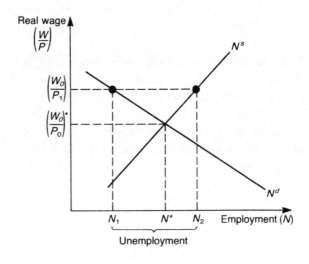

Figure 5.5

Unemployment can therefore arise because money wages are inflexible (sticky). Why don't money wages adjust rapidly in order to bring the labour market back into equilibrium at full employment? This is a complex question to answer. From the total economy's point of view it would appear to be rational to have perfectly adjusting money wages. But from the point of view of individuals supplying labour or businessmen hiring labour it need not be rational. This is an example of individual rationality not squaring up with collective (group) rationality.

Employment Investment

Employment is an important investment decision for the firm. A business firm invests many resources in hiring, selecting and training its workforce. It also invests in goodwill with its workforce in order to create a climate of good morale. Equally, employees in a company invest in their employment with that company.

They will have spent time searching (ie. job search) for a job that offers them a wage and working conditions that they prefer. Also, they will have invested their own time in being trained in skills that are very specific to the company and they will have purchased houses in the locality. Employees, therefore, get tied into a specific company because their skills are specific to that company and they get tied into a local community.

It is for these reasons that firms and individuals will not wish to make frequent adjustments to the money wage rate. If a firm responds to a change in the price level by adjusting the money wage of its employees then it will gain a reputation of poor industrial relations, morale will be low, and it will lose its best (productive) workers who will go off and work for other firms (probably competitors). Thus, there tends to be an implicit agreement (sometimes called an implicit contract), based on an 'invisible handshake' between a company and its key employees, which states that money wages will not adjust rapidly in a downward direction.

A number of points now need to be clarified. If real wages are slow to adjust because money wages are inflexible, how can the firm respond?

(1) It tends to be the money wages of key workers (i.e. those who are important to the long-run profitability and survival of the company) that are inflexible.
(2) As real wages rise then the firm lays off workers. This means that overtime is cut back and low-skilled non-essential staff are paid off.
(3) Inflexible money wages doesn't mean that money wages don't adjust. Rather it means that they adjust slowly, relative to the price level. It is not a rapid flexible adjustment as happens in the classical model.

The Keynesian Aggregate Supply Curve

Let us now try to put what we have learned into an aggregate supply diagram. Figure 5.6 shows an aggregate supply curve made up of three

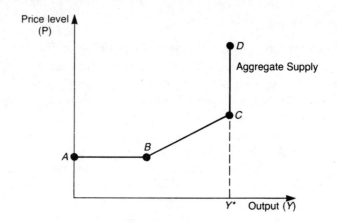

Figure 5.6

segments AB, BC and CD. The segment along CD is the full-capacity or full-employment aggregate supply curve. This corresponds to the physical limits in the economy. Because labour and capital are fully employed, the economy cannot produce any more output beyond this point. Keynesians recognise this limit.

Before the full-employment limit is reached, Keynesians argue that there is a segment of the aggregate supply curve, BC, which is upward-sloping. Along BC, money wages do not adjust as quickly as the price level. Firms can therefore adjust by producing more output and hiring more labour. Along AB, prices are completely inflexible. Output and employment change without prices changing.

Let us now put the aggregate demand and aggregate supply curves together in Figure 5.7. Take an aggregate demand curve AD_0. Suppose investment spending increases. This will increase expenditures and demand in the economy, so the aggregate demand curve moves from AD_0 to AD_1. As aggregate demand increases, firms produce more output to meet this extra demand and also hire more labour. Output rises from Y_0 to Y_1. But prices will also be rising and this is shown as the move from P_0 to P_1. Why do price levels rise? The extra demand in the economy puts pressure onto markets and prices are bid upwards. But if the price level rises faster than money wages then the real wage will fall and firms will hire more labour. Thus, an increase of aggregate demand over the range BC will result in both an increase in output and an increase in the price level.

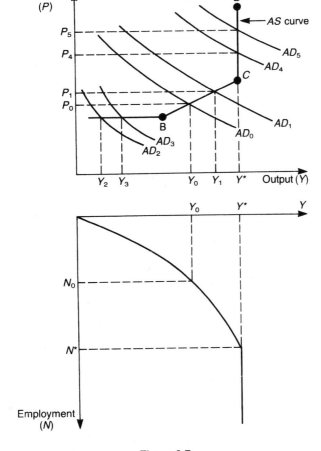

Figure 5.7

Compare this with a shift in demand from AD_2 to AD_3 over the range AB of the aggregate supply curve. In this case, because prices are inflexible, all of the increase in demand comes through as an increase in output, i.e. Y_2 up to Y_3. This is in contrast to the full-employment range CD. Because the economy has reached its physical capacity constraint – it cannot increase output beyond Y^* – then all of the pressure of the increase in demand from AD_4 to AD_5 shows up as a price-level increase from P_4 to P_5.

By recognising that different prices (including money wages) adjust at different speeds, the Keynesian theory of aggregate supply produces a much wider range of supply responses, which are shown by the different segments of the aggregate supply curve. If we want to know what happens to the economy following a change in aggregate demand, it is necessary to know where the economy is located on the aggregate supply curve.

Self-Assessment Questions

(a) Show what will happen to the price level and the level of output following a cut in taxes if the economy is located along the segment AB of its aggregate supply curve.
(b) What will happen if the money supply is increased and the economy is located along the segment AB of its aggregate supply curve?
(c) What will happen if investment spending is increased and the economy is located along the segment BC of its aggregate supply curve?
(d) What happens if government spending is cut and the economy is located along the segment BC of its aggregate supply curve?

Keynesian Unemployment

In the classical model unemployment was caused because real wages were too high. Look back at Figure 5.5. The real wage (W_0/P_1) lies above the equilibrium real wage $(W_0/P_0)^*$.

Full employment is restored by a reduction in the real wage. Keynes, however, argued that because money wages are inflexible it will probably take a long time for the economy to adjust to full employment via real wage adjustments.

However, an inappropriate real wage is not the only cause of unemployment. If the level of demand is too low then the actual level of unemployment will be below the full-employment level. Firms produce output and hire labour to meet the market demand for their products. The aggregate demand curve is the addition of all individual demands in the economy and the aggregate supply curve is the addition of all supply responses by firms. A low level of demand in the economy will mean that many individual firms will have excess capacity (unused capital). If demand was to increase, these firms could hire more labour and use up the excess capacity. Thus in Figure 5.7, if aggregate demand is AD_0, then the level of output is Y_0 and the level of employment is N_0 which is below the full-employment level N^*.

Unemployment is, therefore, $N^* - N_0$. Unemployment in this Keynesian model is caused by demand deficiency. It could be reduced if aggregate demand was increased to AD_6.

By concentrating upon demand deficiency, therefore, the Keynesian theory of unemployment suggests that governments can have a role in macroeconomic policy-making by adjusting the level of aggregate demand – this is called 'demand management' policy and is developed later when we discuss fiscal and monetary policies. In the meantime you should consider using the aggregate demand and aggregate supply model to analyse what might happen if the government does certain things. In essence, you have already done this with the last Self-Assessment Questions. Now go through the exercise again but this time think about the government introducing the changes in order to manage aggregate demand and affect the level of employment.

Self-Assessment Questions

What will happen to aggregate demand, output and employment over the segment BC of the aggregate supply curve if the government:

(a) increases government expenditures?
(b) reduces taxation?
(c) increases the money supply?

Are Prices and Wages Inflexible?

If we observe the way in which actual prices are determined in an economy we find that it is not as simple as elementary economics suggests. This will come as no surprise to decision-makers who are in the business of making prices. The demand and supply model of the market-place either tells a very short-run story of price determination in auction or commodity markets (e.g. for raw materials such as peanuts, wheat, tin, copper, etc.) or it gives an idea of where the long-run price of a commodity will settle once the forces of demand and supply have worked their way through the system.

Prices do not adjust instantly. Demand and supply are seldom equal to one another. The plans of consumers (demand) do not match up to the plans of producers (supply). In a simple world we might expect prices to adjust in order to bring them into line, but what Keynesian economists (in comparison to classical economists) argue is that in the short run prices will not adjust; it is quantities that will adjust. Prices will adjust in the longer run.

Why might prices be slow to adjust? A number of reasons can be given. First, there are costs of making adjustments. Setting prices is an activity that is costly. It involves obtaining information about the imbalance between demand and supply and computing that information. Search for data and the computation of data are time-consuming and costly. Once the new prices have been determined, employees have to be informed. In a complex organisation, which has many branches spread over many different locations, informing employees is not a costless exercise. Restaurants cannot afford to print revised menus every few minutes, and mail order companies cannot send out new catalogues every day.

Having changed prices, firms cannot be sure that they have got it right. Demand and supply are changing all the time. In order to cope with this uncertainty and the risk of getting the price too wrong, firms make incremental adjustments. Moreover, they adjust slowly. Thus, sluggish prices may be the result of risk-reducing tactics. In an attempt to reduce risks some firms may enter into long-term contracts. Buyers agree to purchase certain quantities at specified prices and times and sellers agree to do likewise. Such long-run agreements mean that neither side to the buyer/seller relationship exploits temporary swings in demand or supply. It also means that prices are inflexible in the short run.

Implicit labour contracts, based upon an 'invisible handshake', characterise many parts of the labour market. Wages do not adjust quickly in response to variations in demand and supply. We have already seen that, for reasons of maintaining good morale amongst the workforce and good industrial relations, firms will not make frequent adjustments to wage rates. This does not mean that *incomes* (i.e. hours worked multiplied by the wage rate) do not fluctuate. Hours worked, especially overtime, can be and are adjusted.

Market Structure

Another reason for price rigidity is market structure. Flexible prices are associated with perfect markets. However, in monopolies and oligopolistic markets we would expect prices to be less flexible. Many large sections of modern economies seem to be characterised by oligopoly or monopoly. Thus, steel companies and automobile companies have considerable discretion in setting their prices. Oligopolistic firms set prices in order to serve the long-run interests of the industry. Prices are not set so high that excess profit will invite entry of new competitors, nor are they set so low that shareholders will get upset. The pricing rule used in such markets is usually a mark-up on costs that maintains healthy but not excessive profits. Costs, rather than demand and supply, are the main determinants of price. Price changes that are unrelated to costs produce knock-on effects that are damaging to firms in the industry. Such price rises, which swell profits, anger consumers and thereby threaten to erode goodwill, and also signal to employees that demands for higher wages should be made. Price rises which make significant increases in profits will also attract new entrants into the industry.

What about price reductions in oligopolistic markets? If one firm reduces its price then all others in the industry will follow; market shares remain the same and the industry as a whole ends up with lower prices and lower absolute profit levels. Price wars in oligopolistic markets tend to be self-destructive. So the battle for market shares focuses on non-price factors such as advertising and product innovations.

Flexible Prices

Suppose that prices were flexible and did fluctuate. Consumers would simply wait until prices were at their lowest. Indeed, by postponing their consumption, the firm's demand would be at its weakest and prices would fall. A rational firm will maintain stable prices despite daily fluctuations in demand. This discourages consumers adopting strategies of the kind described above.

For the reasons given above, prices are likely to be much less flexible than is commonly supposed in those macroeconomic models which are based upon the classical assumptions of perfectly competitive markets.

Classical versus Keynesian Theories of Aggregate Supply

When choosing between classical and Keynesian models we need to be clear about our beliefs as to how we think the economy behaves. In the short run is it prices that adjust first, followed by quantity adjustments, as in the classical model? Or do quantities adjust in the short run whilst prices eventually adjust in the long run, as Keynesians believe?

The Keynesian view is that the economy is always out of equilibrium (i.e. is always in disequilibrium). To be always in equilibrium requires that decision-makers have a lot more information upon which to base their consumption and production plans than generally exists. Information is not perfect because to be informed is costly – information is not free. Resources are spent on gathering data and computing and analysing results. Information is a scarce commodity which gives some groups a competitive advantage. This means that they will not give away the information to all groups.

Decision-makers are not perfectly informed, which is another way of saying that they do not have information about the plans of other decision-makers. Firms do not know exactly what the consumption and savings plans of households are. Therefore, firms plan output in a climate of uncertainty, not knowing exactly if they will be able to sell all of their output at the prices they have chosen. Equally, when households make spending and savings decisions they do not know what their incomes will be, which is another way of saying that they do not know if firms will purchase all of the labour that the household has to sell at the prevailing wage rate.

If the plans of firms and households do not fit together then the outcome will be disequilibrium: planned consumption and savings will not be equal to actual consumption and savings; planned output and investment will not be equal to actual output and investment. When the economy is out of equilibrium, utility-maximising individuals and profit-maximising firms will adjust in order to improve upon their situation and get closer to the desired objectives of their plans. It is this continuous search for improvement upon the current situation which drives the economy through time.

5.5 THE NEW CLASSICAL THEORY OF AGGREGATE SUPPLY

We finally turn to the theory of aggregate supply proposed by monetarist and New Classical economists. One assumption, which lies at the heart of many models used by economists, is that individuals are perfectly informed. When making decisions and plans about how much to produce, how much to consume, how much labour to supply and how much to invest, those who are taking these decisions are assumed to have all of the relevant information at their disposal. This is another way of saying that information is freely available – its cost is zero or almost zero. Clearly this is not so. Information is not freely available. Some individuals in the decision process have information that gives them a competitive advantage and they are not going to give that up to others. Thus, there is not an equal distribution of information throughout the economy. Also, information is costly to acquire. There are search costs, i.e. the basic costs of time and effort involved in data collection; then there are the computing costs of relating bits of data in order to generate information. What does the fact that individuals are not perfectly informed mean for macroeconomic models?

Those who supply labour know the money wage rate (W) but not the price level (P). Therefore they do not know the real wage (W/P). Why do they not know the price level? The price level ruling in the current time-period can only be known in future time-periods (e.g. next year), once the statisticians have collected all the data on prices and computed the price level. Stop and ask yourself, do you know the index of prices that will enable you to compute your real income today? If the real wage rate is not known then the labour supply decision might be wrong. Recall that the supply of labour depends upon the real wage. Suppose individuals estimate what the price level (P) might be and further suppose that it is below the actual price level. Then the real wage will be overestimated and there will be an oversupply of labour. Firms hire the labour. When the overestimated real wages are spent in the shops, workers quickly find that they have made a mistake.

They learn about the true level of real wages and then cut back their supply of labour. This, according to the New Classical economists, explains the expansions and contractions in the economy.

Let us see this in more detail in Figure 5.8. In Figure 5.8 the long-run aggregate supply curve for the economy is shown ($LRAS$). This corresponds with the natural level of output (or full-employment level of output) Y_f. The line SAS_0 is the short-run aggregate supply curve, which now needs to be explained. Workers form expectations about what the price level is. Assume we start in equilibrium with a price level of P_0. Individuals' expectations are that the future price level will be P_0^e, where e stands for 'expected'. Now, suppose that for whatever reason the price level rises. If workers keep to their expectation (P_0^e) then the real wage is wrong, they will overestimate the price level and oversupply labour. This means that the economy moves along the SAS, (P_0^e) line up to a point such as Y_1 when workers discover the mistake that they have made, i.e. that the price level is P_1 and not P_0. They then adjust by cutting back on their labour supply and so the economy moves back to Y_f to some point such as A. They form new expectations of the price level (P_1), so that if the price level again rises to P_2, this time the economy will move along the new SAS (P_1^e) line, and so on.

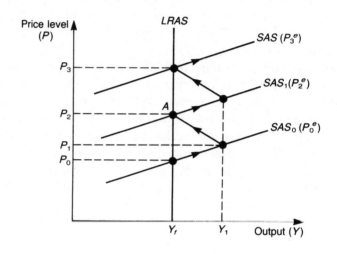

Figure 5.8

The Role of Expectations

The previous discussion depended upon the concept of expectations. What do we mean by expectations, how are expectations formed and what role do they play?

When individuals make decisions they face complex and uncertain environments. They do not know how the economy is going to unfold over time. Decisions taken today have important implications for the future and yet the future is only known imperfectly. Not only do decisions made today affect the future but that future will affect the decisions that are made today. How do decision-makers cope with this uncertainty? One way is to take a view about what the future might look like, i.e. to form an expectation of future events. What do we expect the price level to be in 12 months' time: What do we expect interest rates and exchange rates to be next month? If we are to understand decision-making, we must understand how individuals form expectations.

Adaptive Expectations

Studies of individuals' expectations tend to suggest that their know-ledge of what is happening to economic variables is less than perfect. Whilst they might have a sense of what is happening to the direction of change in a variable such as unemployment or the inflation rate (i.e. is it going up or down), they generally do not know by how much it has changed (i.e. was it + 5% or − 10%?). One approach to thinking about expectations is to view them as being **adaptive expectations**, i.e. individuals form expectations about the values to be placed upon future economic events by looking at past values. Thus, if we were to decide what we expect the rate of inflation is gong to be in six months' time we might look at values for the rate of inflation for each month over the past two years. In forming our expectations we would pay more attention to what has been happening to inflation in the more recent months, over our two-year period, than the earlier months. Our expectations are thus formed as a weighted average of previous values of the variable about which we are forming expectations, with greater weight being given to more recent values. Thus we *adapt* our expectations as more recent information becomes available. In this approach, expectations of the future depend upon our knowledge of the past and our presumption is that the future will not be radically different from the past. This approach to the modelling of expecta-tions is favoured by monetarist economists like Milton Friedman.

Rational Expectations

Individuals using adaptive expectations will, by definition, make errors. The future does not always turn out as we expect. One question is why? Individuals learn from their mistakes and if there is a systematic error, rather than just random error, then it is rational for individuals to take this knowledge of the systematic error into account when forming expectations. Adaptive expectations would, therefore, be adjusted to take into account our knowledge of the systematic error. Expectations which take into account as much information as the decision-maker has at his disposal are called **rational expectations**. This information will include information about the past but it will also include forecast information. Decision-makers do have models (no matter how simple and crude) which summarise their beliefs about how the economy behaves. It is from these models that they work out the systematic error. It would be foolish to ignore the information that such models provide when individuals form expectations.

Some approaches to rational expectations are somewhat extreme and it is a mistake to criticise the notion of rational expectations rather than these extreme approaches. New Classical economists have assumed that, when making decisions, economic agents have more information than they possess in reality, in particular that they have models of the economy which will provide forecast information. Whilst this might be true of some decision-makers, the majority have highly imperfect or non-existent models to help them to predict the future. Nevertheless, individuals can form rational expectations by taking into account highly imperfect forecasts of the future. Rational expectations do not imply perfect information, although more extreme versions do.

One extreme version of rational expectations is that used by the New Classical economists, who couple the assumption of perfectly informed rational expectations with the flexprice model of perfect competition. In this case individuals have a perfect forecasting model and are able to form expectations of future values of economic variables such as the price level. There are no systematic errors in their forecast of the price level – these have been learned from in the past and have been incorporated into the model. Thus, expectations of the price level are consistent with the actual price level and the economy lies along the long-run aggregate supply curve. An economy in which perfectly informed decision-makers make rational expectations will always be in equilibrium.

If the perfect information assumption is dropped and individuals are assumed to make mistakes, and if, furthermore, markets are not assumed to be perfect but are instead characterised by sticky prices, then the economy will be out of equilibrium and will only adjust slowly to its equilibrium. Out-of-equilibrium behaviour is that which describes real economies and the reasons for this can now be stated simply:

(1) Individuals do not have perfect information when they make decisions and design their plans.

(2) Individuals' knowledge of the future is incomplete. When they form expectations they make mistakes. One person's mistake is another person's information and so mistakes become compounded.

(3) Whilst individuals learn from their mistakes it might take some time to do so and having learned from them there is no guarantee that future mistakes will not be made because the structure of the present economy is constantly changing, which means that the future is always unknowable.

(4) Prices are not flexible but are, for all the reasons given earlier, sticky. This means that the speed at which the economy adjusts is slower than the flexprice model would predict.

Anticipated versus Unanticipated changes in Aggregate Demand

If economic agents form the expectations adaptively, then following an increase in aggregate demand, the economy will initially move from P_0, Y_f, to P_1, Y_1 in Figure 5.9, as the actual price level moves above the expected price level. As expectations gradually adjust, so the SAS schedule will move upwards from SAS (P_0^e) with the economy finally settling at P_2, Y_f, where actual and expected prices are once again equal, i.e. $P^e = P_2$.

If expectations are formed rationally, however, this process of adjustment will apply only to an unanticipated change in aggregate demand, i.e. a change which could not have been forseen by rational

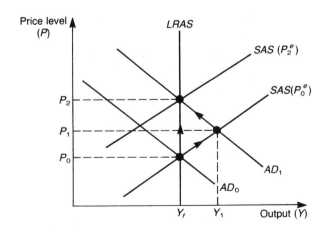

Figure 5.9

agents, so causing their rational expectation of the price level to be an underestimate of the actual price level.

If, on the other hand, the increase in aggregate demand from AD_0 to AD_1 is fully anticipated, then agents will immediately revise their expectation of the price level from P_0 to P_2, so that the SAS schedule shifts from $SAS(P_0^e)$ to $SAS(P_2^e)$ without prices first having to rise. In this latter case, the change in aggregate demand has no impact on output, but only leads to a rise in the price level.

Self-Assessment Question

Using this analysis, show the effects on output and the price level in the short run *and* the long run of an unanticipated fall in aggregate demand, assuming rational expectations.

5.6 SUMMARY

The analysis of aggregate demand and supply has taken us a long way from the simple income and expenditure model that we started off with. What we learned from the income and expenditure model is contained in the aggregate demand curve. We now have a model which shows the interdependencies in an economy. If we change one part of the economy, this sets up a chain reaction of changes that work their way through the economy via multipliers. We have seen how the level of output and the rate of interest are determined in the IS/LM model and how output, employment and the price level are determined in the AD/AS model.

We have also seen that the outcome of changes in aggregate demand depends critically upon the flexibility of prices and wages and the way in which expectations are formed. At one extreme, Keynesians assume price and wage rigidity below full employment, so that only quantities (output, employment) adjust. At the other extreme, New Classical economists assume price and wage flexibility and rational expectations, with the result that anticipated changes in aggregate demand affect only nominal magnitudes (prices, wages), leaving quantities unaffected. Only in the most extreme situation, however, in which all prices and wages adjusted instantaneously and agents had perfect information about the future (in effect, perfect foresight) would the economy be continuously in equilibrium at Y_f. In general, therefore, the economy will tend to be in disequilibrium, with economists from different schools of thought divided over the speed at which equilibrium is reattained.

Further Reading

Gordon, R. (1987) *Macroeconomics*, Little, Brown and Company, Boston.
Brown, W. (1988) *Macroeconomics*, Prentice-Hall, New Jersey.

Part III

DOMESTIC MACROECONOMIC PROBLEMS

6

Business Cycles

Chapter 5 concluded with the idea that an economy is usually out of equilibrium and that decision-makers seek an improvement upon their current situation. If we examine time series of economic data, what we tend to observe are cyclical fluctuations in unemployment, the change in *annual* real output, interest rates, etc. These fluctuations are referred to as the **trade cycle** or the **business cycle**. Economists have examined such cycles in the hope that they might find a regularity in the pattern of the cycles. For example, is the distance between the peaks of the cycle five years? If there is a regular occurrence to the cycle then it would be possible to predict when the economy is going to move into a slump.

Unfortunately, no regularity in cycles has been found. This is not too surprising. Economies are highly complex interactive systems. They are not mechanical models with built-in physical laws just waiting to be discovered. Indeed, if such regular patterns did exist, decision-makers would learn about these regularities and this would influence the timing of their decisions, i.e. they would not wish to be caught in a slump and so would stop investing before the slump takes place. The very act of not investing would bring about the slump earlier and, therefore, destroy the regularity of the pattern. Information influences *expectations* of the future and expectations shape decisions.

6.1 THE PHASES OF THE BUSINESS CYCLE

The phases of a business or trade cycle are shown in Figure 6.1. As an economy moves through time it passes from slump through recovery and boom into recession. The level of real output fluctuates over time. The upward-sloping straight line shows potential output (full-employment output) which indicates that the full-employment level of output grows over time. In the analysis of the previous section the full-employment level of output (potential output level) was fixed. The size of the labour force, capital stock and the level of technology were all assumed to be fixed. Over time, however, these factors change. Population growth, investment in new capital goods and new scientific discoveries all add to the productive potential of the economy.

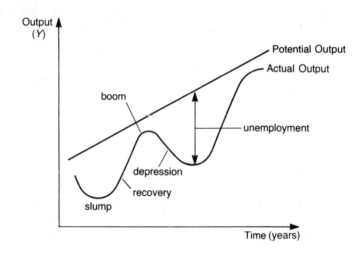

Figure 6.1

   Comparing the difference between the actual level of output and the potential level of output gives an index of unemployment. The greater the difference, the higher is unemployment. It can be seen that as the level of output fluctuates, the level of unemployment fluctuates also.

   When an economy moves into a slump or depression then aggregate demand falls and demand-deficient unemployment rises. Businessmen's expectations are that the recession will continue; they cut back on investment plans, cut back on output in order to reduce their inventories of unsold goods and cut back on employment. Profits fall and because the demand for borrowing for investment has declined, the rate of interest falls also. Businessmen's depressed expectations will keep the economy in a slump. Interest rates might reach such a low level that it becomes worthwhile investing again. The new investment stimulates demand, the economy begins to pick up momentum slowly; expectations of improvements emerge; more new investment takes place and so the economy comes out of the recession and moves into the recovery phase.

An economy can, however, get stuck in the depths of a slump for many years during which expectations are so depressed that the economy cannot pull round. The economic history of many countries records long periods of depression. During the 1920s and 1930s Britain was caught in the depths of a depression. In these instances a government will intervene and use increases in government spending and reductions in taxation in order to stimulate demand and create expansionary expectations.

As the economy passes through the recovery phase the level of output increases, unemployment falls, profits improve and firms, and hence the economy, get close to their capacity limits. At the top of the boom everyone is competing for loanable funds, and therefore interest rates rise, which choke off investment. As investment spending falls, the economy moves into the deflation phase and so the business cycle is set up. Also, in the boom phase because the economy is reaching its capacity limit everyone is competing for scarce resources and prices rise. Labour becomes more expensive as money wages chase rapidly rising prices. The boom withers out in inflation.

Business Cycles and the IS-LM Model

Cycles in the various variables can be illustrated using IS/LM analysis as in Figure 6.2. The economy starts off at the initial equilibrium (Y_0, r_0) at the point where the IS_0 and LM_0 curves intersect. Now shift the IS curve out to IS_1. This gives a new equilibrium which is plotted. Now shift the LM curve, first to LM_1 and then to LM_2. When LM_2 intersects the IS_1 curve it does so at full employment. Plotting the different equilibrium values of Y, r and N against time reveals the beginnings of a cycle.

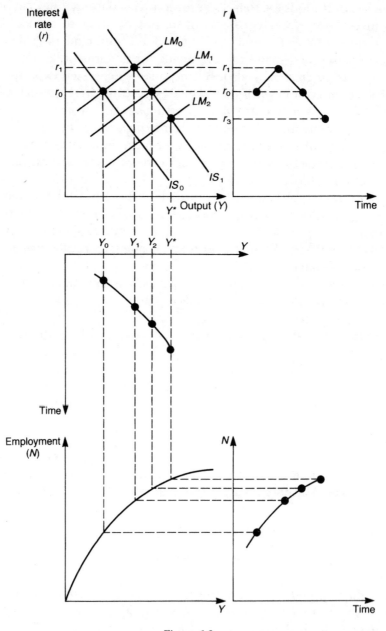

Figure 6.2

A number of different theories have been put forward to explain the existence of business cycles. We will concentrate on the Keynesian theory of the multiplier-acceleration interaction which was first proposed by Paul Samuelson in 1939.

6.2 MULTIPLIER-ACCELERATOR INTERACTION

The concept of the multiplier has already been introduced. Changes in autonomous spending, such as investment, cause changes in income. The concept of the accelerator is that investment depends on changes in income. Therefore, if we put the multiplier and accelerator theories together, we get an important interdependency in the economy. Changes in income depend upon changes in investment, and changes in investment depend upon changes in income. Both income and investment feed upon each other.

Let us now see how this interaction might generate cycles. A number of assumptions are necessary:

(a) The consumption function: consumption in the current period (t) depends on income in the previous period $(t - 1)$. This can be written most simply as:

$$C_t = c\, Y_{t-1}$$

In this simple consumption function c is both the average and the marginal propensity to consume.

(b) The accelerator: investment depends upon the change in national income, i.e. the difference between the income of the last period $(t - 1)$ and the income of the period before that $(t - 2)$. This can be written as:

$$I_t = I_0 + v\,(Y_{t-1} - Y_{t-2})$$

where I_0 is autonomous investment and v is the value of the accelerator.

Consider a very simple economy with no government and no foreign trade. Thus:

$$Y = C + I$$

Assume that, when we begin the model, income (Y) is 1 000 units, $c = 0.5$, $v = 0.5$, $I_0 = 500$ units. Therefore:

$$C_t = 0.5 \ Y_{t-1} = 500$$

$$I_t = 500 + 0.5 \ (Y_{t-1} - Y_{t-2}) = 500$$

$$Y_t = C_t + I_t = 1000$$

Now assume that, for whatever reason, autonomous investment increases by 10 units to 510. Then,

$$Y_{t+1} = C_{t-1} + I_{t+1}$$

$$= 500 + 510 = 1010$$

The rise in income from period t to period $t + 1$ causes consumption and investment to rise in the next time-period $(t + 2)$:

$$C_{t+2} = 0.5 \ Y_{t+1} = 505$$

$$I_{t+2} = 510 + 0.5 \ (Y_{t-1} - Y_t)$$

$$= 510 + 5 = 515$$

Thus:

$$Y_{t+2} = C_{t+1} + I_{t+2}$$

$$= 505 + 515 = 1020$$

This further rise in income will cause consumption and investment to rise further in period $(t + 3)$:

$$C_{t+3} = 0.5 \ Y_{t+2} = 510$$

$$I_{t+3} = 510 + 0.5 \ (Y_{t+2} - Y_{t+1}) = 515$$

Therefore:

$$Y_{t+3} = 510 + 515 = 1025$$

The next stages, up to $(t + 12)$, are shown in Table 6.1. After four time-periods income begins to fall and so investment falls and, via the multiplier, income will fall. A cycle has been set up. As you work your way through the example in the table you will observe that the cycle converges on a new equilibrium level of income equal to 1020. This is called a **convergent cycle** and is graphed in Figure 6.3.

Now consider an example in which the value of the accelerator (v) is 1.5. This is set out in Table 6.2. In this example the cycle does not converge on an equilibrium level of national income. Instead it is an **explosive cycle**.

Table 6.1

Time-period	Consumption $C_t = 0.5Y_{t-1}$	Investment $I_t = I_0 + 0.5\,(Y_{t-1} - Y_{t-2})$	National income $y_t = C_t + I_t$
t	500	500	1 000
$t + 1$	500	510	1 010
$t + 2$	505	515	1 020
$t + 3$	510	515	1 025
$t + 4$	512.5	512.5	1 025
$t + 5$	512.5	510	1 022.5
$t + 6$	511.25	508.75	1 020
$t + 7$	510	508.75	1 018.75
$t + 8$	509.375	509.375	1 018.75
$t + 9$	509.375	510	1 019.375
$t + 10$	509.6875	510.3125	1 020
$t + 11$	510	510.3125	1 020.3125
$t + 12$	510.15625	510.15625	1 020.3123
etc.	etc.	etc.	etc.

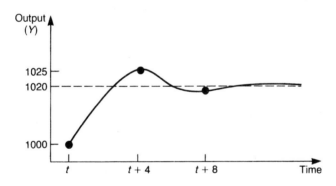

Figure 6.3

Self-Assessment Questions

Draw the graph of Y_t against time as set out in Table 6.1, and see for yourself that it is a convergent cycle that is set up.

Using the multiplier/accelerator model, trace out the time path of national income over 12 years, assuming that (a) $c = 0.8$ and $v = 0.1$;

Table 6.2

Time-period	Consumption $C_t = 0.5Y_{t-1}$	Investment $I_t = I_0 + 1.5(Y_{t-1} - Y_{t-2})$	National income $y_t = C_t + I_t$
t	500	500	1 000
$t + 1$	500	510	1 010
$t + 2$	505	525	1 030
$t + 3$	515	540	1 055
$t + 4$	527.5	547.5	1 075
$t + 5$	537.5	540	1 077.5
$t + 6$	538.75	513.75	1 052.5
$t + 7$	526.75	472.5	999.25
$t + 8$	499.63	430.12	920.75
$t + 9$	464.88	405.75	870.63
$t + 10$	435.31	421.31	856.62
$t + 11$	428.31	489	917.31
$t + 12$	458.66	601.03	1 059.69
$t + 13$	529.84	652.38	1 182.22
$t + 14$	591.11	693.8	1 284.91
$t + 15$	642.45	664.03	1 306.48
$t + 16$	653.24	542.37	1 195.61
$t + 17$	597.80	343.69	941.49
$t + 18$	470.75	255.9	726.65
etc.	etc.	etc.	etc.

(b) $c = 0.5$ and $v = 4$. Are the cycles convergent (damped) or explosive?

From the examples that have been examined it should be clear to you that whether or not a cycle is explosive or convergent (i.e. damped) depends upon the relative values of the marginal propensity to consume (c), i.e. the value of the multiplier and the value of the accelerator (v).

Further Reading

Matthews, R. C. O. (1959) *The Trade Cycle*, Cambridge University Press, Cambridge (particularly chapters 1–3).

Rowan, D. C. (1983) *Output, Inflation and Growth: An Introduction to Macroeconomics*, 3rd edition, Macmillan, London.

Samuelson, P. (1939) 'Interactions between the Multiplier Analysis and the Principle of Acceleration', *Review of Economics and Statistics*, Vol. 21.

Levacic, R. and Rebmann, A. (1982) *Macroeconomics: An Introduction to Keynesian-Neoclassical Controversies*, 2nd edition, Macmillan, London.

7

Inflation

The previous chapters have examined the factors that determine employment, output, the interest rate, the wage rate and the price level. We now turn to inflation, which can be described as a tendency for the price level to rise over time. Inflation is distinguished from the *rate of inflation*, which is the rate (speed) at which the increase in the price level takes place. Inflation is a flow concept whilst the price level is a stock.

From these definitions it should be clear that the price level can rise whilst the rate of inflation is falling. For example, if the price level in some initial time-period is $1 000 and if between years one and two it rises by 20%, then at the end of year two the price level will be $1 200. Now, if the rate of inflation falls to 15% between years two and three the price level will still rise – this time to $1 380. Again, if the inflation rate falls to 10% between years three and four, the price level will rise to $1 418.

When individuals are asked about the rate of inflation they often confuse this with the price level. Thus, if someone is asked what they expect to happen to the rate of inflation in the future they might reply that they expect it to rise if they have, in fact, thought about the price level rising. But clearly they could still have consistent expectations if they expected the rate of inflation to fall whilst they still expected the price level to rise.

Inflation influences individual behaviour, and expectations about inflation can play a crucial role. Whether or not you expect the rate of inflation to rise or fall will determine your purchasing behaviour – do you buy today or wait until tomorrow? It is because inflation has an influence upon decision-makers' behaviour that we are interested in the likely factors that cause its rate to change.

7.1 MEASURING INFLATION

Before considering the determinants of inflation let us remind ourselves about how we measure it. Table 7.1 shows a series of figures for a retail price index based on 1990 = 100. Thus, the value of the index is 100 in 1990 and 116.5 in 1991. This means that between 1990 and 1991 prices rose by 16.5% per annum.

Table 7.1

Year	Retail Price Index (1990 = 100)	Annual Inflation Rate (%)
1987	63.6	
1988	69.4	9·14
1989	80.5	16·00
1990	100.0	24.2
1991	116.5	16.5

To calculate the annual increase in prices generally we use the formula:

$$\text{annual inflation rate} = (P_t - P_{t-1})/P_{t-1} \times 100$$

where P_t is the value of the price index for year t.

Thus the rate of inflation between 1989 and 1990 is:

$$(P_{1990} - P_{1989})/P_{1989} \times 100 = \left(\frac{100.0 - 80.5}{80.5} \right) \times 100 = 24.2$$

Self-Assessment Question

Calculate the rate of inflation between 1987 and 1988 and between 1988 and 1989.

7.2 THE MONETARIST EXPLANATION OF INFLATION

One popular explanation of the causes of inflation is 'too much money chasing too few goods'. This is the monetarist explanation of inflation which focuses upon the money supply and is associated with the name of Milton Friedman. What view of the economy lies behind this approach?

You will recall that the price *level* is determined by the intersection of the aggregate demand and aggregate supply curves (as in Figure 7.1). In the monetarist model of the economy the long-run aggregate supply curve is vertical at the level of full-employment national output (Y_N). An increase in the money supply will increase the aggregate demand curve from AD_0 to AD_1 and the result is that, as expectations adapt over time, the price level will rise from P_0 to P_1. From this analysis an increase in the money supply causes the price level to rise without any lasting increase in output or employment. The

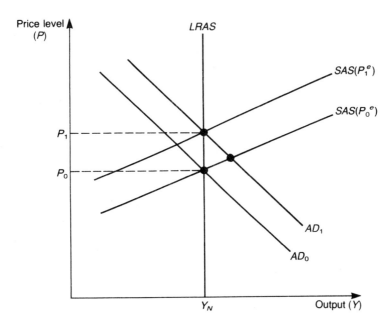

Figure 7.1

reason for this result is clearly due to the monetarist assumptions of a vertical long-run aggregate supply curve and adaptive expectations. (Note that in the New Classical case where expectations are formed rationally, a change in aggregate demand which is anticipated leads directly to a rise in the price level.)

The same result is also demonstrated using the famous quantity theory equation

$$MV = PY$$

where M = the nominal money stock, V = the velocity of circulation, i.e. the number of times a dollar passes hands during a specific time-period, P is the price *level* and Y is the level of real output produced by the economy (which in the long run is constant at Y_N).

If we further assume that V is fixed by institutional factors, then any change in M must be translated into a change in the price level (P) in long-run equilibrium. A 10% increase in the money supply will cause a 10% increase in the price level. The price level, adopting this approach, is simply determined by the money supply and nothing else.

The money supply equation can be rewritten and expressed in terms of changes:

$$\left\{\begin{array}{c}\text{\% change in}\\\text{price}\end{array}\right\} = \left\{\begin{array}{c}\text{\% change in}\\\text{money supply}\end{array}\right\} + \left\{\begin{array}{c}\text{\% change in}\\\text{velocity}\end{array}\right\} - \left\{\begin{array}{c}\text{\% change in}\\\text{output}\end{array}\right\}$$

Monetarists assume that velocity is constant (or at least, relatively stable over time). Therefore whether or not prices change depends upon whether the change in the money supply is greater or less than the change in output. As output changes, individuals will demand more money for the greater number of transactions which the extra output implies. If the transactions demand for money increases at the same rate as the money supply (and if velocity is constant) then there will be no inflation. On the other hand, if the increase in the demand for money is less than the increase in the supply of money then individuals will be left holding surplus money balances which they do not want. They try to get rid of these unwanted money balances by spending them, with the result that demand for output rises. Since the supply of output is fixed at the full-employment level, an increase in aggregate demand causes prices to rise in the long run.

To summarize: in the monetarist model, with full employment and constant velocity, the level of the money supply determines the price level; while the rate of growth of the money supply and the rate of growth of velocity relative to the growth of output determines the rate of inflation.

7.3 ALTERNATIVE THEORIES OF INFLATION

This monetarist explanation of the rate of inflation applies to the long run when the economy is at full-employment capacity constraint and when velocity is fixed. In the short run (and the long run is a series of short runs), velocity might change and the economy is unlikely to be at full employment. Thus, an increase in the money supply, which increases aggregate demand, also has the possibility of causing quantities of output produced to change rather than the price level. A non-classical aggregate supply curve is shown in Figure 7.2.

It will also be recalled that aggregate demand can shift for reasons other than a change in the money supply, e.g. an increase in

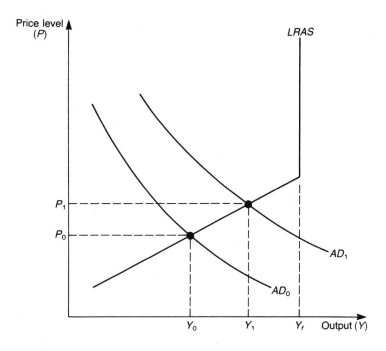

Figure 7.2

government spending, or an increase in private investment spending, etc. In this case as aggregate demand increases, the price level increases but not in proportion to the increase in the money stock. The level of output increases also. This provides us with an explanation of inflation in the short run. It is only in the long run that the economy gets close to full employment Y_f, especially since the full-employment capacity constraint of the economy is growing over time due to population growth, investment and improvements in productivity.

What does the empirical evidence tell us about the relationship between changes in the money supply and the rate of inflation? If we examine data for a large number of countries for a greater number of years there is nothing other than a very loose relationship. The rate of inflation is not explained by changes in the money supply and we have to look elsewhere for other explanations.

Price Fixing

To understand what determines the rate of inflation we need to return to a consideration of how prices are determined. We have already distinguished between flexprice and fixprice models. Empirical studies of price determination reveal that many business executives use a mark-up formula when setting prices, i.e. costs plus a mark-up on costs to obtain a target profit rate. This can be expressed as follows:

$$\text{Total revenue} = \text{Price} \times \text{Quantity produced} = PY$$
(assuming all output produced is sold)

$$\begin{matrix} \text{Total} = \\ \text{costs} \end{matrix} \quad \begin{matrix} \text{Wage rates}\,(W) \times \text{Number employed}(n) + \\ \text{Non-labour costs}(C) \times \text{Quantity} \\ \text{of non-labour inputs, taxes, raw} \\ \text{materials, etc.}(m) \end{matrix} \quad = (W.n) + (C.m)$$

Putting everything together we obtain:

$$PY = (1 + k)(W.n + C.m)$$

where k is the mark-up on costs that will give the required rate of profit. This mark-up equation can be rewritten as follows:

$$P = (1 + k) \left[\frac{Wn}{Y} + \frac{Cm}{Y} \right]$$

$$\text{or} \quad P = (1+k) \left[\frac{W}{(Y/n)} + \frac{C}{(Y/m)} \right]$$

Why write it this way? (Y/n) is output per unit of labour input, i.e. labour productivity. Thus, the price of a commodity will depend upon the wage rate (W) relative to labour productivity. Likewise it will also depend upon the productivity of non-labour inputs (Y/m) relative to their costs(C).

This now tells us how a business executive goes about determining the prices of individual products. It depends upon the costs of inputs $(W$ and $C)$ and the productivities of inputs. It also depends upon the profit mark-up. In the short run, productivities are constant so that if prices change then it is most likely going to be due to a change in costs. Higher input costs show up in higher prices because the aggregate supply curve shifts upwards and to the left (see Figure 7.3). As the economy gets closer to full employment, more and more pressures are placed upon inputs and their prices rise and demand increases, thereby pushing the aggregate supply curve upwards.

Over the range AB of the aggregate supply curve in Figure 7.3, product and factor prices are constant. There is so much excess capacity in the economy because, at levels of output over the range AB, the economy is operating well below its productive potential or full-employment level of output (Y_f). Any increase in demand results

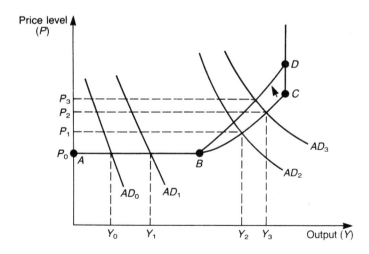

Figure 7.3

117

in a quantity change rather than a price change. For the reasons already given, prices are inflexible. Over the range BC, however, as the economy gets closer to full employment, the pressure of demand causes prices to rise – product prices rise but input prices are assumed to remain constant. The closer we get to the productive potential, the faster prices rise.

Hence, the curve BC becomes progressively steeper. If wages and other input prices also change, then the aggregate supply curve actually shifts from BC to BD.

Let us now combine all of this. If aggregate demand in the economy increases from AD_0 to AD_1 then, because there is a great amount of slack in the economy, the price level stays constant at P_0 and output increases from Y_0 to Y_1. If aggregate demand increases from AD_2 to AD_3 then the price level rises from P_1 to P_2; this might cause wages to rise (in order to maintain the real value of wages) so that the aggregate supply curve moves up and the price level rises to P_3. This is higher than expected – real wages will be eroded and wages will start to chase after rising prices. A wage-price spiral has been set in motion.

The aggregate supply curve will move upwards if any input price (not just wages) increases. Thus, if the price of imported goods increases, this will be passed on. Inflation can be imported.

Now we have two explanations of inflation in the short run: (i) an increase in aggregate demand due to increases in spending arising from an increase in the money supply or an increase in some component of spending such as investment or consumer spending; (ii) an upward shift in the aggregate supply curve caused by an increase in input prices relative to any change in productivity.

The former is **demand pull inflation** and the latter is **cost push**.

7.4 INFLATION AND UNEMPLOYMENT

Wage costs are usually the largest element of any organisation's total costs. If wage costs rise faster than productivity this puts pressure on product prices, and market share and jobs could, therefore, be lost. There is a potential relationship between inflation (wage inflation) and unemployment. This was studied by the British economist W. Phillips, who found that a trade-off existed between the rate of change in wages and unemployment. This is shown in Figure 7.4.

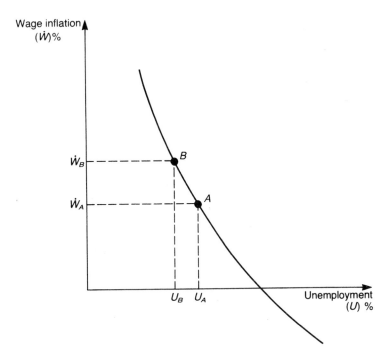

Figure 7.4

As unemployment falls and, therefore, the pressure of aggregate demand in the economy increases, this pressure is passed through into labour markets and higher wages. If wages rise faster than productivity, then the economy will experience real wage inflation and product prices will rise.

In general:

$$\dot{P} = \dot{W} - \dot{q} \tag{7.1}$$

where $\dot{P}$ is the rate of price inflation, $\dot{W}$ is the rate of (money) wage inflation, and $\dot{q}$ is the rate of labour productivity growth.

Equation (7.1) allows us to respecify the Phillip's Curve shown in Figure 7.4 in terms of inflation ($\dot{P}$) rather than $\dot{W}$. Figure 7.5 shows that there is a unique rate of unemployment, U_N, at which there is no inflation (i.e. where $\dot{W} = \dot{q}$). This rate of unemployment is variously known as the **natural rate of unemployment** or the **non-accelerating-inflation rate of unemployment**.

119

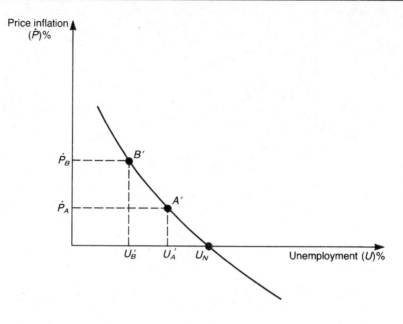

Figure 7.5

The Importance of Inflationary Expectations

The role of expectations has already been explored in a static context in Chapter 5. In terms of the relationship between wage inflation and unemployment in Figure 7.4, and hence the relationship between inflation generally and unemployment in Figure 7.5, it is clear that, if the expectation that inflation would occur became widespread and built into wage bargains, the position of the Phillip's Curve would be fundamentally altered.

Milton Friedman first formally explored this possibility in 1968, when he pointed out that workers bargain for *real* wages, not money wages. If, for example, inflation were widely expected to be 5% p.a., then when the labour market was in equilibrium (with the supply of, and demand for, labour in balance), workers would press for, and employers willingly concede, money wage increases of 5% p.a. over and above the rate of growth of labour productivity. In general, the relationship between wage inflation and unemployment would shift vertically upwards by the amount of the expected inflation (see Figure 7.6).

$$\dot{W} = f(U) + \dot{P}^e \qquad (7.2)$$

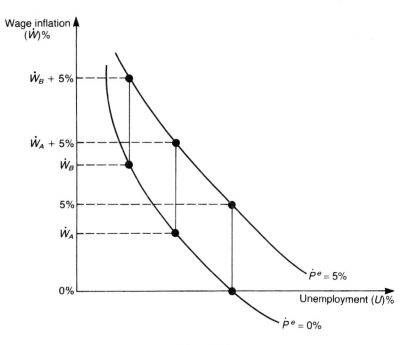

Figure 7.6

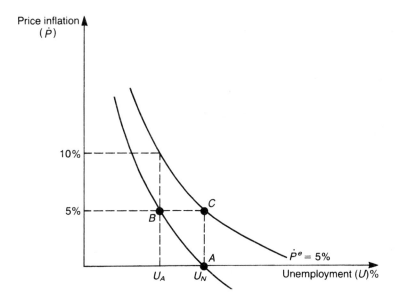

Figure 7.7

where $f(U) = $ 'is a function of the rate of unemployment' and $\dot{P}^e = $ expected rate of inflation.

Incorporating this modification into the relationship between price inflation (as opposed to wage inflation) and unemployment by combining equations (7.1) and (7.2) gives us:

$$\dot{P} = f(U) - \dot{q} + \dot{P}^e \qquad (7.3)$$

U_N is now the rate of unemployment at which actual inflation equals expected inflation, rather than zero, as Figure 7.7 illustrates. Suppose initially the economy is at point A, with inflation equal to zero (i.e. $\dot{W} = \dot{q}$). The rate of growth of aggregate demand now increases and supply-side bottlenecks begin to emerge, forcing the rate of price inflation up to 5%. With workers expecting prices to remain stable ($\dot{P}_e = 0\%$), the increases in money wages caused by the excess demand for labour are misperceived as *real* increases and the economy slides up its Phillip's Curve to point B. However, if expectations are formed adaptively (as Friedman argues), then in time the expected rate of inflation will be revised upwards to 5%, and this 'cost-of-living allowance' will gradually become built into wage settlements. As this happens, the rate of unemployment consistent with 5% inflation will increase, until (assuming the new, higher rate of growth of aggregate demand is maintained) the economy settles at point C, on the new Phillips Curve ($\dot{P}_e = 5\%$).

In the 'expectations-augmented' Phillips Curve model, it follows that each Phillips Curve is a short-run phenomenon, which describes the relationship between unemployment and *actual* inflation, for a given rate of *expected* inflation. Because the expected rate steadily converges on the actual rate of inflation, these short-run Phillips Curves are applicable only to disequilibrium situations. In the long run, when expected and actual rates of inflation are equal, the economy is at its natural rate of unemployment (U_N). In other words, there is no long-run trade-off between unemployment and inflation in the expectations-augmented version of the Phillips Curve model – the long-run Phillips Curve is vertical at the natural rate of unemployment, as shown in Figure 7.8.

A number of important conclusions follows from the incorporation of adaptive expectations into the Phillips Curve:

(1) The only way of keeping unemployment below its natural rate is by continuously increasing the rate of growth of aggregate

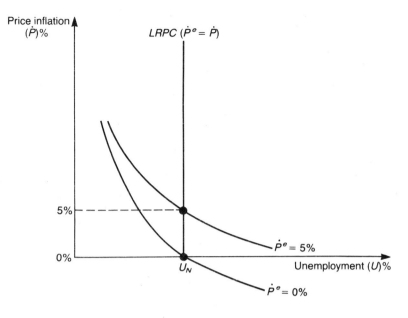

Figure 7.8

demand, so that actual inflation always exceeds the expected rate. This implies that governments would have to be prepared to allow the rate of inflation to accelerate without limit.

(2) Conversely, governments could achieve price stability (zero inflation) by closely controlling the growth of aggregate demand, provided they were prepared to accept the transitional costs in terms of higher unemployment. The longer it takes inflationary expectations to adjust to the experience of lower-than-expected inflation during a deflationary period, the greater these transitional costs will be. Governments seek to speed up this adjustment process by 'talking down the rate of inflation' (i.e. making announcements designed to moderate inflationary expectations).

To talk down inflation governments must have some credible threats. For example, wage restraint is likely to be exercised on both sides of the bargaining table because of the fear of recession. Business executives do not want to grant large wage increases just before their markets are cut back in a recession. Likewise, labour does not wish to price itself out of a job. To break inflation expectations governments, therefore, need to signal to business decision-makers that they will not bail them out; that if they set

123

wages too high then they will have to live with the consequences –
i.e. higher rates of inflation and a loss of markets to foreign
competition.

But this approach to inflation psychology makes some strong
assumptions about human behaviour. It assumes that everyone
will conform rationally to the threat. In practice, individuals play
games and try to beat the system. When bargaining for a wage
increase one group might argue that if everyone else believes the
threat that government will not bail out the economy by
stimulating demand in a recession, and the rate of inflation is cut
from 10% to 5% as a result, then they could still press ahead with
a 10% increase in money wages and be 5% better off in real terms.
However, if each group plays this game then the outcome will be a
10% rise in the rate of inflation and no one will be better off!

(3) Trade unions cannot independently cause inflation, as is widely
thought. If the government maintains tight control of the growth
of aggregate demand, then if unions successfully achieve higher
wage increases, which their employers try to pass on in the form of
higher prices, the result will be higher unemployment. This
happens because with total spending fixed, the firms conceding
wage rises will lose business to domestic and foreign competitors
which resist, forcing them to cut jobs. Only if the government
reacts to the rise in unemployment by increasing the rate of
growth of aggregate demand, allowing spending to increase by
enough to 'validate' the wage increases won by trade unions, will
inflation increase.

While trades unions are therefore still very involved in the
inflationary process, according to the expectations-augmented
Phillips Curve model, they can only cause inflation indirectly, if
the government stands ready to passively counter any rise in
unemployment by increasing aggregate demand. Not
surprisingly, this conclusion is very controversial and economists
remain divided on this subject.

Self-Assessment Questions

Use the expectations-augmented Phillip's Curve model to show the
effects of:

(a) a reduction in the rate of inflation when expected inflation is 20%.

(b) an increase in trade union power which results in higher wage settlements that are not validated by an increase in aggregate demand.

7.5 COUNTER-INFLATION POLICIES

What policies might be used to reduce the rate of inflation?

(1) Reducing government spending.
(2) Increasing taxes.
(3) Reducing the money supply.

Each of these policies will reduce demand in the system and shift the aggregate demand curve to the left. But they are not without problems. Reducing demand will obviously cause a reduction in output produced. Initially this will be done by firms cutting back on the amount of overtime working, but eventually they will lay workers off and make them redundant.

An increase in taxes might spark off new inflationary expectations. If sales taxes (indirect taxes) are increased, then this will raise the aggregate supply curve and, therefore, weaken the effect on prices of a cut in demand. Likewise, if income taxes are increased this will reduce personal disposable incomes and demand but it will also cause workers to increase their pressure for an increase in money wages in order to maintain their living standards.

A reduction in the money supply has an obvious impact on aggregate demand. It increases interest rates, which will reduce consumption and investment demand because of the increase in the costs of borrowing. A rise in interest rates should also help to strengthen the exchange rate (as we shall see later), which will make imports cheaper and therefore help to keep the price level down. The danger with this policy is that cheap imports will displace domestic manufacturing output, with the result of 'deindustrialisation' of the country.

Each of these policies highlights the short-run inflation/unemployment trade-off. Reducing aggregate demand brings about a recession – output declines and unemployment rises – and this situation persists until inflationary expectations moderate. In a democracy, in which governments may have to face re-election before the transitional costs of reducing inflation have worked through the economy, this makes counter-inflation policy particularly problematic.

The policies outlined above are demand-management policies – they focus attention on moving the aggregate demand curve. Another set of policies focuses upon the aggregate supply curve. In particular they try to shift the aggregate supply curve to the right. This will then offset the deflationary impact of demand-management policies on employment and output levels.

A shift in aggregate supply to the right requires an increase in the potential (full-employment) output of the economy. How might this be done?

(a) Improving the labour force: via education and training programmes; improving the flow of information given to workers about job vacancies and helping them to relocate in areas where jobs are to be found; increasing labour productivity will reduce costs.
(b) Providing tax incentives to stimulate investment in new plant and machinery: e.g. accelerated depreciation. This increases the depreciation (capital consumption) rate allowed for tax purposes and increases the cash flow from investment.
(c) Improving the infrastructure: i.e. increasing investment on capital items such as roads, ports, communication systems, etc.

Prices and Incomes Policies

Finally, another type of policy designed to control the rate of inflation are **prices and incomes policies**. These policies influence prices and wages directly and can take a variety of forms. They are aimed at moving the aggregate supply curve downwards. They involve one or both of the following:

(1) Price controls – these place a ceiling on the prices of selected items.
(2) Wage controls – wage increases are limited to a specific rate of increase (note that it is wage control not income control because many sources of income, such as from interest or profits, are difficult to control).

However, these controls on prices or wages dam up the pressure in the economy. They do not necessarily eliminate the inflationary pressures which are not being tackled directly. Individuals tend to know (and expect) that the controls will be relaxed or completely lifted in the future, so they know they will be able to catch up. When they do catch up, the rate of inflation will be just as high as it would have been without the controls. During a period of price control, firms will delay the completion of orders for as long as possible. It is in their interest to hold back from completion at the current prices because if the controls were to be relaxed tomorrow they would then transact at a higher price. During a period of price controls, therefore, a backlog of orders will build up without an increase in GNP.

Self-Assessment Questions

During the 1970s many economies suffered from a condition called 'stagflation', i.e. increasing rates of inflation coupled with stagnating or falling levels of real output. This was blamed on the sudden increase in the price of oil in 1973.

(a) Using the aggregate demand and aggregate supply diagram, illustrate stagflation.
(b) What policies might a government have adopted to get an economy out of stagflation?
(c) What impact would such policies have upon the performance of firms in that economy?

7.6 THE IMPACT OF INFLATION

Why is inflation of importance; why do governments worry about inflation? One answer is that inflation has distributional consequences; it does not influence everyone equally. Some contracts, including labour contracts, are fixed in nominal terms. Thus, during periods of high rates of inflation, those on fixed nominal contracts will lose in real terms. During a period of inflation not all prices rise at an equal rate. The large hike in oil prices transferred purchasing power (income) to oil-exporting countries during the 1970s. Increases in prices hurt creditors and help debtors. Suppose you borrow $100 and agree to pay it back one year later with 5% interest, so that you would pay back a total of $105. If inflation is 10% over that year, in real terms you will only pay back $94.5.

Inflation and Real Rates of Return

We define the nominal rate of return as the sum received next year, minus the sum invested now, divided by the sum invested now, i.e.

$$\text{nominal rate of return} = \frac{\text{sum received next year} - \text{sum invested now}}{\text{sum invested now}}$$

If we invest $100 today and expect $110 tomorrow then the nominal rate of return is:

$$\text{nominal rate of return} = \frac{110 - 100}{100} = 10\%$$

To calculate the real rate of return we want to take into account the purchasing power of the dollar, i.e. what bundle of commodities (real output) can be purchased? We can approximate an answer to this question by the following formula:

$$\text{real rate of return} = \text{nominal rate of return} - \text{rate of inflation}$$

Thus, if the nominal rate of return is 10% whilst the rate of inflation is 10% then the real rate of return is 0%. If the rate of inflation is greater than the nominal rate of return, the real rate of return will be negative.

Inflation Expectations and Nominal Rates of Return

If we expect the rate of inflation to be 10% then nominal rates of return must be at least 10%. Higher expected rates of inflation will result in higher nominal interest rates. But an increase in the expected inflation rate does not automatically raise nominal interest rates by an equal amount, thereby leaving interest rates constant. The reason is that real interest rates are determined by demand and supply in the money and capital markets.

Why will individuals keep their funds in savings accounts offering low, even negative, real rates of interest? The plain answer is that it is possibly the best alternative available to them. Other assets offering higher real rates carry more risks, and have high brokerage costs that are fixed costs and act as a disincentive to investors of small sums of money.

Once a financial contract has been agreed, the rates of interest on borrowing and lending are fixed. They are fixed and determined on the basis of the expectations of the future rates of inflation held by borrowers and lenders. The actual outcome for the rate of inflation will, in all probability, not equal expectations. Errors in inflation predictions mean that the actual rate of inflation will diverge from the expected rate of inflation. If the actual rate of inflation is higher than expected then the real rate of inflation will be less than expected, and vice versa.

Taxes and Real Yields

If R is the nominal interest rate, t is the tax rate and the after-tax nominal rate is R_t then

$$R_t = (1 - t)\, R$$

If the rate of inflation is r, the after-tax real rate of return (RR_t) is

$$RR_t = (1 - t)\, R - r$$

During inflation the gap between before-tax and after-tax real returns widens because taxes are paid on nominal rather than real returns. A 1% increase in the rate of inflation requires more than a 1% increase in nominal interest rates for real returns to be constant.

Any contract that is stated in nominal terms will have its real value altered by inflation. Examples are taxes, pensions, leases and social security payments. Inflation reduces the burden on the payer and the benefit to the payee.

Unless income-tax brackets are adjusted during inflation then, as individuals' nominal incomes rise, they could find themselves being pushed into a higher marginal income-tax bracket. This increases their real tax burden.

During inflationary periods corporate profits are overstated. Using a system of historic cost accounting, production costs are understated. Firms also overstate their profits during inflation if they use FIFO (First In, First Out) inventory accounting. Businesses keep an inventory of unsold items that were produced at different times and at different costs. When one of these items is sold, which cost should be used when calculating profits? With the FIFO accounting method the cost of the good produced earliest and still in the inventory is used. Thus, during inflation, FIFO accounting understates current production costs and overstates profits.

The fact that inflation is usually unexpected means that agreements that seemed like good deals at the time they were made suddenly turn into bad deals. Inflation produces haphazard and indiscriminate wealth transfers.

The impacts of inflation can be reduced by **indexing**, i.e. tying the value of contracts to some price index such as the retail price index or the GNP price deflator. Indexation does not mean that the value of the contract necessarily tracks the chosen index, percentage point for percentage point. Instead it might be of the form: GNP index minus k%. Thus, if the GNP index rises by 10% and $k = 4$%, then the value of the contract will rise by 6%.

7.7 INFLATION AND ECONOMIC GROWTH

There is no obvious direct link between inflation and economic growth. Any relationship that does exist arises indirectly via government intervention in the management of the economy. It is the nature of the response of governments to inflation (both actual rates of inflation and expected rates) that will determine the impact on growth and productivity. Inflation might lead to slow growth or stagnation because governments use restrictive demand policies to bring inflation under control. Such policies often lead to high rates of unemployment, low rates of capacity utilisation, low rates of investment and poor productivity growth.

Is it, therefore, inevitable that a country cannot achieve near full employment in the short run without creating inflationary pressures and the need for restrictive demand-management policies? The answer is no – much depends upon the nature of the institutional arrangements prevailing in that country. Those countries which tend to have an inflationary bias also have adversarial industrial relations systems and decentralised trade unions. They also have governments who respond to inflations by using strongly deflationary demand-management policies (the USA, the UK, Canada, France and Italy fall into this category).

In contrast there is another group of economies, called 'corporatist economies', which is characterised by a high degree of co-operation and collaboration between the major economic groups when it comes to policy formation; an industrial relations system that is co-operative; and a disbelief that an economy, when out of equilibrium, will rapidly adjust to equilibrium via a flexprice response. These corporatist economies have been able to implement relatively successful voluntary incomes policies. This means that whilst inflation has not been eliminated, nevertheless it has been sufficiently moderated through the co-operation between governments and unions. Because inflation has been kept under control by methods that do not deflate the economy, unemployment has been kept low by demand-management policies.

Further Reading

Parkin, M. and Bade, R. (1988) *Modern Macroeconomics*, 2nd edition, Philip Allan, Oxford.

Anderson, P. S. (1989) *Inflation and Output*, BIS Economic paper No. 24, Bank for International Settlements, Basle.

Laidler, D. E. W. and Parkin, J. M. (1975) 'Inflation – a Survey', *The Economic Journal*, Vol. 85, December.

Dornbusch, R. and Fischer, S. (1987), *Macroeconomics*, 4th edition, McGraw-hill International, New York.

8

Unemployment

In the theoretical models discussed in Part II, unemployment was seen as a disequilibrium situation, in which there was excess supply of labour for some reason. There are, however, additional causes of unemployment which can be classified in the following way:

(1) **Frictional unemployment.** This occurs when individuals are between jobs but are actively searching for a new job. Sometimes it is called 'search unemployment'. This unemployment is of a temporary nature and is of no social significance because it simply demonstrates the functioning of the labour market: it is the flow which takes place as the stock of employment adjusts. In this case there are vacancies and there are unemployed workers searching to fill them.

(2) **Structural unemployment.** This arises when individuals find their skills are not in demand. They are not employable because they have become technologically redundant. Vacancies exist in the economy but the unemployed cannot fill them because they have the wrong skills.

(3) **Seasonal unemployment.** At particular times of the year specific industries suffer a fall in demand. When this occurs they lay off labour and rehire them again when demand picks up. Examples are found in agriculture where the weather and harvesting seasons determine the demand for labour.

8.1 THEORETICAL PERSPECTIVES ON UNEMPLOYMENT

These categories of unemployment are not in dispute. Controversy does, however, abound amongst economists who try to account for the remaining unemployment.

One group of economists (nowadays called the New Classical economists) argues that unemployment is mainly caused by the real wage failing to adjust to make the demand for labour equal to the supply of labour. Profit-maximising firms demand labour up to the point at which the marginal cost of employing labour is equal to the marginal revenue obtained from selling the extra product which is produced by that labour. If the real wages cost sticks and is too high then profit-maximising firms will reduce their demand for labour, and employment in the economy will be lower than it might otherwise be.

If the supply of labour exceeds the demand for labour at the prevailing real wage then the classical economist's solution is to advocate a reduction in real wages.

Why might the real wage not adjust? We have already looked at this and so we will now be brief. If information is costly to obtain and/or if there are monopoly elements in the labour market, then competition will not bring about an adjustment of real wages. A solution frequently advocated to lower the 'natural' rate of unemployment is to remove market imperfections. Another reason that the real wage might not be at the appropriate level which makes the demand for and supply of labour equal, is that workers have incorrect expectations with respect to the rate of inflation. Workers bargain for a money wage and if their expectations of the rate of inflation (and, therefore, where the price level will be in the future) are incorrect then they will end up with a real wage which deviates from the equilibrium. Unanticipated inflation, for example, will cause individuals to make mistakes when bargaining over wages.

The Keynesian View

The Keynesian interpretation of the causes of unemployment are significantly different from those of the New Classical economists. Whilst Keynesians do recognise that unemployment will arise if the real wage is too high, they argue that this is not the complete story.

Unemployment also arises if there is a deficiency of aggregate demand for commodities because this feeds back into the labour market. If the order books of profit-maximising firms are empty, they will not hire labour. Why might demand be deficient? The answer given by Keynesians is that, because the future is uncertain and because information is difficult and costly to obtain, the consumption and production plans of all individuals in the economy will not be compatible. That is to say, they will not be in equilibrium. The prices that prevail, including real wages, will not be the prices that bring about equilibrium, and given that prices are slow to adjust then individuals will adjust the quantities that they purchase (i.e. demand) and this feeds back to the demand for labour (employment). There is, therefore, a role for Keynesian demand-management policies.

Cyclical Unemployment

Unemployment over the business cycle ('cyclical unemployment' as opposed to frictional or structural unemployment) therefore arises for a variety of reasons:

(a) The real wage is incorrect – this might be due to incorrect expectations about inflation or unanticipated inflation.
(b) Demand is deficient either because of random shocks to the economy or because of disequilibrium prices in the market (due to uncertainties and information costs) which result in the plans of different groups in the economy being incompatible.

The problem is not that one view of unemployment is correct and the other is wrong; it is that either is a perfectly valid explanation but which reason prevails at which point in time is the problem. There is, in fact, a good deal of agreement now amongst economists about the causes of unemployment. Unemployment arises because of imperfect information in the system and unemployment persists because prices are slow to adjust. The disagreements centre around issues such as (a) just how imperfect is the information; (b) just how slow are prices to adjust; (c) what causes information to be imperfect and prices slow to adjust – is it government intervention in the economy which is the source of these problems?

Both Keynesian and New Classical economists argue that there is a natural or equilibrium rate of unemployment. Keynesians, however, refer to the non-accelerating rate of unemployment (NAIRU) – this is the level of unemployment where inflation is anticipated. But Keynesians and New Classical economists are in dispute over where this equilibrium rate of unemployment actually occurs.

Policies designed to reduce the equilibrium rate of unemployment are referred to as **supply-side policies**. This distinguishes them from Keynesian demand-side policies. Frictional or search unemployment is affected by the existence and level of unemployment (social security) benefits. If unemployment benefits are high in the sense that they do not differ much from the wage that an individual might earn if employed then this will lengthen the period of search, which means that the length of time associated with frictional unemployment is extended. Improvements in the flow of information about job vacancies will tend to reduce this period – and hence the level of frictional unemployment. Additional policies to improve 'matching' between job vacancies and job-seekers include:

(1) Improving the geographical mobility of labour so that individuals can migrate to areas where vacancies are to be found.
(2) Training programmes which retain workers whose skills have become redundant and which update existing skills to keep them apace with technological change.

Why do we worry about unemployment? To answer this we must look at the associated costs of unemployment.

8.2 THE COSTS OF UNEMPLOYMENT

We have already distinguished between voluntary and involuntary unemployment. A person who is voluntarily unemployed must be better off being unemployed than being employed. Income from their savings (wealth) or some other source (government social security payments) are obviously, in this case, sufficient to keep them happy while out of work. For the majority, however, unemployment is not voluntary. We do not count as voluntarily unemployed those who are temporarily out of work but who are actively searching for another job (i.e. frictional or search unemployment).

Involuntary unemployment means that individuals would like to work at the going wage but cannot find a job because there is excess labour supply at the existing wage. These individuals are worse off as a result of being unemployed. The private costs of unemployment are the benefits forgone (opportunity cost) because individuals have a lower income than they otherwise might. Also there are search costs whilst individuals look for work, e.g. costs of postage, purchasing newspapers to find advertisements, etc. In addition to the private costs of unemployment there are wider social costs. Individuals who are not working are not producing goods and services. Society is denied this output and the benefits that derive from it. This loss of benefit is counted as a 'social cost' of unemployment.

Further Reading

Layard, P. R. G. (1986) *How to Beat Unemployment*, Oxford University Press, Oxford.

McKenna, C. J. (1985) *Uncertainty and the Labour Market: Recent Developments in Job-Search Theory*, Wheatsheaf, Brighton.

Minford, A. P. L. *et al* (1985) *Unemployment: Causes and Cure*, 2nd edition, Basil Blackwell, Oxford.

Greenhalgh, C. A. *et al.* (1983) *The Causes of Unemployment*, Clarendon Press, Oxford.

Part IV

MACROECONOMIC POLICY

9

Basic Principles of Macroeconomic Policy

Part II introduced us to the operation of the macro-economy. By now you should be familiar with the way in which developments in one part of the economy can be transmitted through, *inter alia*, changes in interest rates, to affect another. Understanding the complex linkages which tie together the different sectors of the macro-economy is clearly important for a business seeking to anticipate both adverse and beneficial economic trends. For example, a forecasted upturn in consumer spending may bode well for sales, but it may also cause a rise in interest rates, and this is an additional factor which may heavily influence the future strategy of an expanding business.

However, in seeking to make sense of forecasted changes in, say, consumer spending or investment, it is not sufficient just to understand the way in which private economic agents interact with one another to produce macroeconomic outcomes. This is because one of the biggest players in the macroeconomic game, namely the government, is motivated by a range of political considerations, rather than responding passively to price and output signals in the same way as the private sector. The government may, at certain times, decide to counter a forecasted downturn in investment with an increase in government spending and at others with an expansion in the money supply calculated to reduce interest rates; under different circumstances, the government may react to a predicted surge in consumption by raising taxes. In each case, the final impact on business sales revenues and debt servicing costs will be very different from estimates which failed to allow for the behaviour of the government.

The aim of Part IV is to introduce you to the government's macroeconomic role, so that you can learn both the means by which the government intervenes in the economy and, perhaps more important, the reasons why it chooses to intervene in different ways at different times. By the end of Part IV you should be familiar with the objectives and instruments of macroeconomic policy and understand the various constraints (both real and perceived) which limit the government's scope for manoeuvre in the macroeconomic sphere.

9.1 MACROECONOMIC POLICY OBJECTIVES

From our knowledge of the macro-economy acquired so far, it should already be clear that the government has considerable scope to influence macroeconomic variables. Increasing income taxes, for example, leaves households with less disposable income and is hence liable to depress consumer spending; while raising government spending on final goods and services is analytically identical to increasing investment in terms of its impact on real incomes and interest rates. Boosting the money supply tends to reduce interest rates, thus stimulating investment. In embarking on our investigation of macroeconomic policy, the first question which springs to the fore is not, therefore, 'how can the government affect the macro-economy?', but rather 'what motivates the government when it intervenes in the macro-economy?'

Before going on to answer this question, ask yourself why consumers buy electric drills. They buy electric drills not for the satisfaction derived from ownership *per se*, but because they want the services ownership offers, namely the ability to drill holes in their houses. Similarly, the government operates macroeconomic policy not as an end in itself, but rather to provide benefits for the electorate, thereby improving its own prospects for re-election. In other words, the government intervenes in the macro-economy with the aim of altering the behaviour of certain key macroeconomic variables in a way which enhances the welfare of its citizens. Generally speaking, the variables with which the electorate – and so the government – are most concerned are:

(1) The price level.
(2) The rate of unemployment.
(3) The balance of payments.
(4) The rate of growth of real output.

These variables are known as **policy objectives.** The theoretical framework we have developed so far has tended to concentrate on a 'closed' economy, that is an economy which does not trade either goods or financial assets with the outside world. We shall therefore reserve discussion of policy objective (3) until Part V, when the international dimension is more fully considered. Our model is also a 'static' one, in the sense that it abstracts from questions of economic growth. This leaves us to focus on (1) the price level and (2) the rate of unemployment, for present purposes. Just what do these two policy objectives amount to in operational terms?

Inflation

The government's policy objective for prices is relatively straightforward and, in an ideal world, it would aim for a zero rate of inflation. It is, however, worth pointing out that much of the economic damage caused by inflation arises when it is *unanticipated*, so that agents are unable to interpret correctly the meaning of changes in prices, wages and interest rates. As a result, the signals about relative price changes are distorted by the 'noise' from the inflation broadcast, causing the misallocation of resources. The implication is that a stable rate of inflation, which reduces the scope for expectational errors, is also important.

Indeed, a rate of inflation which is stable at 4% p.a. might be preferable to a rate which is 3% on average, but which fluctuates unpredictably between 0% and 6%. Nevertheless, with this caveat in mind we shall assume that the government's objective for the price level is zero inflation.

Unemployment

The rate of unemployment is a more elusive concept. Indeed, it is far from clear what a 0% unemployment rate, the apparently self-evident objective for unemployment, actually means. Should it mean that everyone who could work is working? And should it mean they are working full time (35 hours a week, 40 hours a week)? Or should it mean that everyone who would like to work, given the present level of wages, is working? Or that everyone who would like to work, given what they feel to be a 'fair' wage, is working? Most countries choose to define as unemployed any person not working and actively seeking either part-time or full-time work, which fits most closely with the third of these classifications. The problem is that this excludes large numbers of people, notably married women and older men, who are not interested in working at present wage levels, but who would be at higher wage levels. During an economic upswing, rising real wages therefore tempt more and more of this group into the labour market, so that 0% unemployment, on this definition, could never be achieved until everyone who could, in principle, work is, in fact, doing so.

Moreover, this difficulty aside, it is also debatable whether 0% unemployment (however defined) is an economically sensible objective. In a dynamic market economy, the 'invisible hand' is continuously reallocating resources in response to changing consumer demand. This implies that labour must be released from declining, 'sunset' industries and drawn into expanding, 'sunrise' sectors. Such transfers take time, partly because searching for new jobs is a time-consuming process in itself and partly because the labour being shed may be in geographic areas remote from, or possess skills inappropriate to, the sunrise industries, so further increasing the change over time. Suppose that, on average, 20% of the labour force change jobs each year and spend an average of ten weeks between jobs. It follows that, at any one time, there is an average of 4% of the labour force 'unemployed'. (See Chapter 8 above.)

Generally, therefore, an appropriate objective for unemployment is a target rate which, given the characteristics of the national labour market and the rate of structural economic change, means that supply of labour (i.e. the employed plus job-seekers) is broadly in balance with the demand for labour (i.e. the employment plus unfilled job vacancies). This rate, which varies from country to country, might be anywhere from 2–6% and is sometimes called **full employment**. It is closely related to the concept of the **natural rate of unemployment**, which is the rate of unemployment at which there is neither excess supply of, nor excess demand for, labour and although there are some technical differences between the two, both convey the key idea that the target rate of unemployment is significantly above 0%.

Unemployment versus Inflation

Moving on from the difficulties of actually specifying operational policy objectives for the price level and the rate of unemployment, the other fundamental problem which faces policy-makers is that, in the short run at least, the two objectives may actually be mutually inconsistent. As we discovered in Chapter 7, while there are theoretical grounds for believing that inflation and unemployment may be independent of each other in the long run (i.e. when inflation is fully anticipated), in the short run there is, typically, a trade-off between the two: lower unemployment means more rapid inflation, and vice versa.

Given the time-frames within which many democratic governments operate, which require them to face re-election before long-run equilibria are ever established, they have a natural predisposition to exploit short-run trade-offs. The relative weight given to inflation and unemployment by national electorates, not unsurprisingly, varies from country to country depending on a host of historical, social and cultural characteristics. West Germany, for example, suffered very rapid inflation in the 1920s and consequently has tended to make the attainment of stable prices an overriding objective. The United States and the United Kingdom, in contrast, have historically been more concerned to avoid a return to the very high levels of unemployment endured during the 'Great Depression' of the 1930s and, until recently, assigned priority to achieving low rates of unemployment. Many developing countries similarly place greater store by full employment than price stability.

Political priorities change over time, of course, not least because electoral perceptions of the relative ills of inflation and unemployment may alter in the light of experience. In the United Kingdom, for example, the very low levels of unemployment enjoyed in the 30 years after the Second World War and the unprecedented rates of inflation suffered in the mid-1970s caused many voters to reverse their long-standing priorities. The changing climate of academic opinion also played its part, with many becoming convinced that the inflation-unemployment trade-off was a purely transitory phenomenon and that, by implication, the government could control inflation, but not unemployment, in the long run. This sea-change in British political opinion during the late 1970s was not unique, with similar changes taking place in many developed countries.

Self-Assessment Question

All four of the policy objectives set out on page 141 are simply proxies, or indicators, of social welfare, by which electors judge the macroeconomic performance of their government. But in what ways might the unbridled pursuit of either zero inflation or full employment by the government actually reduce social welfare?

9.2 MACROECONOMIC POLICY INSTRUMENTS

As noted above, the government has enormous power to influence the economy, by, *inter alia*, altering its tax and spending plans, influencing monetary conditions and using its legislative power to change the behaviour of private-sector agents. These various policy instruments affect, in their turn, the policy objectives with which governments are concerned in one of two different ways. Consider the very simple *AS–AD* diagrams shown in Figures 9.1(a) and 9.1(b).

Since output and employment are related (via the aggregate production function), we can think of this diagram as mapping out the trade-offs between inflation (indicated by a movement up the vertical axis) and unemployment (measured by a movement from right to left along the horizontal axis).

In Figure 9.1(a), suppose the government wants to increase the level of employment. It could achieve this goal – in the short run – by boosting aggregate demand (from AD_0 to AD_1) through tax cuts, expenditure increases and an expansion in the money supply. Alternatively, it could tackle the same problem from the supply side, using tax reforms to increase the incentive to work and subsidies to boost investment, so increasing the supply potential of the economy (shifting AS_0 to AS_1).

Now consider Figure 9.1(b) and imagine that the government wants to reduce prices (remember this is a static model – in dynamic context, this would be equivalent to reducing inflation). It could either cut aggregate demand (from AD_0 to AD_1) by increasing taxes, cutting its expenditure or reducing the money supply, or it could try to engineer a rightward shift in the aggregate supply schedule (from AS_0 to AS_1). Rather than using tax and industrial policy to increase the efficiency of

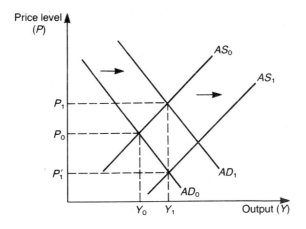

Figure 9.1(a)

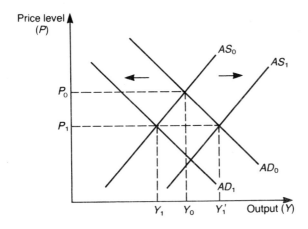

Figure 9.1(b)

the economy (as in Figure 9.1(a)), if the government is primarily concerned to combat inflation, it could cut producers' costs directly by imposing an incomes policy, ensuring wage reductions by force of law.

In discussing macroeconomic policy, it is important to distinguish between policies which are intended to achieve an objective primarily through their effect on aggregate demand and those which work through the supply side. In practice, of course, almost any policy instrument has implications for both demand and supply (e.g. a tax cut affects consumer spending *and* the incentive to work; while tighter monetary policy reduces interest-sensitive investment expenditures *and*, in the longer term, implies a lower capital stock and hence a reduced supply potential). But categorising policy instruments by reference to their main, intended impact nevertheless remains a useful convention.

Demand-Management Policy

In what follows, Part IV is concerned only with macroeconomic policy which works by affecting aggregate demand, that is **demand-management policy**. Sometimes this is also known as **stabilisation policy**, since the government is often seeking to stabilise aggregate demand at some target level (by making continuous policy adjustments to offset exogenous changes in private-sector spending) rather than trying to achieve sharp, stepwise changes in its level of growth.

In managing aggregate demand, there are two main groups of policy instruments which the government has at its disposal. Firstly, it can break directly into the circular flow of income by altering the size, composition and timing of its withdrawals (in the shape of taxes, net of transfer payments) and expenditures, the generic term for which is **fiscal policy** (see below). In principle, it could also use legislative controls to achieve the same effects. Although rare in peacetime, laws to impose specific saving and spending patterns on the private sector are occasionally adopted at times of national crisis (e.g. during a war). In the UK, rationing during the Second World War (which restricted consumers' purchases of goods to individual, preset weekly limits) artificially restrained aggregate consumption, easing the inflationary pressures which would otherwise have arisen, and providing an interesting example of demand management by government edict.

Secondly, government can indirectly influence private-sector demand by altering the monetary conditions which frame spending, saving, borrowing and lending decisions. The government can manipulate both interest rates and the money supply through a variety of techniques. Less subtly, the government can use its legislative powers to outlaw various financial activities or instruct banks to behave in a certain fashion. Taken together **monetary policy** therefore embraces all policy instruments primarily intended to affect the macro-economy by modifying the behaviour of financial intermediaries and so, in turn, the spending of their private-sector customers.

Self-Assessment Question

Given that the government could pursue its macroeconomic objectives either through the demand side or the supply side, under what circumstances is stabilisation policy likely to conflict with, rather than complement, supply-side policy?

9.3 OUTSIDE LAGS, INTERMEDIATE TARGETS AND INDICATORS

Imagine you are formulating macroeconomic policy. The task you face is difficult in practice, but conceptually simple. You must adjust the various policy instruments at your disposal – taxes, government spending, monetary growth and interest rates, etc. – to achieve the best attainable mix of inflation and unemployment rates, given the relative preferences of the electorate and the nature of the trade-offs between these two objectives. Once the policy is up and running, a little fine-tuning is all that is needed, surely? If inflation starts to accelerate, a rise in taxes and interest rates should take the steam out of the economy, while a rise in unemployment should be the signal for more government spending.

Sadly, this cosy picture of policy making is spoiled by the existence of **outside lags,** that is, there are often considerable time-lags between changes in policy instruments and subsequent changes in policy objectives. If raising interest rates instantly curbed expenditure and inflation, it would be very straightforward to keep the economy on course. In reality, it will take months, or even years, before the effect becomes noticeable. This then begs a vital question? Given that there are time-lags between a change in instruments and objectives, how are policy-makers to judge precisely what change in instrument settings is appropriate?

Making Adjustments

Suppose interest rates are 5% and inflation begins to accelerate. What increase in interest rates is necessary to bring inflation back to its original rate – 6%? 10%? 20%? Suppose interest rates are, in fact, raised to 10% but, over the following month, inflation continues to accelerate even faster. Does this mean that the earlier rise in interest rates was ineffectual, suggesting that a much larger rise is called for? Or does it simply reflect the fact that the original rise will take time to have its effect, so that if the government sits tight and waits inflation will ease in due course?

To illustrate this problem, imagine you are driving a car along a twisting mountain road. You are continuously turning the steering wheel from one side to another to keep the car on the road and so avoid disaster (i.e. the lag between adjustments to your instrument – the steering wheel – and its effect on your objective – to keep the car in the middle of the road – is negligible). Suddenly, to your horror, the steering becomes sluggish. Now when you turn the wheel there is a five-second delay before the car responds. The road starts to bend sharply to the left. You turn the steering wheel. Nothing happens. The edge of the precipice looms. Frantically you spin the wheel hard to the left. Just as disaster seems unavoidable the car turns to the left and you round the bend safely. But the road then makes a sharp turn to the right. You turn the wheel the opposite way, but alas, to no avail. The car is still responding to your earlier panic-stricken wrenchings on the wheel and completes its left turn into empty space . . .

The moral of this story is that the policy-maker needs some way of gauging whether or not the instruments of policy are set appropriately. One way of doing this is to return to economic theory and specify the transmission mechanism by which it is believed that the policy objective will be achieved. Consider, for example, one version of the transmission mechanism by which monetary policy (e.g. in the shape of changing the amount of reserves the commercial banks have to back their deposits and loans) affects inflation:

$\triangle$ **Bank Reserves** $\rightarrow$ $\triangle$ **Bank Lending** $\rightarrow$ $\triangle$ **Money Supply** $\rightarrow$
$\triangle$ **Interest Rates** $\rightarrow$ $\triangle$ **Expenditure** $\rightarrow$ $\triangle$ **Inflation**

Since it is by changing the money supply (and so interest rates and expenditure) that the instruments of monetary policy ultimately have their effect on inflation in this story, one means of getting early feedback on the likely effectiveness of policy is to monitor changes in the money supply. Indeed, provided that the relationship between monetary growth and subsequent inflation is sufficiently stable and predictable (as 'monetarists' argue it is), monetary policy could actually be conducted by altering the instrument settings in order to keep money supply growth on a target path consistent with the inflation objective.

Intermediate Targets

Suppose, for the sake of argument, that an x% rise in monetary growth results in an $(x-3)$% increase in the rate of inflation, with a time-lag of approximately two years. And suppose further that changes in bank reserves impact on monetary growth within a space of, say, one month. Month by month, therefore, instruments could be adjusted to keep the money supply growing at an annual rate of 3%, secure in the belief that, in the medium term (two years plus), this will ensure stable prices. In such a situation, the money supply is serving as an **intermediate target**. Intermediate targets are macroeconomic variables which are not objectives in their own right, but which are operational goals in the sense that limiting them to certain values guarantees the desired performance of ultimate policy objectives like inflation and unemployment.

The choice of intermediate target depends upon the policy-maker's perception of the transmission mechanism linking instruments and objectives, both in terms of the way in which the component variables are linked together and the strength and stability of the relationships involved. The widespread popularity of monetary targets in many developed countries, for example, was associated with monetarist theory – which postulates a central role for the money supply in the transmission mechanism – and statistical evidence for a stable relationship between monetary growth and inflation. Previously, governments had been persuaded by Keynesian economists that changes in the money supply had little implication for inflation and used other intermediate targets for monetary policy (e.g. bank lending).

Indicators

Intermediate targets must be distinguished from **indicators**, which perform a similar function, but work in a somewhat different way. An indicator is a macroeconomic variable which (like a target variable) is stably related to the policy objective, but which does not stand somewhere along the transmission mechanism linking instruments and objectives. In other words, the indicator does not determine the objective, but it is closely correlated with it. This may be because the objective determines the indicator, or because both are co-determined by the policy instrument. Diagrammatically, it is not that:

Policy Instrument → Indicator → Policy Objective

but either that:

Policy Instrument → Policy Objective → Indicator

or that:

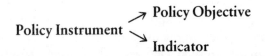

But how could a variable which was either determined by the objective itself, or co-determined by the policy instrument, possibly be of any guide to policy-making? Surely data about the indicator would be available no sooner than statistics for the objective itself, in which case the outside lag would have worked itself out by definition. A simple example may help to resolve this apparent dilemma.

Suppose the government's objective is to increase the number of couples getting married. One way of doing this might be to offer tax incentives, by giving larger tax allowances to married than to single people. Suppose further that, on average, most couples intending to get married buy an engagement ring three months before the wedding itself. Monitoring retail sales of engagement rings therefore provides the government with an early indication of its success in promoting marriage via fiscal policy: more generous tax breaks result in higher ring sales and, in due course, in more weddings. But in no sense do sales of engagement rings cause weddings and this is, of course, the fundamental difference between an intermediate target and an indicator. (Imagine the bizarre results if the government believed that engagement ring sales determined marriages and sent its civil servants out to buy caseloads of rings!)

Just because indicators do not determine policy objectives does not mean that movements in the former cannot precede the latter. Therefore, even where the causality runs from objective to indicator, and even where they are co-determined simultaneously, the fact that reliable, statistical data are more rapidly available for the indicator than for the policy objective itself makes it a useful policy guide (although inflation and unemployment data are available on a monthly basis, statistics for other policy objectives, like the balance of payments and economic growth, are subject to very long lags and major revisions over time).

In the real world, indicators play an important role in fiscal policy, where, unlike monetary policy, theory provides no compelling candidate for the role of intermediate target. Tax cuts, for example, filter through only slowly into higher consumer spending, thereby increasing output and employment. In trying to assess the effects of a tax cut on, say, unemployment, policy-makers may monitor the behaviour of an economic variable which indicates the likely impact that the fiscal changes will ultimately have on the labour market.

For example, the government may measure the number of hours of overtime being worked by the existing workforce and the level of industrial stocks, both 'leading' indicators of forthcoming changes in the demand for labour (i.e. if the higher consumer spending triggered by the tax cuts is forcing employers to use its labour more intensively and meet demand by running down stocks, they are likely to take on more workers in due course). Similarly, ex-factory and wholesale prices are good leading indicators for retail price inflation.

Macroeconomic indicators are discussed in more detail in Chapter 15.

Self-Assessment Question

In circumstances where outside lags are very long and there is no reliable intermediate target or indicator, is it possible that demand-management policy might actually destabilise the economy?

9.4 INSIDE LAGS AND MACROECONOMIC FORECASTING

It would be comforting to think of macroeconomic policy being designed along the lines of an aeroplane's 'automatic pilot', with various intermediate targets and indicators providing continuous feedback to policy-makers on the progress of the economy, thereby allowing them to make regular, 'fine-tuning' adjustments to their policy instruments. In practice, of course, our knowledge of the macroeconomic system is very far from perfect and the links between instruments, targets, indicators and objectives far from precise. At the same time external shocks, like the huge oil price hikes of the 1970s and – for many developing countries – the international debt crisis of the 1980s, can blow the economy deep into unchartered territory, scrambling previous macroeconomic regularities in the process. But there is a more fundamental reason why macroeconomic policy cannot be run on automatic pilot and that is that the instigators of policy changes are not inanimate chips in an aeroplane's computer, but human beings working within a complex institutional structure. The various bureaucratic and political processes which must take place between an adverse development on the macroeconomic front taking place and corrective adjustments to policy instruments actually being made, accordingly give rise to a second source of lag, the **inside lag**.

While the role of targets and indicators is to act as an early warning system, setting the alarm bells ringing whenever they deviate from their desired values, it still takes time to collect and process the relevant statistical data, which must then be analysed to determine whether the observed disturbance is minor and self-correcting or requires a policy response. This type of inside lag is usually known as the **recognition lag**. Once undesirable macroeconomic developments have been identified, there is then a **decision lag**, while the government decides what action to take. This lag arises in part because there may be different options to discuss. For example, an acceleration in inflation may be variously tackled by slower monetary growth, higher taxes or government spending cuts. Different factions in the government may hold different views as to the appropriate mix of policies which should be used and these must be debated and agreed. In the mid-1960s the British Labour Government tried a range of different measures to curb its balance of payments deficit, and devaluation of the exchange rate in 1967 was only finally sanctioned after three years of internal discussion.

Decision lags also result from the institutional framework within which they are taken. In most countries, monetary policy is conducted on behalf of the government by the central bank and actually formulated by a small committee of senior central bank officials. Accordingly, a decision to change the setting of monetary policy instruments can normally be made very rapidly. In contrast, even where the government is clear what it would like to do, changes in fiscal policy normally have to be ratified by the country's legislature before they can actually be implemented, a process which may take months or even years. The famous Kennedy tax cuts in the United States, introduced by President Kennedy in the early 1960s to boost a flagging economy, were not finally passed into law by Congress until after his assassination. In some countries, the legislative timetable may not allow for adjustments to fiscal policy except at discrete intervals. In Britain, for instance, major tax changes can only normally be made once a year in the spring budget, precluding mid-year changes except in exceptional circumstances.

The final type of inside lag is the **administrative lag,** which refers to the time taken for the executive actually to implement a policy decision. Just as central banks can normally decide policy changes quickly, they can also execute them in the time it takes to telephone the various bank staff involved. Adjustments to fiscal policy may take much longer to set in train. Imagine a change in the basic rate of income tax, intended to stimulate consumer spending. The government department or ministry responsible for collecting taxes has to reassess the tax liability of millions of the country's citizens and it may take several months before taxpayers begin to feel the benefit of the tax cuts. In Britain, it is typically three months before most taxpayers notice the effect of a tax change announced in the spring budget on their take-home pay.

Taken together, the various inside lags and outside lags may result in the policy changes actually being destabilising rather than stabilising. In Figure 9.2 the thick, unbroken line illustrates the course that

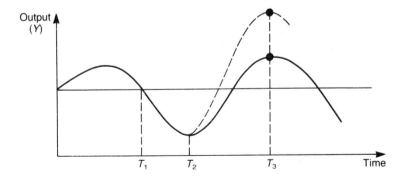

Figure 9.2

output would have followed over time in the absence of government intervention. At time T_1, the government recognises the slowdown in the economy, but the remaining inside lags before the policy changes are implemented do not work themselves out until T_2. Gradually the policy begins to take effect (note that the outside lag is a **distributed lag**, in the sense that it is distributed over time, rather than there being months of zero effect and then one day in which the full effects are delivered in a rush), having its full impact by T_3. Between T_1 and T_3, however, the economy has spontaneously recovered, so that the effect of the 'stabilisation policy' is actually to push output further away from its target level!

Forecasting

The existence of lags mean that forecasting plays a central role in macroeconomic policy. Refer to Figure 9.3. If the government could have forecast the forthcoming downturn at T_1', rather than after it had already started, as in Figure 9.2, then it could have begun the process of implementing the necessary policy changes at that point, so that they would have had their full effect by T_2', thus stabilising the economy as intended.

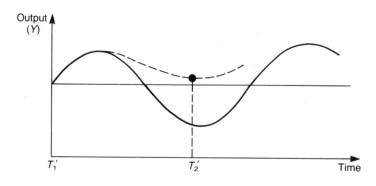

Figure 9.3

There would still remain a role for targets and indicators, to provide feedback for the fine-tuning of policy instruments, but, by accurately predicting major fluctuations in income long enough in advance, the problems of time-lags could be greatly moderated. To this extent, the success of macroeconomic policy clearly depends heavily on the precision of the government's forecasting. Despite the large-scale computer models which most governments use, however, there are many economists who fear that the various inside and outside lags are so long and variable that stabilisation policy will always be counter-productive. They argue instead for fixed **policy rules** (e.g. a constant rate of monetary growth and a balanced budget), designed to serve the economy best in the long run and completely lacking any feedback mechanism. This important debate is considered further later.

Self-Assessment Question

How could the inside lags associated with fiscal policy be reduced, or even eliminated, by designing tax structures and expenditure programmes which respond automatically and counter-cyclically to changes in output?

9.5 CONSTRAINTS ON MACROECONOMIC POLICY

There is a variety of theoretical and practical difficulties which be-devil macroeconomic policy-making and, where appropriate, these are discussed later during the more detailed consideration of monet-ary and fiscal policy. However, these are essentially technical prob-lems which beset any goverment which has decided to implement a particular policy in a particular way. It is important to realise that macroeconomic policy is not made in a vacuum and there are many political, social and cultural factors which may militate against the success of a policy, however technically perfect it may be.

Most obviously, in a world which is becoming increasingly inte-grated, international agreements and relationships constrain the government's room for manoeuvre and, in some cases, rule out the use of certain policy instruments entirely. For example, the UK is a member of the European Community. By 1992, the Community intends to have 'completed the internal market', by abolishing all the remaining 'non-tariff barriers to trade'. These include, notably, the different indirect tax rates levied by different member governments. Harmonisation around central, Community-wide rates by 1992 means that thereafter member governments will be unable to use this major arm of fiscal policy for domestic stabilisation purposes. Recently, the Community has also begun to discuss moving towards the adoption of a common currency, a step which, if taken, would mean the transfer of responsiblity for monetary policy from national central banks to a new European central bank.

For many developing countries currently experiencing external debt problems, macroeconomic policy is often formulated under the supervision of the International Monetary Fund (IMF) and/or the World Bank, since it is only by agreeing a mutually acceptable package that the debtor countries can ensure access to the credit facilities these institutions offer. International trade agreements, like the General Agreement on Tariffs and Trade (GATT), and exchange-rate targeting arrangements, like the Bretton Woods system (which ended in 1973) and the European Monetary System (EMS), also have profound implications for the conduct of macroeconomic policy.

Internally, political, social and cultural forces also mean that some policy instruments are simply unacceptable, even though they may work well to achieve the policy objective. For example, a government which shot any bank manager lending more than a prescribed ceiling might be able to exercise very precise control over monetary growth, but is unlikely to enjoy continued electoral support. Output could be increased by working 12 hours every day, but such a policy is likely to encounter resistance from labour unions (concerned for the welfare of their members) and religious groups (seeking to protect holy days). It is important, therefore, when considering the macroeconomic policies pursued by a rational government, to be aware of the unique combination of external and internal forces which shape their formulation.

Self-Assessment Question

Is optimal monetary policy possible in a parliamentary democracy with regular general elections?

Further Reading

Greenaway, D. and Shaw, G. K. (1988) *Macroeconomics: Theory and Policy in the UK*, 2nd edition, Basil Blackwell, Oxford (especially chapters 16–17).

Vane, H. R. and Thompson, J. L. (1989) *An Introduction to Macroeconomic Policy*, 3rd edition, Harvester Wheatsheaf, Hemel Hempstead.

Levacic, R. (1987) *Economic Policy-making: Its Theory and Practice*, Harvester, Brighton.

10

Fiscal Policy

Across the world, governments tax away from their citizens significant proportions of the national income, either redistributing the receipts in the form of transfer payments (e.g. grants, unemployment benefits, etc.) or using them collectively to provide certain goods and services (e.g. public highways, defence, health care, etc.). Such intervention massively distorts the operation of the economy, which is of course one of its primary aims. While governments must necessarily provide certain, so-called 'public' goods which the market is incapable of providing (because, for example, non-payers cannot be excluded from enjoying the benefits), in most countries the scale of state intervention goes far beyond this minimalist level.

Taxation and expenditure are used, for example, to make the distribution of wealth and income more equitable, by levying higher average rates of tax on the rich and wealthy and providing 'safety net' benefits to the poor. Taxes and subsidies are also widely used to manipulate relative prices in order to discourage some activities (e.g. the consumption of tobacco and alcohol) and promote others (e.g. industrial investment). And at the macroeconomic, rather than the microeconomic, level, the balance of taxation and expenditure can be altered to influence the overall amount of spending in the economy. All other things being equal, tax cuts which leave households with higher disposable incomes tend to stimulate aggregate demand, while reductions in government spending have the opposite effect.

We shall begin by reviewing the theory of fiscal policy within the context of the closed economy $IS-LM$ model, going on to consider the design and measurement of fiscal policy and concluding with an examination of the major theoretical controversy in this area, namely 'crowding out'.

10.1 FISCAL POLICY IN THE *IS–LM* MODEL

You should recall from Part II that, in purely analytical terms, taxation can be viewed in the same way as saving (that is, as a withdrawal from the circular flow of income) and government spending on goods and services as comparable to investment (that is, an exogenous injection into the circular flow of income). What about transfer payments, often one of the largest items in a government's budget? Since these are basically tax receipts which have been taken from one (richer) household and returned to another (poorer) one, the easiest way of incorporating them neatly into the model is to think of them as negative taxes; in other words, to regard only taxes net of transfers as constituting a leakage from the circular flow.

This fudges the issue slightly, to the extent that richer and poorer households typically have different marginal propensities to consume (so that taking $100 from the former and giving them to the latter is unlikely to be neutral in its effects on demand), but it is a convenient simplification for what follows.

Figure 10.1 shows the four-quadrant derivation of the *IS* curve, when taxes (net of transfers) and government spending on final goods and services are added to the model. Taxes were assumed to be a simple, linear function of income ($T = tY$, where T is tax revenue and t is the average and marginal tax rate) and government spending (G) is exogenous.

The mechanics of the diagrams suggest that while the *IS* curve (and hence the level of income) can be influenced by altering either tax rates or government spending, the precise effects of each are not identical. Specifically, a $100 tax cut will not have exactly the same impact on income as a $100 increase in government spending. At an intuitive level, it is easy to see why. Part of a $100 tax cut will be saved by the recipient households, so that the first-round impact on national income is only that part of the $100 which is actually consumed; in contrast, the whole of a $100 increase in government spending adds to

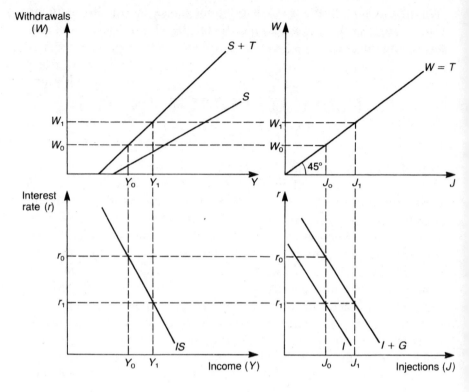

Figure 10.1

income in the first instance, by definition. In other words, as a means of manipulating aggregate demand, changing its spending plans is more cost-effective than altering tax revenues by the same amount.

One interesting implication of this effect is that an increase in government spending, which is matched dollar for dollar by higher taxes, will actually be expansionary! This is because part of the extra taxes taken would otherwise have been saved, so that households' consumption falls by less than government spending rises, giving a boost to demand in net terms. The leverage effect of a tax-financed increase in government spending is known as the **balanced budget multiplier** ($\triangle Y / \triangle G$, where $\triangle G = \triangle T$).

To illustrate this point, imagine a simple, closed economy (i.e. one which does not trade with the outside world). Ignoring the complications of induced changes in interest rates for a moment, we can focus on the goods market to show the effect of a balanced increase in government spending and taxes. In this economy, consumption (C) is a linear function of disposable income (Y_d), such that $C = 0.8Y_d$ and (because we are assuming fixed interest rates) we take investment (I) as given at $100. To begin with, the average tax rate (t) is set at 25%, so that $Y_d = (1-t)Y$, and government expenditure at $100. Equilibrium income can easily be calculated from these figures:

$$Y = C \qquad + I \quad + G$$
$$= 0.8(1-t)Y + 100 + G$$

rearranging

$$Y = \frac{100 + G}{1 - 0.8(1 - t)}$$

and with $t = 0.25$, $G = 100$,

$$Y = 500$$

and tax revenue (T) $= tY = 125$.

Now consider the effect of an increase in government spending of $250. All other things being equal, this will lead to a multiplied increase in income (which rises to $1 325), where the size of the multiplier is $1/[1 - 0.8(1-t)]$ or in this case, 2.5. Although tax revenues will rise (by $0.25 \triangle Y$) they will increase by only $156.25, almost $100 less than the increase in government spending. Suppose instead that the government is concerned to ensure that the extra spending is financed, dollar for dollar, by increased tax revenues. Government spending has more than trebled, but given the expansionary effect this will have on income, the necessary increase in the tax rate will not be of the same magnitude. What happens if the tax rate is raised to 50%? The new equilibrium level of income is now $750 (much lower than before, since the higher tax rate has reduced the size of the multiplier from 2.5 to 1.67) and tax revenues rise from $125 to $375 (i.e. $0.5 \times \$750$), increasing by precisely the $250 needed to match the increase in government spending.

The critical point is that while government spending and taxes have both risen by the same amount, they have had a net expansionary effect on income, increasing it from $500 to $750. Note that the size of this increase is identical to the increase in tax-financed expenditure. In other words, the numerical value of the balanced budget multiplier ($\triangle Y$/taxed-financed $\triangle G$) is unity.

Crowding Out

Of course, changes in government spending, whether matched by tax increases or not, only have a multiplied impact provided that there are no other 'knock-on' effects. Interest rates and the money market, which were omitted from the example above for simplicity, are likely to be affected, inducing changes in investment which counteract the expansion in income.

Figures 10.2(a) and 10.2(b) illustrate two possible limiting cases. In the first (Figure 10.2(a)), the fiscal stimulus (assume, for the sake of argument, an increase in government spending, with no change in tax rates) has the full impact that the basic multiplier analysis would suggest, since with a horizontal LM curve there is no change in interest rates and hence no knock-on changes in investment. In the second (Figure 10.2(b)) the extra government spending shifts the IS curve out to the right as before, but because the LM curve is vertical, the only result is a rise in interest rates. Income is unchanged, since the rise in interest rates has caused a reduction in investment of precisely the same magnitude as the original increase in government spending. The multiplier has been suffocated by the rise in interest rates, so that, ex-post, its value $(\triangle Y / \triangle G)$ is zero. As a general rule, unless the LM curve is perfectly horizontal, the incorporation of the money market into the analysis means that the government expenditure and balanced budget multipliers will always be less than they would at first appear.

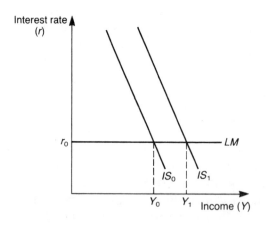

Figure 10.2(a)

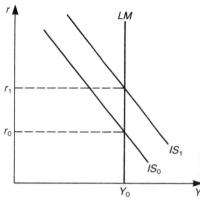

Figure 10.2(b)

What causes this choking-off effect? Remember that the slope of the *LM* curve depends on the income-sensitivity of the demand for transactions, or active money, balances and the interest-sensitivity of the demand for asset, or idle, balances (refer back to Chapter 4 if you are unclear about this). As the extra government spending starts to increase income, the demand for active balances rises and, with a given money supply, interest rates must rise to induce wealth-owners willingly to release idle balances to be used for spending purposes. Another way of looking at this process is to consider the way in which wealth-owners acquire the higher active balances they demand, which is by selling fixed-interest securities, so pushing down their market price and increasing interest rates. The rise in interest rates has two effects: firstly, it reduces the demand for idle balances; secondly, it depresses investment, so slowing the expansion in income triggered by higher government spending.

The more reluctant wealth-owners are to give up idle balances (i.e. the more interest-insensitive the demand for idle balances and hence the steeper the *LM* schedule), the higher interest rates must be driven and the less income will rise. At the limit, when the demand for idle balances is completely insensitive, interest rates simply continue rising until income (and hence the demand for active balances) returns to its original level. The net result is simply that the composition of aggregate demand has altered, with government spending (x) dollars higher and investment (x) dollars lower, but income unaltered. The extent to which fiscal policy **crowds out** private expenditure is clearly critical to the success of fiscal stabilisation policy. Crowding out through higher interest rates, often termed **financial crowding out** is, moreover, only one way in which consumption and investment may be adversely affected. Accordingly, this central controversy in fiscal policy is considered in more detail below.

Self-Assessment Questions

Using the four-quadrant derivation set out in Figure 10.1 above, show:

(a) the effect of a reduction in the tax rate.
(b) the effect of an increase in government spending on the slope and position of the *IS* schedule. Given an upward-sloping *LM* schedule, what are the implications of (a) and (b) respectively for the composition of aggregate demand ($C + I + G$)?

10.2 THE ROLE OF AUTOMATIC STABILISERS

If the government is concerned to stabilise aggregate demand via activist fiscal policy, the approach it should follow seems straightforward enough: if private-sector demand falls (e.g. because of an exogenous fall in investment), it should cut taxes to stimulate a recovery in consumption while at the same time expanding its own expenditure, and vice versa if private-sector demand is judged to be overly buoyant. In the real world, things are not so simple. The inside lags discussed above mean that it takes time for the government to recognise an unwelcome change in private spending and then to decide upon and implement the appropriate fiscal responses. Such inside lags may be considerable: much government spending (e.g. road building, construction, etc.) cannot be altered in the short run; tax rate changes may require legislative approval before they can be put into effect.

Expenditure Stabilisers

One way of overcoming such difficulties is to design fiscal policy in such a way that the counter-cyclical fiscal adjustments required are triggered automatically, rather than requiring deliberate policy action. On the expenditure side, this means finding forms of spending which are demand-led and increase (decrease) as income falls (rises). In fact, many of the demands made upon the state for goods and services are related to the level of income. In most countries, the government seeks to provide some form of social safety net, into which the poorer in society fall. During an economic recession, as incomes fall and unemployment rises, increasing numbers of people become eligible for public housing, health care and education. The government may also operate agricultural support programmes, which oblige it to buy larger quantities of produce to prop up market prices during a recession. Such counter-cyclical features are naturally present in many spending policies, but can be deliberately exaggerated in the interests of building automatic feedback mechanisms into the fiscal system.

Taxation Stabilisers

On the taxation side, the objective is to devise a structure which works to reduce (raise) the average rate of tax as income falls (rises). Note that while a proportional tax rate, t (where $T = tY$), reduces the size of the multiplier (see above) and so moderates the absolute fluctuations in income caused by exogenous shifts in, say, investment, this phenomenon of **fiscal drag** does not actively counteract downswings and upswings. In considering the effect of taxes, it is important to remember that taxes have been defined net of transfer payments (i.e. money payments from government to households for which no goods and services are received, for example unemployment benefits, pensions, etc.). Making transfer payments to low-income families is an alternative way of alleviating many of the same problems as direct public provision of goods and services and, in consequence, the numbers eligible for such support tend to rise (fall) during a recession (boom). In most countries, the actual tax system itself is usually *progressive*, with marginal rates that vary with income and so give rise to a variable average tax rate.

Consider the following simple example of the structure facing a typical income-earner: there is a tax-free allowance of $5 000 p.a.; between $5 001 and $10 000, the marginal rate of tax is 20%, rising to 30% between $10 001 and $15 000, 40% between $15 001 and $20 000 and 50% thereafter. Table 10.1 shows the marginal and average tax rates at different levels of income. Only in the tax-free band and at infinitely high incomes are the two the same, with the average rate of tax rising continuously from 0% towards 50% once the taxable threshold is crossed.

Table 10.1 Marginal and Average Rates of Taxation

Pre-tax income ($)	Marginal rate of taxation (%)	Total tax payable ($)	Average rate of taxation (%)
5 000	0	0	0
10 000	20	1 000	10
15 000	20	2 500	16.7
20 000	40	4 500	22.5
25 000	50	7 000	28
50 000	50	19 500	39
5 000 000	50	2 494 500	49.9

Indirect tax structures also provide a counter-cyclical thrust. Most governments tend to tax so-called 'luxury' goods like alcohol, tobacco and electronic consumer durables more heavily than 'basic essentials' like food, clothing, energy and housing. Almost by definition, luxury goods tend to be the things households buy during times of prosperity and the first things to be sacrificed when times are hard; in technical terms, they have a high income elasticity of demand while essentials have a very low income elasticity. As a result, when incomes are high and rising, an increasing proportion of consumption is devoted to purchasing heavily taxed luxuries (i.e. so increasing the ratio of indirect taxes paid to income), while the proportion slumps during a recession when incomes are low and falling (so reducing the ratio of indirect taxes paid to income).

Stabilisers and Outside Lags

Taken together, the presence of automatic stabilisers which increase (reduce) government spending and reduce (increase) the average tax rate during a downswing (upswing) ease some of the problems caused by inside lags, by making at least part of the fiscal adjustments needed automatic. It is important to understand that this leaves unaddressed the issue of outside lags. The automatic changes in G and t cannot be triggered until income itself has changed and these are then subject to the normal time-lags before their effects begin to bite. It is possible, therefore, that such automatic 'stabilisation' could actually be destabilising if the outside lags are sufficiently long that the economic cycle naturally passes its turning point (i.e. recovering after a recession, slowing down after a boom) before they work themselves out.

Self-Assessment Question

The economy is 'overheating', with unemployment falling very rapidly and inflation accelerating. The government is experiencing a growing budget surplus as a result and the finance minister claims that this is evidence that the government is using fiscal policy to stabilise the economy. Under what circumstances might the finance minister be correct?

10.3 MEASURING THE STANCE OF FISCAL POLICY

If the government is concerned with policy objectives which can be influenced by demand management, the foregoing suggests that it should alter its tax and spending plans in order to keep the level of income at some optimal level (or, in a dynamic setting, on some optimal growth path). Deviations of income from the desired level (or growth rate) can, accordingly, be corrected by appropriate changes in either taxes or spending, or both. It is clear that by operating such a *feedback rule*, the budget $(T - G)$ is only likely to balance by accident, so that the government must be prepared to accept whatever budget surplus (where $T - G > 0$) or deficit (where $T - G < 0$) arises as a by-product of its demand-management policy.

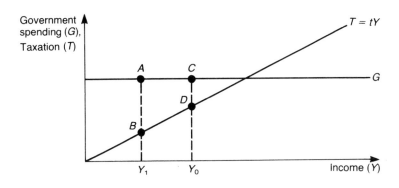

Figure 10.3

Crude statistics for the budget deficit or surplus say very little about the stance of government policy, however; that is, the extent to which it is expansionary or deflationary. As already noted, with fixed government spending and a constant, proportional average tax rate (t), total tax revenues (tY) vary over the economic cycle and so the size of the budget deficit is inversely related to the level of income (see Figure 10.3). At Y_1 the budget deficit (AB) is larger than at Y_0 (CD), not because of any discretionary change in policy (i.e. a deliberate change in G or t), but simply because the economy is depressed. In no sense is the stance of fiscal policy at Y_1 more expansionary than at Y_0

in fact, it is exactly the same and the larger deficit is simply a passive response to changes in the level of income.

The implication of Figure 10.3 is that it is impossible to infer from the statistics shown in Table 10.2 that Japan, for example, was operating a tighter fiscal policy than Canada, or even Italy, in 1991. In order to make this judgement, it is necessary to find some means of dissecting the crude figures to isolate, on the one hand, the effects of the economic cycle and, on the other, discretionary changes in government policy. One simple way to do this is to express the government's finances in terms of the budget balance it would have at some given level of income (e.g. the level of income consistent with, say, 6% unemployment). The level chosen is entirely arbitrary, since it serves as nothing more than a reference point for comparing one year with another and one country with another. In Figure 10.4 it is clear

Table 10.2 Budget Balances Around the World, 1991

	Budget Balance (% of GNP)
United States	−2.0
United Kingdom	−0.2
Germany	−4.0
France	−1.2
Italy	−9.5
Japan	+3.3
Canada	−4.0

Source: Goldman Sachs.

that, following policy changes, the government's fiscal stance in Year 2 is actually more restrictive than in Year 1, despite the fact that the recorded budget deficit is larger (i.e. the increase in the deficit due to cyclical forces more than offsets the reduction due to policy changes).

The distinction between exogenous (i.e. policy-determined) and induced changes in the budget balance can be illustrated by looking at the changing structure of the US budget deficit in Table 10.3. The last column shows the actual deficit recorded in each year this decade, while the **structural deficit** measures the size the deficit would have been had the economy been at 'full employment' (equivalent to about 6% unemployment) – Y^* in Figure 10.4. The

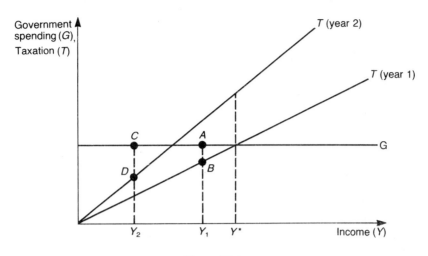

Figure 10.4

difference between the two is the **cyclical deficit**, that part of the deficit attributable to purely cyclical factors.

Table 10.3 The Changing Structure of the US Budget Deficit ($bn)

	Cyclical deficit	Structural deficit	Actual deficit
1980	4	55	59
1981	19	39	58
1982	62	48	110
1983	95	101	196
1984	49	126	175
1985	46	163	209
1986	34	187	211
1987	32	118	150
1988	27	130	157
1989	−18	166	148
1990	−90	310	220
1991	−73	358	285

Source: Congressional Budget Office; Goldman Sachs

Although this approach to the measurement of fiscal policy has certain attractions, it also has some serious limitations. You will recall that one way of circumventing the inside lag problem is to design fiscal policy so that changes in spending and tax rates are automatically triggered by changes in income, thereby reducing the need for discretionary adjustment. The effect of such automatic stabilisers is to render the government spending schedule negatively sloped and the tax schedule curvilinear (because its slope, which is the tax rate t, increases with income). The new schedules are set out in Figure 10.5, where the solid lines represent spending and tax revenues with automatic stabilisers and the broken lines show those without. The sensitivity of the budget deficit to changes in income is much greater under these circumstances, but the direction of causation is no longer simply from the latter to the former: when income falls, it causes changes not just in the budget deficit, but in government spending and tax rates which feed back to influence income.

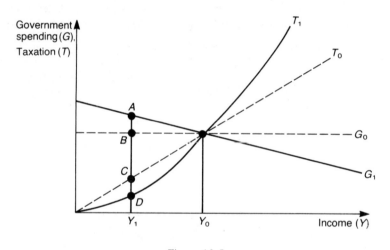

Figure 10.5

To the extent that automatic stabilisers are designed to mimic the discretionary policy changes which would otherwise be made, is it useful to ignore these by focusing on a structural deficit? In Figure 10.5 the budget is balanced at Y_0 and it is clear that the budget deficit with automatic stabilisers is very much bigger at Y_1 than it would be in their absence, by $AB + CD$ (AB due to the higher government spending and CD due to the lower tax rates). Both sets of spending and tax plans (i.e. one with automatic stabilisers and one without) give the same structural zero-balance at Y_0 yet to deliver the same expansionary stimulus to the economy at Y_1 in the absence of stabilisers, discretionary changes which shift G and T vertically apart by $AB + CD$ would be required. In other words, at Y_1 the system with automatic stabilisers and a structural, balanced budget is equivalent to the basic, discretionary system with a structural deficit of $AB + CD$ (and at $Y < Y_1$ an even larger structural deficit). Imagine, moreover, that this system of automatic stabilisers is perfect, so that discretionary changes in policy are never needed to keep aggregate demand stable. The government's structural budget therefore always shows precise balance, despite the fact that the fiscal automatic pilot is continuously tightening and loosening policy in response to changing macroeconomic conditions. Under such circumstances, cyclical adjustment is a pointless exercise.

In the real world, however, automatic stabilisers have only a modest feedback effect on income and typically require significant reinforcement by discretionary changes. However progressive the overall tax structure, unless the average tax rate rises to 100%, the government can only claw back a proportion of any exogenous rise in private-sector spending, so that income must change. Similarly, when a household's income falls (e.g. due to unemployment) to the extent that it qualifies for income-contingent public services and transfer payments, the **replacement ratio** (value of services and benefits when out of work relative to income in work) is generally much less than unity, so that again there is a net fall in demand and income. Because discretionary fiscal changes must, accordingly, always play the leading, rather than the supporting role in stabilisation policy, the concept of structural budget balances is therefore generally useful, despite the widespread use of automatic stabilisers; but for the reasons discussed above, it should be interpreted with caution.

Self-Assessment Question

Given what you know about the way the macro-economy works, does it follow that if the government's objective is to stabilise national income at the full-employment level, it should run a structurally balanced budget (i.e. where $G = T$ at full employment)?

10.4 FISCAL POLICY AND THE NATIONAL DEBT

When the budget is not in exact balance (i.e. so that tax receipts do not precisely cover government expenditure), the government must be either accumulating (if there is a budget surplus) or running down (if there is a budget deficit) its stock of net financial assets (i.e. financial assets net of financial liabilities). The essence of the **government budget constraint** can be expressed in various ways:

Expenditure + lending = Tax receipts + borrowing

Expenditure + increase in financial assets = Tax receipts + increase in financial liabilities

Budget surplus = Tax receipts − expenditure
= Increase in financial assets − increase in financial liabilities
= Increase in net financial assets

Most governments in most years run budget deficits, rather than budget surpluses (for example, until 1989 the British Government had had only one budget surplus – in 1970 – during the whole postwar period), and for this reason it is sometimes more useful to recast the budget constraint in deficit terms, that is:

Budget deficit = Increase in financial liabilities – increase in financial assets
= Increase in net financial liabilities

Ignoring for a moment the question of transactions in financial assets, which for most governments are negligibly small, consider now the various ways in which a government may finance a budget deficit. Essentially, it can only do so by selling financial claims on itself. The power to issue currency (i.e. legal tender, notes and coin) gives it a unique opportunity to sell a non-interest-bearing, irredeemable liability (in effect, the government sells newly printed notes and newly minted coinage to the banking system at face value, so profiting by the difference between production costs and face value), but in most developed economies the demand for additional currency is small relative to the size of the deficits to be financed.

The balance of the deficit must thus be covered by the sale of fixed-interest securities, variously known as Treasury bills, Treasury notes, bonds and gilt-edged stock, depending on the term of the security –

which may be from three months to eternity, for a perpetual or 'consolidated' security – and the issuing government.

The National Debt

The stock of outstanding government liabilities is generally known as the **national debt**. Britain's national debt dates back to 1694, when the government of the day was forced to run a large budget deficit to prosecute the country's war with France. Over the intervening period, it has risen from £11m to £170 bn ($300 bn). America's national debt has its origins in the 1776 War of Independence and had reached $3000 bn by 1990. Since governments rarely run persistent budget surpluses, fixed-term securities must be refinanced rather than repaid when they reach maturity. Normally, official statistics for the national debt exclude currency issue, which neither requires servicing (i.e. the payment of interest) nor redemption. The less widely used concept of **public debt**, which embraces both the national debt and currency issue, is therefore a more precise reflection of the accumulated effects of past budget deficits, but given the relative unimportance of currency, the difference between them is small (e.g. for Britain, currency outstanding is only in the order of £15 bn).

Abstracting from the question of currency, and continuing to ignore dealings in financial assets for the time being, a simple relationship between the budget deficit (BD) and the national debt (D) can be derived:

$$BD = \triangle D$$

and adding time subscripts:

$$BD_t = D_t - D_{t-1}$$

In other words, the difference between the national debt at the end of time-period $t - 1$ (D_{t-1}) and at the end of the period t (D_t) results from the budget deficit incurred by the government during time-period t (i.e. BD_t). The link is not just one-way, however. The size of the national debt also influences the size of the budget deficit, since interest on the debt has to be paid. Analytically, debt interest is a transfer payment by the government to bond holders, so that, given the way taxes have been defined net of transfers, the larger the outstanding debt, the smaller (net) tax revenues will be. To focus attention on debt interest, it is useful to separate out this item from the other tax and expenditure flows so that:

Budget deficit (BD) = Expenditure (G) − tax receipts (T) + debt interest (rD)

where r = average interest rate on outstanding national debt. Adding time subscripts as before,

$$BD_t = (G - T)_t + rD_{t-1}$$

This equation shows that not only will the national debt continue to grow as long as there is a budget deficit, but that there will be a budget deficit unless tax receipts exceed expenditures by more than the interest payments on the existing debt. Clearly, the larger the national debt, the higher the interest payments, and, all other things being equal, the larger the budget deficit. In this sense, the national debt feeds on itself and the larger it becomes, the more painful the expenditure cuts and tax increase needed to arrest its growth. It is clearly possible to envisage a situation in which the debt grows in an uncontrolled, explosive fashion. In Table 10.4 the government is actually in **primary balance** on its non-interest expenditure and taxes, and the rapid growth of the budget deficit and the national debt arise wholly from the fact that interest payments are financed by new borrowing.

Table 10.4 An Explosively Growing National Debt

Year	G_t	T_t	rD_{t-1}	BD_t	D_t
0	–	–	–	–	1000
1	100	100	100	100	1100
2	100	100	110	110	1210
3	100	100	121	121	1331
4	100	100	133	133	1464
5	100	100	146	146	1610
6	100	100	161	161	1771
7	100	100	177	177	1949
8	100	100	195	195	2143
9	100	100	214	214	2358
10	100	100	236	236	2594

Note. Interest rate (r) = 10%.

In general, this does not happen in a dynamic, real world setting where economic growth means that tax revenues grow continuously over time, allowing the government to generate a growing, offsetting surplus on its primary budget to set against the rising cost of debt service. Table 10.5 sketches out an alternative scenario, in which tax revenues increase steadily each year.

Table 10.5 shows that with an annual rate of growth of income (Y) – and thus tax revenues (tY) – of 10%, the primary surplus builds up, reducing the budget deficit by more than the growing interest payments swell it, and so eventually halting the growth of the national debt. Discretionary changes in G and t apart, whether the budget deficit grows or falls over time therefore depends upon, *inter alia*, the size of the inherited national debt, the average interest rate paid on outstanding securities, and the rate of growth of income.

Table 10.5 A Stabilising National Debt

Year	G_t	tY_t	rD_{t-1}	BD_t	D_t
0	100	–	–	–	1000
1	100	110	100	90	1090
2	100	121	109	88	1178
3	100	133	118	85	1262
4	100	146	126	80	1342
5	100	161	134	73	1415
6	100	177	142	65	1480
7	100	195	148	53	1533
8	100	214	153	39	1593
9	100	236	157	21	1593
10	100	259	159	0	1593

Note. Interest rate (r) = 10%. Annual rate of growth of income (Y) = 10%.

It might be thought that the illustrative figures used in Table 10.5 are somewhat unrealistic, particularly the assumption of a rate of growth of income of 10% p.a., since 10% interest rates are commonplace, but most developed economies average only 2–3% p.a. economic growth. Why are they not universally experiencing severe debt problems? The confusion arises from mixing up real and nominal variables. You will recall from Chapter 7 that interest rates are normally expressed in nominal terms, but in real terms the return paid is less than the nominal return by the rate of inflation:

Real interest rate = nominal interest rate − inflation rate

Conversely, economic growth conventionally refers to the rate of growth of real income and so the rate of inflation has already been deducted:

Real economic growth = nominal economic growth − inflation rate

For purposes of simplicity, most *IS–LM* analysis is conducted on the assumption that the inflation rate is zero (so real variables equal nominal variables). On this basis, the 10% figure assumed for real economic growth in Table 10.5 is undoubtedly unrealistic, but so too is a 10% real interest rate: historically, real interest rates have tended to shadow real growth rates in most countries (at around 2–3%), but with the advent of rapid inflation in the 1960s and 1970s, have often been strongly negative. If, on the other hand, the figures in Table 10.5 are interpreted as nominal figures, a 10% rate of growth for nominal income is highly representative of the experience in many countries. At the time of writing, for example, real income in Britain is expected to grow by approximately 3%, while inflation is running at about 7%, so giving growth of 10% for nominal income.

This distinction between nominal and real variables brings us to another important perspective on budget deficits and the national debt, namely the effect of inflation. During an inflationary period, nominal interest rates rise to reflect an inflation allowance. This so-called **Fisher effect** arises because lenders demand compensation for the expected fall in the real value of their capital over the term of the loan, and borrowers accede in view of the reduction in their real debt the inflation is expected to cause. However, the Fisher effect only applies to current interest rates. Buyers of fixed-interest government securities have contracted to lend their money at interest rates prevailing at the time they bought the assets. From the government's point of view, inflation works to boost their tax revenues (as nominal income grows) but leaves their interest payments on all except newly issued debt unaltered. Another way of looking at this process is to say that inflation leaves their real tax revenues unchanged, but cuts the real value of the national debt. This erosion of the real national debt is sometimes called the **inflation tax** because it transfers real wealth from the private owners of government securities to the government.

Let P_t be the price level at the end of time t and D_t be the nominal national debt at the end of time t. Between one time-period and the next, the size of the inflation tax is simply the amount by which the existing nominal national debt should have been increased to maintain its real value:

$$\text{Inflation tax} = (P_t / P_{t-1}) \, D_{t-1} - D_{t-1}$$
$$= [P_t - P_{t-1}/P_{t-1}]D_{t-1}$$
$$= \dot{P_t} D_{t-1}$$

where $\dot{P_t}$ is the rate of inflation during time t. Hence the real increase in the national debt is not simply the mirror of the budget deficit, but rather the budget deficit less the amount of the inflation tax. That is, measured in prices at end time t, the increase in the real national debt (RD) is:

$$\triangle RD_t = BD_t - P_t D_{t-1}$$

Thus, the faster the rate of inflation and the larger the national debt, the larger the nominal budget deficit which can be accommodated without increasing the real indebtedness of the government. Changes in the real indebtedness of the government offer a measure of the **real budget deficit**. In many countries during the 1970s, despite running quite large nominal deficits, the real budget was strongly in surplus as a result of the high inflation tax. (The counterpart was a real deficit on the part of the private sector, whose real wealth was eroded by inflation.)

Self-Assessment Question

In 1945, the ratio of the national debt to nominal gross domestic product (i.e. national income) in the United Kingdom was 200%, since which time it has fallen to 50%, despite the fact that successive governments have run budget deficits in all but three years. Explain.

10.5 FISCAL POLICY AND CROWDING OUT REVISITED

As noted above in 'Fiscal Policy in the *IS–LM* Model', unless the demand for money is perfectly interest-elastic (i.e. the *LM* schedule is horizontal), any fiscal stimulus to the economy will put upward pressure on interest rates, so crowding out investment and reducing the size of the increase in income. However, this is not the only possible route by which the expansionary effects of fiscal policy may be dissipated. Crowding out is, in fact, the generic term for any mechanism whereby higher government spending (or lower tax rates) lead to offsetting contractions in private-sector spending. (NB: for simplicity, in what follows a rise in government spending will be used as the means of stimulating the economy, but you should be aware that, bearing in mind the slight differences discussed on pp. 159–61, a reduction in tax rates would have similar effects.)

One simple way of categorising different types of crowding out is to distinguish between those that operate through the demand side of the economy and those that work through the supply side. In other words, crowding out may take place if:

(a) The higher government expenditure is partially or wholly offset by an induced fall in one or both of the private-sector components (i.e. consumption and investment) or aggregate demand; or

(b) The increase in aggregate demand (however large) fails to call forth an equivalent rise in output (aggregate supply), so that instead the government simply succeeds in bidding up the average price level (i.e. causing inflation), thereby diverting resources away from the private sector in the process).

The latter possibility could arise only under circumstances where any form of demand management, whether fiscal or monetary policy, was futile (e.g. if the economy was already at full employment or if the economy always rapidly returned to a vertical, long-run aggregate supply schedule following a change in aggregate demand). The design of macroeconomic policy under such conditions is discussed further below, but for present purposes it will be assumed that provided the fiscal stimulus actually causes an increase in aggregate demand, this will have the desired effects on the real economy.

Crowding Out and the Multiplier

Before reviewing the various ways in which an increase in government expenditure might reduce consumption and/or investment, it is useful to clarify the relationship between crowding out and the multiplier. In a very important sense the two concepts are mirror images. Simple income-expenditure theory postulates that exogenous changes in government spending trigger sympathetic changes in consumption (i.e. *crowd in* consumption), so that the final change in aggregate demand is some multiple of the original exogenous change. Crowding out, on the other hand, implies that changes in government spending induce opposite, offsetting changes in private spending.

The link between the multiplier and the degree of crowding out can be most easily illustrated algebraically:

$$\text{multiplier } (k) = \triangle Y / \triangle G$$

$$\text{percentage crowding out} = (\triangle G - \triangle Y) / \triangle G \times 100$$

hence,

$$\text{percentage crowding out} = 100 \, (1 - k)\%$$

$$
\begin{array}{ll}
k > 1 & \text{negative} \, (< 0\%) \text{ crowding out (i.e. crowding in)} \\
k = 1 & \text{zero} \, (0\%) \text{ crowding out} \\
0 < k < 1 & \text{partial} \, (0 - 100\%) \text{ crowding out} \\
k = 0 & \text{complete} \, (100\%) \text{ crowding out} \\
k < 0 & \text{super} \, (> 100\%) \text{ crowding out}
\end{array}
$$

Crowding Out Consumption and Investment

Turning first to consider the routes by which a rise in government spending may cause an offsetting reduction, rather than a multiplied expansion, in consumption, it is worth noting in passing that there are a number of mainstream theories of consumption which suggest that households may not automatically increase their spending following an increase in their incomes brought about by higher government spending. But while this would stop the expansionary effects of the fiscal stimulus after the first round, the initial rise in income would nevertheless have taken place. Another way of looking at this is that, with a marginal propensity to consume of zero, the multiplier would be unity and the degree of crowding out would be precisely zero. This still leaves unanswered the key question, is there any basis for the proposition that households may actually consume less following a rise in income?

One possibility is that the extra government spending goes to provide or improve services that some consumers may hitherto have been buying from the private sector (e.g. health care, education), so causing them to switch to the publicly provided service. This is sometimes termed **direct crowding out**. Another explanation for a fall in consumption is offered by the **Ricardian equivalence theorem,** which postulates that households are ultra-rational and increase their savings in anticipation of the higher taxes that will be required in future to service and repay the increased national debt.

The equivalence theorem is so called because government borrowing to finance higher expenditure is said to constitute deferred taxation and is accordingly equivalent to higher taxes today in terms of its net effect on aggregate demand. Because households do not live for ever, the equivalence theorem requires that individuals are not only ultra-rational, but also that they take a strong view about the appropriate stock of net assets (i.e. net of both actual, personal liabilities and future tax liabilities) that they should pass on to their descendants and that they make concerted efforts to adjust this stock out of current income in response to changes in fiscal policy. It also presupposes that none of the higher government spending goes on programmes which add to the supply potential of the economy, so generating the extra tax revenues needed to service the higher national debt by increasing the level of income.

Analytically, the crowding out of consumption through the channels just outlined implies that the rightward shift in the *IS* curve caused by the increase in government spending would be reversed by the fall to autonomous consumption. Accordingly, 100% crowding out would mean that the reversal was complete, so that the *IS* curve would not move at all following an exogenous change in government spending. In contrast, the crowding out of investment spending, which operates in a variety of ways, involves a rise in interest rates which slides the economy back up a new *IS* curve.

The standard form of financial crowding out has already been reviewed. In this version the higher government spending causes an increase in income, which increases the demand for active balances, pushing up interest rates (with an unchanged real money supply) and thereby choking off investment. There is, however, a second source of upward pressure on interest rates. The sales of government securities required to finance the extra spending add to the private sector's financial wealth and, to the extent that the demand for idle balances is a function of the total stock of financial wealth, this leads to a rightward shift in the relevant demand schedule (see the bottom-right quadrant of Figure 10.6). The *LM* function consequently shifts to the left, raising interest rates and reinforcing what might be termed the 'active balances' effect on investment.

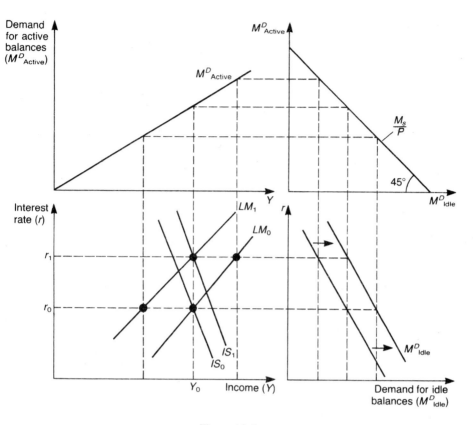

Figure 10.6

The Keynesian View

Keynesian economists, who argue that money and financial assets like securities are very close substitutes (so that the demand for idle balances is very interest-sensitive), doubt that this latter 'idle balances' or 'portfolio balance effect' is likely to exert very much upward pressure on interest rates, pointing out further that unless the demand-for-money function is stable over time – which they deny – this effect will not be predictable either. Some Keynesians have also pointed out that consumption, as well as the demand for idle balances, is also a function of financial wealth, while interest payments on government securities are transfer payments which, in our analytical framework, manifest themselves as a fall in the net tax rate. Hence, government bond sales will tend to make the *IS* schedule shift to the right (as financial wealth increases) and become flatter (as the net tax rate falls), so offsetting the leftward movement of the *LM* curve.

Proponents of the crowding-out view counter by claiming that households do not view government securities as net wealth (in the sense that, following the spirit of the equivalence theorem, households will anticipate higher taxes in future as a result of government borrowing), pointing out, moreover, that the idle balances' effect is, unlike the active balances' effect, not a once-for-all phenomenon. As long as the higher government expenditure is maintained, the associated borrowing continuously adds to financial wealth and the leftward drift of the *LM* curve persists. If anything, the process accelerates, since the gradual fall in income leads to an ever-larger budget deficit (for the reasons discussed above on pages 167–71) and ever-heavier sales of securities.

This controversy continues to divide the economics profession and its resolution is clearly of great importance to fiscal policy-makers. To the extent that there is a consensus view, it is that there will be some degree of crowding out and that this will increase over time, but that the actual effects of fiscal policy cannot be predicted in isolation from the monetary stance. Clearly, financial crowding out in both forms could be easily avoided by increasing the money supply, in order to accommodate the increased demand for money and prevent interest rates rising, thereby allowing the full, multiplied effects of the higher government spending to take effect. However, this moves us beyond the discussion of 'pure' fiscal policy into the issue of macroeconomic policy co-ordination and this development must await the review of monetary policy to which we now turn.

Self-Assessment Question

Can you envisage any circumstances under which higher government spending might crowd in exogenous private-sector spending, inducing a rise in investment, for example?

Further Reading

Shone, R. (1989) *Open Economy Macroeconomics: Theory, Policy and Evidence*, Harvester Wheatsheaf, Hemel Hempstead.

Gowland, D. H. (1985) *Money, Inflation and Unemployment: The Role of Money in the Economy*, Harvester, Brighton.

Hillier, B. (1991) *The Macroeconomic Debate: Models of the Closed and Open Economy*, Basil Blackwell, Oxford (especially chapter 5).

Brown, W. S. (1988) *Macroeconomics*, Prentice-Hall, New Jersey.

11

Monetary Policy

In many developed economies, monetary policy has become almost synonymous with the doctrine of monetarism in recent years. With varying degrees of success, almost all major Western governments have experimented with targets for monetary growth, in the belief that such monetary 'rules' would assist them in their battle against inflation. Many developing countries, too, often at the behest of the International Monetary Fund, from whom debt problems have forced them to borrow, have also adopted monetary targets in one form or another. But although monetarism assigns overriding importance to monetary policy, it has always been an important arm of demand management and remains so for those governments which either tried and abandoned monetarism, or were never converted to it.

As noted in Chapter 9, monetary policy basically embraces all government measures directed at the financial system with the objective of influencing the behaviour of its private-sector customers (e.g. deterring companies and individuals from borrowing via high interest rates). This section recalls first the role of the money in the economy and then turns to consider the various ways in which the government can intervene in the process of money creation to further its macroeconomic policy aims.

11.1 MONETARY POLICY IN THE *IS-LM* MODEL

Chapter 4 introduced you to the role of money in the *IS-LM* model and this section explores the various transmission mechanisms more fully. You should ensure that you are familiar with the derivation of the *LM* schedule before continuing and, in particular, that you understand the significance of the interest rate and income sensitivity of the demand for real money balances. Figure 11.1 sets out the four-quadrant derivation of the *LM* schedule, which maps out (for a given price level, P) those combinations of interest rates (r) and income (Y) which ensure that the demand for real money balances, M^D, is equal to the real money supply, M_s/P:

$$M_s/P = M^D = f(Y,r)$$

Remember that a higher level of income increases the demand for transactions, or active, balances, and so must be offset by a higher interest rate to reduce the demand for asset, or idle, balances, so that overall equilibrium between the demand for, and an unchanged real supply of, money is maintained. An increase in the real money supply (i.e. an increase in the nominal money supply M_s, assuming fixed prices) shifts the *LM* schedule to the right (the actual process by which this increase takes place will be discussed below).

Consider briefly the nature of the transmission mechanism in this simple model. When the *LM* schedule shifts to the right, it slides down the *IS* schedule which is downward-sloping. The equilibrium level of income (at the intersection of the new *LM* curve and an unchanged *IS* curve) is higher than before, with interest rates lower than before. But how is this new equilibrium attained? The immediate effect of the increase in the money supply is that wealth-owners have excess real balances, given current incomes and interest rates. Their immediate response is to switch this unwanted money into interest-bearing assets. But while individual wealth-owners can successfully restore their portfolios to equilibrium, at the level of the economy these adjustments are like a game of 'pass the parcel', with someone holding excess balances every time the music stops. A direct consequence of this increased demand for interest-bearing assets, however, is a gradual rise in asset prices (i.e. a fall in interest rates) and it is through this route that the effects of the monetary expansion are transmitted to the goods

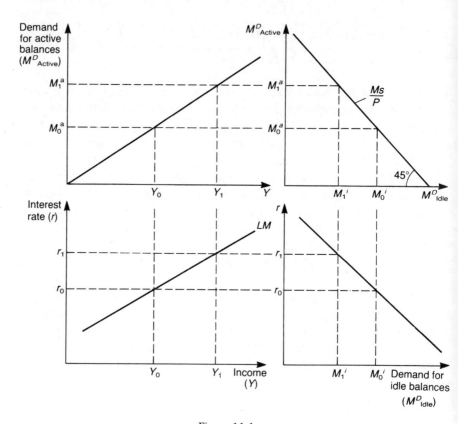

Figure 11.1

market. Investment is interest-sensitive and, as interest rates fall, firms begin to borrow more and increase their capital spending, which has the familiar impact on income through the usual multiplier channels.

As income rises (so increasing the demand for active balances) and interest rates fall (boosting the demand for idle balances), the demand for money increases until eventually wealth-owners in aggregate are induced to hold the higher money balances willingly. In equilibrium, therefore, interest rates are lower and investment, (induced) consumption, savings, taxes and income are all higher. The transmission mechanism, sometimes called the **cost-of-capital channel**, can be summarised thus:

$$\uparrow M_s \rightarrow \downarrow r \rightarrow \uparrow I \rightarrow \uparrow Y \rightarrow \uparrow M^D$$

The potency of monetary policy thus turns on the strength of the

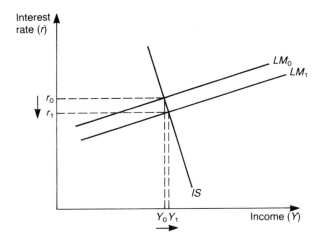

Figure 11.2(a)

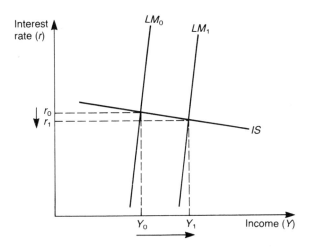

Figure 11.2(b)

various links in the cost-of-capital chain of causation. If, for example, the demand for money were highly interest-sensitive, then the rate of interest would not have to fall very far before wealth-owners were once again in equilibrium; consequently, the first link would be very weak and the effect of the money supply change would fizzle out before it reached the real economy. Alternatively, investment might be very interest-insensitive, so that however large the change in interest rates eventually brought about, there was little subsequent increase in autonomous expenditures (and so income). The third link, which depends on the value of the income multiplier, has implications for the leverage effect of any change in injections, however caused, and so is not specifically relevant to the discussion of monetary policy *per se*.

Early 'Keynesian–monetarist' debates between, on the one hand, Keynesian economists who argued that monetary policy was ineffective as a tool of demand management and, on the other, monetarists who claimed that monetary policy was extremely powerful, tended to be conducted in terms of these two interest elasticities. The two respective positions can be conveniently summarised using *IS-LM* diagrams. The Keynesian position is set out in Figure 11.2(a), which has a flattish *LM* schedule (which follows from the assumption of a high interest sensitivity of investment). Because the first two links in the cost-of-capital channel are thus weak, the effect of a change in the money supply is slight.

Figure 11.2(b) sets out the opposite monetarist viewpoint, with a steep *LM* curve (because money and other financial assets are considered poor substitutes, the interest sensitivity of the demand for idle balances is very low) and a shallow *IS* curve (based on the proposition that financial and real assets are close substitutes, so that investment expenditures are highly interest-sensitive). Unsurprisingly, changes in the money supply have a powerful effect on income.

The Keynesian View of Monetary Policy

Theoretical debates about the nature of the monetary transmission mechanism have since moved on from this point, which was reached during some very acrimonious academic exchanges during the 1960s. Keynesians, for their part, have tended increasingly to stress the instability of the demand for money. Both the demand for active balances and the demand for idle balances depend, in their view, on expectations of an uncertain future: if there is a general feeling of unease about likely developments in the economy, with fears of possible inflation and/or unemployment, the demand for active balances may rise as people seek security in larger money balances; if there is a widespread view that interest rates are likely to rise, the demand for idle balances may increase, since wealth-owners will want to switch out of fixed-interest securities which seem set to fall in value (remember that the market price of a fixed-interest bond is inversely related to interest rates). If the demand for money is unstable, fluctuating unpredictably in response to changing sentiment in the money market, the *LM* will shift in the absence of changes in the money supply; by the same token, increases in the money supply may coincide with changes in the demand for money which sometimes reinforce, and sometimes cancel out, the expansionary effects which would otherwise result. On this basis, Keynesians argue that not only is monetary policy generally weak in its effects on income, but the effects are highly unpredictable.

In contrast, monetarists, who assert that the demand for money is highly stable, also invoke an additional transmission mechanism, which supplements their (strong) cost-of-capital channel and means that monetary policy will have a major impact on income. As already noted, monetarists believe that real and financial assets are close substitutes (e.g. in Britain, a very high proportion of household wealth is held in the form of residential housing, rather than securities or bank deposits), so that faced with excess real balances, wealth-owners switch not only into bonds, but also into real assets (e.g. housing, real estate, automobiles and other consumer durables). Hence, the effect of an increase in the money supply extends beyond pushing down interest rates (which stimulates investment), directly increasing consumer expenditure as well.

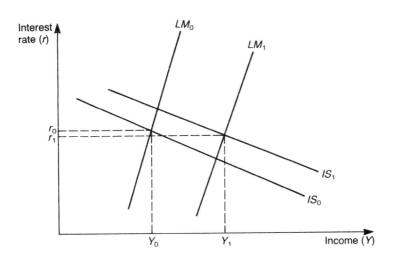

Figure 11.3

Analytically, this appears as a shift to the right in the *IS* schedule (See Figure 11.3), providing a further boost to income. Clearly, these debates about the potency of monetary policy are extremely important and we shall return to them later.

Self-Assessment Questions

The slopes of the *IS* and *LM* schedules are very important for the effectiveness of monetary policy. Under what circumstances would money policy have *no* effect on income? Can you conceive of a situation where these circumstances are likely to arise in the real world?

11.2 THE MONEY SUPPLY PROCESS

Since monetary policy involves altering the money supply – whether with the intention of determining the quantity *per se* or the rate of interest on other financial assets – a useful point of departure is to consider the nature of the money supply process. 'Money', to paraphrase the famous monetarist economist Milton Friedman, 'is whatever does the work of money'; in other words, money is that collection of financial assets which serves as a medium of exchange. Broadly speaking, in most countries currency and bank deposits (chequing accounts, or chequing accounts plus time deposits if the latter can easily be converted into the former) jointly perform this central function. Where does this money come from?

Currency is issued by the government, normally through the central bank which acts on its behalf in this regard, while bank deposits are the liabilities of the commercial banking system. The two magnitudes are related, since banks must 'back' a certain proportion of their deposits with their own holdings of currency, as insurance against withdrawal by their depositors. In this sense, therefore, the issue of currency sets a limit on the volume of bank deposits which can be created and it is this relationship which is at the heart of monetary policy.

Table 11.1 sets out the balance sheet of the commercial banking system and the money supply identity in a very simple world in which there is a central bank and only one commercial bank. Suppose the central bank issues $1000 of currency, increasing the money supply by this amount dollar for dollar – stage (1). A proportion, say 90%, is eventually deposited at the commercial bank – stage (2). Bank deposits have now increased by $900, but the total money supply (bank deposits plus currency in circulation with the general public) is still only $1000 higher, because the extra bank deposits are offset by the fall in the amount of currency in circulation, $900 of which is now lying idle in the commercial bank's vaults.

Suppose from past experience the commercial bank has found that daily fluctuations in net cash withdrawals (i.e. cash withdrawals less cash deposits) never exceed more than ± 10% of its total deposit liabilities; that is, the extra currency it has taken could safely support increased deposits of up to $9000.

The manager is contemplating this state of affairs when a long-established customer appears to request a loan. In a trice, the manager lends the customer $1000, increasing his deposit by $1000 and booking the loan as a corresponding asset on the bank's balance sheet – stage (3). The money supply has now increased by a further $1000. In due course, the customer spends the $1000, but even if he withdraws currency to do so rather than paying by cheque (which just transfers his $1000 deposit to another bank customer), the bulk of the $1000 is likely to be redeposited at the bank – stage (4). More important, to the extent that some of the newly created bank deposit 'leaks' out of the commercial banking system, resurfacing as extra currency in circulation, this simply alters the form in which the new money is held, rather than changing the amount by which the money supply has increased.

Although this is a very simple model of the money supply process, it nevertheless serves to highlight the key elements in the process: the issue of currency by the central bank (C), the role of the public's 'currency ratio' (c) – the proportion of the money supply the public seeks to hold in the form of currency (C) rather than bank deposits (D) – and the commercial bank's 'reserve ratio' (b) – the proportion of its deposit liabilities the bank needs to hold in the form of currency reserves (C_b). The various links can be summarised algebraically as follows:

$$M = C_p + D$$
$$\text{and} \quad C = C_p + C_b$$

where, $C_p = cD$ and $C_b = bD$,
therefore, $M = cD + D$ and $C = cD + bD$

hence $M/C = (cD + D)/(cD + bD) = (c + 1)/(c + b)$
therefore, $M = C[(c + 1)/(c + b)]$

Table 11.1 Money Creation in a Single Commercial Bank Model (cumulative changes over time)

		COMMERCIAL BANK			
	Liabilities ($)			*Assets ($)*	
Deposits	(1)	–	Currency in vaults	(1)	–
	(2)	+ 900		(2)	+ 900
	(3)	+ 1 900		(3)	+ 900
	(4)	+ 1 810		(4)	+ 810
			Loans	(1)	–
				(2)	–
				(3)	+ 1 000
				(4)	+ 1 000
+ Currency in circulation	(1)	+ 1 000			
	(2)	+ 100			
	(3)	+ 100			
	(4)	+ 190			
= Money supply	(1)	+ 1 000			
	(2)	+ 1 000			
	(3)	+ 2 000			
	(4)	+ 2 000			

The same ideas can be expressed graphically. Figure 11.4 shows the relationship between the volume of currency in circulation (on the vertical axis) and bank deposits (on the horizontal axis). The public's demand for currency is measured going up the vertical axis from C_{po}, while the commercial bank's demand for currency reserves is measured by moving in the opposite direction, namely down the vertical axis from C_{bo}. The distance from C_{po} to C_{bo} represents the total amount of currency available, which the public and the commercial bank must share between them. The schedule C_{pd} maps out the public's demand for currency for different holdings of bank deposits (its slope is the public's currency ratio, c), while C_{bd} shows the bank's demand for currency reserves for different stocks of deposit liabilities (its slope is the commercial bank's reserve ratio, b). The point where the two schedules intersect (at C^1, D^1) represents equilibrium, with the total money stock (currency in circulation plus bank deposits) given by summing the vertical distance $C_{po}C^1$ (currency in circulation) and $C_{po}D^1$ (the stock of bank deposits).

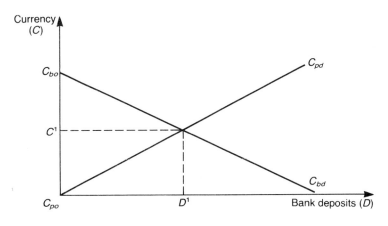

Figure 11.4

Self-Assessment Questions

Referring to Figure 11.4, what would be the effect on the positions and slopes of the schedules, and so on the money supply, of:

(a) an increase in the issue of currency?
(b) a reduction in the public's currency ratio?
(c) an increase in the commercial bank's reserve ratio?

11.3 THE BASIC PRINCIPLES OF MONETARY CONTROL

The so-called **money multiplier** relationship, $M = C[(c + 1)/(c + b)]$, suggests an obvious route by which the authorities could influence the process of money creation, namely by limiting the issue of new currency. Because the currency issue is the 'base' on which the money supply is built, this approach is known as **monetary base control.**

Variations on this theme are used in a number of countries, including Germany and Switzerland.

Notice that this algebraic expression of the link between currency issue and the money supply says nothing explicit about bank lending, the mechanism by which the commercial bank actually expands its deposits following the issue of new currency. The implication is that the bank will simply adjust its lending rate, given the demand for bank loans that it faces, until it has lent all that its holdings of currency will allow. In analytical terms, the supply of bank loans is thus exogenously fixed by the amount of currency reserves the central bank issues, and interest rates simply move to clear the market – see Figure 11.5.

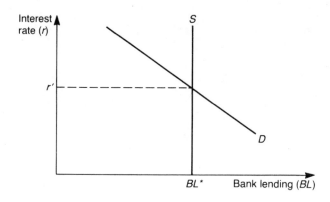

Figure 11.5

Interest-Rate Control

An alternative approach involves turning the spotlight directly on bank lending itself. Suppose that instead of simply issuing predetermined amounts of currency, the mechanism is that the central bank undertakes to lend newly issued currency to the commercial bank – on demand – at an interest rate fixed by the central bank. The commercial bank would then be able to lend, secure in the knowledge that, on request, it could borrow from the central bank all the currency it needed to back the consequent increase in its deposit liabilities. Under this new arrangement, the commercial bank's lending rate would reflect not the demand for bank loans but the cost of acquiring extra reserves. The higher the interest rate charged by the central bank, the higher the rate charged by the commercial bank to its borrowing customers. The supply of new bank loans would be, in effect, perfectly elastic at the interest rate dictated by the central bank. Provided that the central bank has a reasonable idea of the shape and position of the demand for commercial bank loans, it could therefore exercise control over bank lending – and hence monetary growth – by engineering increases or reductions in the commercial bank's lending rate, as illustrated in Figure 11.6.

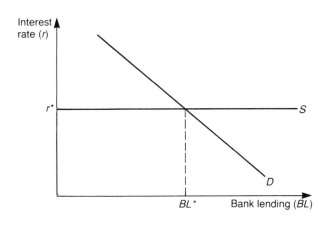

Figure 11.6

Versions of this alternative approach to monetary control are used in a number of countries, including the United Kingdom and Australia. Under such systems, interest rates tend to be more stable than under monetary base control, since they are only altered by the central bank when it becomes convinced that bank lending is behaving in a systematically undesirable way. In contrast, under monetary base control, rigid control of the currency issue means that fluctuations in the demand for bank lending result in greater short-run volatility of interest rates.

A common feature of both systems, however, is that they ultimately control bank lending, and hence the process of money creation, by manipulating the price of, or interest rate on, bank loans. Alternatively, the government could use its legislative power to control the whole process more directly. At a minimalist level, it could enforce regulations which improve its ability to control bank lending using the two techniques already described (e.g. obliging the commercial bank to operate a much higher reserve ratio than prudence alone would require). More radically, the government could oblige the commercial bank to limit its lending to x, regardless of its reserves or the demand for bank loans at prevailing interest rates. The practical implementation of all three approaches to monetary control will be discussed next.

Self-Assessment Questions

What might be the advantages to the government of using direct controls rather than monetary base/interest-rate control to pursue monetary policy? What are likely to be the main drawbacks?

11.4 THE PRACTICE OF MONETARY CONTROL

Although the single commercial bank model allows us to explore the basic mechanics of different monetary control techniques, it has important limitations and in order to discuss monetary control in practice, it is useful to extend our analysis to allow for a multi-bank commercial sector. This is because the almost universal convention, whereby the central bank acts as 'banker' to its numerous, separate commercial banks (e.g. approximately in the United States), makes monetary control techniques in the real world much more sophisticated than our simple analysis so far would suggest.

Why do commercial banks 'bank' with the central bank? In principle, commercial banks could hold currency reserves in their vaults to cover deposit withdrawals, but in a multi-bank system most withdrawals arise because customers need to pay creditors with accounts at other banks. To avoid the large-scale transfer of currency between banks, almost all of which nets out at the end of each day's business, the commercial banks deposit the bulk of their reserves with the central bank which then acts as a clearing house to settle up interbank indebtedness. Under this arrangement we must therefore redefine bank 'reserves' to include both currency in the banks' vaults (as before) plus their deposits at the central bank.

This institutional feature of most banking systems means that currency issue actually has nothing to do with the process by which the central bank alters bank reserves. Apart from reserves and loans to firms and individuals, commercial banks hold a range of other assets, including negotiable stocks and bonds and short-term paper (e.g. Treasury bills) which are actively traded day by day. By intervening in bond and bill markets, the central bank can alter the reserves held by the banking system. If it buys assets from the commercial banks, it pays for them by creating additional central bank deposits and vice versa, if it sells assets. Table 11.2 illustrates a situation in which the central bank buys bills in order to increase reserves.

Table 11.2 The Balance Sheet Implications of Open-market Operations

CENTRAL BANK	
Liabilities	*Assets*
Commercial bank deposits + $10m	Currency Bills + $10m Other Financial Assets

COMMERCIAL BANKING SYSTEM	
Liabilities	*Assets*
Deposits	Currency in Vaults Central Bank Deposits + $10m Bills − $10m Other Financial Assets

If the central bank is trying to control the monetary base, such **open-market operations** will be conducted in order to maintain the volume of reserves at some target level. If the central bank is seeking to manipulate interest rates, this market intervention is designed to peg rates at the desired level: passively lending the reserves needed by the commercial banks at a predetermined rate (the expositional device used above) and supplying them by buying assets at a fixed price are alternative means to the same end and analytically identical in their effects. Most central banks which peg interest rates in fact use a mixture of 'discount window' lending, as it is widely known, and open-market operations and the official rate at which reserves are available go by a variety of names, reflecting which of the two is the more important, e.g. intervention rate (UK, post-1981), minimum lending rate (UK, 1971–81), federal funds rate (US), and so on.

In the real world, therefore, currency is not created out of thin air as we assumed for illustrative purposes above. Rather, commercial banks acquire reserves from the central bank in exchange for other types of financial asset, like bills and bonds, and they are free to switch between the two forms in which these reserves may be held – namely, central bank deposits and currency – at will. Thus only as much currency is actually issued as the commercial banks (reflecting the wishes of their depositing customers) demand and the actual issue itself is irrelevant for monetary control purposes. It is the overall volume of reserves, rather than its composition as between central bank deposits and currency, which matters and it is this magnitude to which open-market operations are directed.

Direct Controls

Open-market operations apart, whether with the aim of influencing either the quantity or the price of bank reserves, the other main way in which monetary control is exercised is through the use of direct controls. The precise form these take varies from country to country. Sometimes the controls are designed to enhance the central bank's leverage over the quantity or price of reserves, or to strengthen the link between the monetary base and bank lending. At other times and places, the controls are intended to supplement normal open-market operations, particularly where a rapid impact on bank lending is required; in some countries, controls are used as a substitute for monetary base/interest rate control.

Consider, first, regulations designed to enhance the central bank's influence over the availability and price of bank loans. In the United Kingdom, commercial banks have historically been required to hold their liquid assets in certain forms (e.g. three-month bills), allowing the Bank of England to concentrate its open-market operations on a single, unnaturally large bill market and thereby making its task of manipulating interest rates rather easier. The Bank of England also has the power to 'freeze' a percentage of the commercial bank deposits it holds, so that they no longer exist for the purposes of balance-sheet accounting. In the United States, a legal (variable) reserve ratio is imposed in order to change the link between the monetary base and bank lending at the authorities' discretion (refer back to Figure 11.4 if you are uncertain about the effect such changes would have).

As an emergency measure, direct controls have been frequently imposed in the United Kingdom as well as many other countries. Their purpose is normally to produce an immediate change in monetary conditions, so avoiding the time-lags otherwise inherent in the system. For example, a rise in interest rates does not reduce bank lending overnight; if the government were concerned to bring about an immediate reduction in bank lending, it might order the commercial banks to restrict their lending activities artificially until its interest-rate changes had time to bite. Such controls were regularly employed in the United Kingdom for short periods during the 1970s and for quite extended periods in the 1960s.

Finally, direct controls are sometimes used as a straightforward alternative to monetary base or interest rate control. **Quantitative controls** involve instructions to commercial banks to limit their lending to some target level. Such directives may be backed by force of law, but often the implicit or explicit threat that the central bank will tighten monetary conditions unless they are obeyed is sufficient. One advantage of direct controls is that they can also be **qualitative**, in the sense that commercial banks can be requested to channel a higher proportion of their lending to, say, manufacturing industry (at the expense of private consumers) during a period of credit restriction. This latter feature of direct controls is typically most developed in countries which use some form of economic planning, where it is important that bank lending be consistent with the plan's objectives.

Self-Assessment Questions

Refer to Table 11.1 above. Suppose there were an increase in the public's demand for currency. What would be the effect on:

(a) bank deposits?
(b) currency issue?
(c) commercial bank reserves? What is likely to be the central bank's response to this development, assuming its monetary targets were previously on course?

Monetary Control and Fiscal Policy

Although currency is released into circulation by the central bank, passively responding to demands by the commercial banks, it is ultimately a liability (albeit a non-interest-bearing, irredeemable liability) of the government. New notes and coin are normally printed by the government and sold to the central bank on request whenever the latter finds its stocks running low. Because new currency is sold at face value, this exercise nets a tidy profit (sometimes termed **seignorage**) for the government and although the proceeds are now small (given the relative unimportance of currency relative to bank deposits) and the currency is provided to the banks – and through them to the general public – on demand, this was not always so.

Historically, the power to create new currency provided governments with an important source of revenue, tempting them to use this device to pay their bills by 'printing money' – that is, by quite literally printing new notes and coin with which to pay creditors directly. The Confederate Government during the American Civil War of the 1860s was a famous exponent of this crude form of 'deficit financing'. But while the institutional structure in most countries prevents modern-day governments from forcing newly printed currency onto its citizens for financing purposes, the links between the government's budgetary finances and the money supply remain powerful.

Normally the government, like the commercial banks, has its account at the central bank, although the nature of the relationship between the two varies from country to country. In the United States, the government and the central bank are constitutionally independent of one another, so that, in principle, the government is a customer like any other; in contrast, the Bank of England is nationalised and therefore the government is both its customer and its owner, making for a rather more intimate relationship.

Refer to Table 11.3. What happens when the government writes a cheque on its central bank account for $10m, for example to pay its school teachers? The recipients pay the cheques into their commercial bank accounts and the commercial banks, in turn, present them to the central bank – stage (1). The central bank credits the commercial banks' accounts and debits the government's account by $10m. The government spending has caused an increase, dollar for dollar, in both bank reserves and the money supply. This is not the end of the story, since this spending must be financed in some way. If it is covered by tax receipts, the whole process is reversed – private firms and individuals give cheques for $10m to the government and both bank deposits and bank reserves fall back to their original values as these are paid into the government's account. In other words, a balanced budget, with spending covered dollar for dollar by taxes, has no monetary implications.

Table 11.3 The Money Supply Implications of a Budget Deficit (changes from one period to the next)

CENTRAL BANK

Liabilities($)			Assets ($)
Government Deposit	(1)	−10m	Currency
	(2a)	+10m	Other Financial Assets
	(2b)	+10m	
Commercial Bank	(1)	+10m	
	(2a)	−10m	
	(2b)	−20m	

COMMERCIAL BANKING SYSTEM

Liabilities ($)			Assets ($)		
Deposits	(1)	+10m	Currency in Vaults		
	(2a)	−			
	(2b)	−10m	Central Bank Deposits	(1)	+10m
				(2a)	+10m
				(2b)	−10m
			Government Securities	(1)	
				(2a)	−10m
				(2b)	−10m
			Other Financial Assets		

Money Supply	(1)	+10m
	(2a)	−
	(2b)	−10m

But suppose the spending is unmatched by taxes (i.e. there is a budget deficit of $10m). Instead, the government sells securities (or Treasury bills) to rebuild its central bank deposit to its original level. In this case, the monetary effects depend on who buys the new securities. If they are purchased by the commercial banks (stage 2a), bank reserves fall back by $10m, but the earlier rise in bank deposits remains; only if the securities are sold to the non-bank private sector is the increase in the money supply also cancelled out − stage (2b). In other words, government expenditure, financed by selling securities to the banking system, has the same effect on the money supply as governments of yore which printed and spent newly created notes and coin. For this reason, deficit spending, paid for by bank borrowing − which is what selling securities to banks amounts to – is still often termed 'printing money' in modern-day economies.

Under a system of monetary base control, while budget deficits do not, of themselves, directly compromise monetary control – since in net terms the monetary base is unchanged, regardless of whether the securities are purchased by the commercial banks or the non-bank private sector – there are important effects on both the level and structure of interest rates. If the extra securities are bought by the banks, this implies that the private sector will be able to borrow correspondingly less within the limits on total bank lending imposed by the ceiling on the monetary base; bank lending rates will, accordingly, be driven up to ration the remaining funds available. Alternatively, if they are bought by the non-banks, the interest rates on securities will be bid up as the government has to compete for available funds with private would-be borrowers in the longer-term capital markets.

Under the alternative system of interest-rate pegging, in which both the monetary base and the money supply move to accommodate the overall demand for bank lending at the policy-set interest rate, the effects of the budget deficit manifest themselves in much the same way. If the extra securities are bought by the banks (adding to bank lending), the central bank must either supply additional reserves, thereby effectively sanctioning the increase in the money supply, or try to claw back this increase by reducing bank lending to the private sector by a comparable amount through higher interest rates. If the extra securities are purchased by the non-banks, of course, the results are as under monetary base control.

Thus, regardless of the system of monetary control in operation, a budget deficit implies either that the money supply increases or that interest rates rise. Moreover, because no central bank can tolerate rising interest rates indefinitely, there must always come a point at which the budget deficit is so large that monetary growth can no longer be contained. When this point is reached, the central bank will be forced to buy government securities, either from the non-banks or the banks direct, so alleviating the upward pressure on interest rates and allowing the monetary base to increase. Hence, irrespective of the constitutional relationship between the central bank and the government, under certain circumstances the government is always able to ensure that its deficits are 'monetised' (i.e. financed by an increase in the money supply).

The Supply-Side Identity

These important linkages between the money supply and fiscal policy can be summarized as follows. As we have already established, to the extent that it is not financed by selling securities to the non-bank private sector ($\triangle GS_p$), the government's budget deficit (BD) must be financed in a way which increases the money supply; that is, in the main by selling securities to the commercial banks and, to a lesser extent, when it is able to sell newly printed currency to match the general public's increased demand for currency ($\triangle C_p$). The only other cause of monetary growth is an increase in bank lending to the private sector ($\triangle BLPS$).

From this can be derived the so-called, 'supply-side identity':

$$\triangle M = BD - \triangle GS_p + \triangle BLPS$$

The value of this identity is that it relates changes in the money supply to fiscal policy (as measured by the budget deficit), to the volume of government securities sold to the non-bank private sector, and to bank lending to the private sector. If the government is attempting to control monetary growth, then, given its intended fiscal stance, it can estimate the implications for bank lending to the private sector and short- and long-term interest rates.

But although this highlights the triangular nature of the relationship between the money supply, the budget deficit and interest rates and the interdependence of monetary and fiscal policy, it is important to realise its limitations. It is a purely *ex-post*, accounting identity, not a behavioural relationship. It does not necessarily imply that reducing the budget deficit would reduce monetary growth. In fact, deep cuts in goverment spending may deflate income, reducing sales of government securities and forcing firms to finance an unexpected build-up in their stocks by extra bank borrowing. The final result may actually be higher monetary growth! Nevertheless, treated with caution, this way of approaching the problem can be helpful in avoiding inconsistent monetary and fiscal policies.

Self-Assessment Question

As demonstrated above, the budget deficit tends to increase automatically during a recession. Should a government that is committed to monetary targets be concerned about such a development?

11.5 PROBLEMS OF MONETARY POLICY

As noted above, monetary policy has in recent years become closely associated with monetarism. This is, perhaps, unsurprising, since monetarist theory assigns overriding importance to monetary policy as a tool of demand management. As the section above showed, monetarists argue both that the cost-of-capital channel is very powerful and that there are also wealth effects at work, whereby an increase in the money supply increases consumption directly. From this, monetarists conclude that governments should use monetary-base control – which is more precise than monetary control through interest rates and less distortionary than direct controls – to achieve pre-determined monetary targets.

Although many countries have experimented with monetarist prescriptions since the mid-1970s, a number of problems have been experienced. First, it has proved very difficult to identify a 'correct' definition of the money supply to target. Although currency and chequing accounts at banks clearly do the work of money, financial innovation across the world has increasingly blurred the distinction between 'money' and 'non-money'. Should instant-access time deposits at banks be included? Should foreign-currency deposits at banks, which can be readily switched into domestic currency, be included?

This leads on to a second problem. If the collection of assets which people regard as 'money' is changing over time in a way which the government cannot predict, it follows that the link between the arbitrary set of assets being targeted and aggregate demand will also change unpredictably. In other words, the demand for any particular monetary aggregate will be unstable. Hence, even if Keynesian economists are wrong in their assertion that the demand for money in general is unstable (due to the volatility of expectations), in a world of financial innovation their conclusion, namely that monetary targets do not provide a reliable means of controlling demand, holds none the less.

A third problem concerns the trade-off between monetary control and interest rates. Whether monetary-base control or interest-rate control is used, it follows that, given the size of the budget deficit, interest rates must rise to whatever level is necessary to achieve the monetary target. In modern economies, however, there are both economic and political constraints on interest-rate movements. On strictly economic grounds, it might be argued that raising interest rates is an inefficient way of curbing aggregate demand (e.g. compared with increasing tax rates), in the sense that a great deal of borrowing is done to finance productive investment in capital and equipment, so that the reduction comes at the expense of distorting the composition of aggregate demand away from investment and in favour of less interest-sensitive consumption. During a period of tight monetary policy, therefore, the business sector tends to bear the brunt of the deflation and this may have implications for longer-term growth. Higher interest rates may also increase the international demand for the currency, pushing up the exchange rate and damaging the competitive position of industry both at home and abroad.

Disintermediation

Politically, high interest rates are extremely unpopular, both with the business community for the reasons already discussed, and with the general public, most notably those who are buying their own homes with long-term variable-rate loans. In many countries, the sensitivity of the electorate to increases in the interest rate on home loans may present the government with a stark choice between monetary control and continued popularity with the voters. Finally, direct controls – often used in an attempt to try to achieve monetary control at lower interest rates by effectively suspending the market mechanism – are not without their problems, most notably the phenomenon of **disintermediation**. This involves the financial system in finding ways to circumvent the direct controls upon it, thus keeping to the 'letter of the law', but acting counter to its spirit.

A good example of disintermediation was the so-called 'bill-leak' in the United Kingdom during the 1970s, when banks responded to a direct control on their own lending activities by arranging loans for their customers which did not appear on their balance sheets. The basic technique involved the banks taking a commercial bill from company X (the would-be borrower) and selling it to an existing deposit customer, company Y, with a guarantee that the money would be repaid at maturity. Company X thus got the bank deposit it wanted to borrow, company Y received a bank-guaranteed, negotiable bill, and the bank earned a fee for guaranteeing the bill and acting as a middleman. Recorded bank lending (and so monetary growth) was lower, but the direct control had not stopped firms borrowing and spending, so that the relationship between the targeted monetary aggregate and spending was simply distorted in the process.

For these reasons, both rigid monetary targets and direct controls have been gradually falling from favour in many countries in the 1990s, with a return to a more discretionary approach to monetary policy taking place. This involves the government monitoring a range of monetary aggregates, rather than just one which may be undergoing structural change as the result of financial innovation, and having regard to both the level and structure of interest rates and the exchange rates. Nevertheless, monetary policy remains a major tool of stabilisation policy in almost every country.

Self-Assessment Question

Given the growing integration of national financial systems – a development graphically highlighted by the October 1987 global stock market crash, during which a slump on Wall Street was rapidly transmitted to other financial centres – what are the implications for the conduct of domestic monetary policy in the 1990s?

Further Reading

Miller, R. L. and Pulsinelli, R. (1986) *Macroeconomics*, Harper and Row, New York.

Greenway, D. and Shaw, G. K. (1988) *Macroeconomics: Theory and Policy in the UK*, Basil Blackwell, New York.

Gordon, R. J. (1987) *Macroeconomics*, 4th edition, Little, Brown and Company, Boston.

Backhouse, R. (1991) *Applied UK Macroeconomics*, Basil Blackwell, Oxford.

12

The Limitations of Macroeconomic Policy

In Chapter 9 we examined both the objectives of macroeconomic policy and the way in which the government intervenes in the macro-economy, using fiscal and monetary policy to achieve these objectives. The discussion highlighted the many theoretical and practical obstacles the government faces in this task, not least the problems of uncertainty, the existence of inside and outside lags and the possibility that, under certain circumstances, both monetary and fiscal policy may be ineffective in changing aggregate demand. These limitations of macroeconomic policy are briefly summarised below.

There is, however, a much more fundamental objection to stabilisation policy and it is that even if the government was able to manage the level of aggregate demand in the economy precisely, this would have no lasting impact on real variables like output and employment. This critique of macroeconomic policy is the focus of our attention in this concluding chapter of Part IV.

12.1 THE TECHNICAL LIMITATIONS OF MACROECONOMIC POLICY

The difficulties which beset a government seeking to manage aggregate demand are various and manifold. The key behavioural relationships (e.g. what determines investment? is the demand for money stable?) through which macroeconomic policy changes are transmitted are only imperfectly understood. Policy-makers can only interpret changing economic reality (what is happening to unemployment?; is inflation accelerating or is the present increase just a temporary 'blip'?) using crude statistical proxies, which are often available only after a particular trend has become well established. Inside and outside lags make the delays between policy changes and changes in policy objectives long and variable. In extreme cases, stabilisation policy may even be destabilising and it will almost certainly distort the structure of the real economy in ways which are not intended (e.g. tight monetary policy may reduce the share of investment in national income; deficit-financed government spending may increase the relative size of the government sector in the economy).

However, these are not arguments against stabilisation policy *per se*. The medical profession has not discovered a cure for cancer and the present treatments are far from satisfactory, but few would suggest – given the suffering endured by cancer victims – that doctors should give up their search for a cure. Similarly, just because the government operates in an uncertain world does not mean that it should not endeavour as best it can to stabilise the macro-economy and try to avoid, or at least moderate, fluctuations in unemployment and inflation. As a general rule, provided that the macro-economy is inherently unstable and that inside and outside lags can be reduced to the extent that policy changes are not destabilising, there will always be a role for demand management policy.

However, suppose the economy were not inherently unstable at all. Suppose, instead, that the private sector responded quickly and efficiently to random demand-side shocks, so that the economy automatically returned to its natural rates of unemployment and output (see Chapter 5). Under such circumstances, 'stabilisation' policy would be at best pointless and at worst counter-productive, needlessly adding to the private sector's efforts to restore balance and thereby causing the economy to overshoot its equilibrium position. It is to this possibility that we must finally turn.

12.2 IS DEMAND MANAGEMENT FUTILE?

The proposition that demand management is futile is closely associated with the theories of expectations formation we encountered in

Chapter 5. Figure 12.1 illustrates the essence of this approach. Remember that the upward-sloping *SAS* schedule is drawn for a given set of price expectations on the part of workers; that is, if employees expect the price level to remain at P_0, then following an increase in aggregate demand from AD_0 to AD_1, employers are able to expand output by offering higher money wages which are misperceived by workers as real increases, although they are in fact real reductions given the contemporaneous, larger rise in the price level.

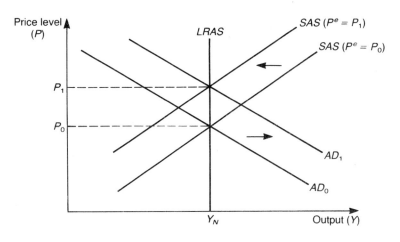

Figure 12.1

In the short run, therefore, an increase in aggregate demand succeeds in increasing output and reducing unemployment at the cost of a rise in the price level (i.e. inflation). This short-run 'equilibrium', however, lasts only as long as it takes for workers to realise they have been fooled. As comprehension dawns, they bargain for higher money wages to compensate them for the rise in prices and the *SAS* schedule begins to drift to the left, a process which continues until workers are content with their money wages, given the level at which prices have settled; in other words, long-run equilibrium is reached only once the price level is fully anticipated, at the natural rate of output (and unemployment). The *LRAS* is accordingly vertical, so that there is no long-run trade-off between inflation and unemployment.

The implication of this model for stabilisation policy are not immediately obvious, since it is the length of the short run – that is, the length of time it takes before price expectations (and thus money wages) fully adjust to a change in prices – that is critical. Suppose the short run were ten years or more. Then an exogenous deflationary shock (e.g. a fall in investment) which shifted the AD schedule to the left and pushed the economy down its SAS schedule, would mean prolonged unemployment and recession, which the government could avoid by using macroeconomic policy to restore aggregate demand to its previous level. This, in a rather crude way, is how most Keynesians would interpret Figure 12.1, although many dismiss the notion that full adjustment is ever achieved (so that the $LRAS$ is steeper than the SAS, but still non-vertical).

Many monetarists, who similarly argue that expectations adjust with a lag to changes in price ('adaptive expectations'), do not deny that it may take several years for the economy to recover from a demand-side shock. However, while they concede that stabilisation policy could perform a useful function in principle, they are concerned that the inside, and more especially the outside, lags are so long and variable that the effort may be counter-productive. Since the economy will automatically return to equilibrium of its own accord, they conclude, why risk further destabilising it with policy changes that may have unpredictable effects?

Policy Rules

Monetarists accordingly advocate setting policy 'rules' which imply that, on average (i.e. over the long run when exogenous, demand-side shocks tend to net out), aggregate demand remains at a constant level, so guaranteeing long-run price stability. Specifically, given their emphasis on the primacy of monetary policy, they advocate setting a rule for monetary growth, which means that, in a dynamic setting, aggregate demand grows no faster than the natural rate of output, leaving the price level stable over time.

The Surprise Supply Function

The 'new classical' school goes further, however, in its attack on the efficacy of stabilisation policy. Its adherents argue that expectations are not formed adaptively, but 'rationally', using all currently available and relevant information. This implies that workers' price expectations will adjust instantaneously to new information about current and future changes in aggregate demand. The implications of this approach are far-reaching. It suggests that economic agents will react very rapidly to random (i.e. unanticipated) demand-side shocks, adjusting their expectations and thereby pushing the economy back to the *LRAS* in a very short period of time (the *SAS* curve is often termed the **surprise supply function**, since the economy only moves up this schedule if the change in aggregate demand comes as a 'surprise', in the sense that it could not have been anticipated).

Following an unexpected, deflationary shock, therefore, the economy moves back to long-run equilibrium as fast as the institutional framework within which wage negotiations, contracts, etc., allows, so that demand-management policy, in this situation, is entirely unnecessary. Indeed, since the private sector is already responding in an optimal fashion to the demand-side shock, it is difficult to see how the government could possibly improve the situation. More startling, however, is the conclusion that, when economic agents form their expectations rationally, then since stabilisation policy is, by its very nature, systematic – and hence predictable – not only is it unnecessary (since the economy will return to its natural rate of output quickly in its absence) but it will also be completely ineffective (since the effects of the policy on aggregate demand will instantly be incorporated into price expectations).

The Policy Ineffectiveness Proposition

The so-called **policy ineffectiveness proposition** states that systematic demand-management policy can never affect output and employment, even in the short run, since its effects will always be incorporated into expectations and thereby neutralised, resulting only in changes in the price level. In operational terms, new classical economists argue for policy rules in much the same way as monetarists, but the theoretical underpinning of their recommendation is radically different, suggesting that however precise demand-management policy could be made, it could never be used in an activist fashion to improve economic welfare.

Although the rational expectations hypothesis has had a major impact on macroeconomic theory – offering as it does an explanation of expectations formation which is consistent with the fundamental economic principle of utility-maximising economic agents – it is probably true to say that most governments remain sceptical. While many now concede that the control of unemployment may be beyond their grasp in the long run, finance ministries and central banks across the world continue to believe that they have a responsiblity to respond to major demand-side shocks in a way which moderates the short-run dislocation to their economies. Practical experience and theoretical developments since 1945 may have helped to highlight the limitations of stabilisation policy, and there is little doubt that since the early 1980s it has generally been operated in a less activist fashion and with far lower expectations of success than hitherto, but it remains a central feature of macroeconomic life which business planners ignore at their peril.

Further Reading

Shaw, G. K. (1984) *Rational Expectations: An Elementary Exposition*, Wheatsheaf, Brighton.

Buiter, W. H. (1980) 'The Economics of Dr Pangloss: A Critical Survey of the New Classical Macroeconomics', *Economic Journal*, March.

Carter, M. and Maddock, R. (1984) *Rational Expectations: Macroeconomics for the 1980s?*, Macmillan, London.

Begg, D. K. H. (1982) *The Rational Expectations Revolution in Macro-economics: Theories and Evidence*, Philip Allan, Oxford.

Part V

THE INTERNATIONAL
MACRO-ECONOMY

13

The Foreign Exchange Market and the Balance of Payments

In Part V, we shall examine the forces behind the demand for, and supply of, foreign exchange. This will necessitate an understanding of the nature of the foreign exchange market. Next we shall discuss the theory of forward exchange, i.e. foreign currency delivered at a given time in the future at a price fixed today. The theory is regarded as important as it implies predicting the future movements of currencies and allows a business speculator in the international financial market to earn profits (or incur a loss!). Next we develop the equilibrium conditions of spot and forward exchange markets. The important institutional developments in the last two decades will then be explained to complete our analysis.

13.1 THE FOREIGN EXCHANGE MARKET STRUCTURE

The business activities of a large number of individuals engender the demand for a supply of foreign exchange. Such agents in the foreign exchange markets comprise traders (i.e. exporters and importers) in goods and services, importers or exporters of capital in the short or long run, travellers, etc. The trading actions of the exporters and importers give rise to buying/selling of foreign exchange. Banks usually try to satisfy the demand/supply needs. If a mismatch occurs between demand and supply, they count on the support of brokers or other banks. Brokers usually specialise in specific currencies. The central bank of any country controls the overall demand and supply situation.

Sometimes the central bank buys or sells foreign currency to influence the rate of exchange. This is called bank intervention in the foreign exchange market. Such intervention is usually made via brokers of foreign exchange. Communications between banks and brokers are usually very quick (e.g. telephone calls within a city/ country or between countries). Since the transaction costs of communication (e.g. telephone calls or telex messages) are very low, information about foreign exchange rates flows very rapidly and rates tend *to be equalised* in all the major international financial centres. If they are not, an **arbitrage**, defined as *simultaneous buying and selling* of a currency, will equalise the rates. Clearly the act of arbitrage allows agents in the foreign exchange markets to make profits.

The price of foreign exchange is defined as the number of pounds sterling required to buy, say, 1 US dollar or 1 Malaysian ringgit. Hence, the rate of foreign exchange is given by £:$ or £:MR where the pound (£) is the home currency and the other symbol stands for the foreign currency. The other definition of the rate of foreign exchange is given by the number of foreign *currency* units per UK pound sterling or Malaysian ringgit. For analytical purposes, there is no difference between the two.

The Spot and Forward Markets

In economics or business news, some currencies are quoted in terms of a 30- or 90-day forward rate. Alternatively, rates are quoted for **spot** delivery of foreign exchange. It simply means that the buyer can draw on the funds bought two 'clear' or 'business days', after the purchase. With a spot purchase, a business person in Kuala Lumpur can buy £2 million sterling from the KL Bank on Monday, 5 March 1989. The bank can then write a draft against a London bank payable on 9 March to settle any pound sterling debt. Clearly, spot rate refers to current rates of exchange.

The quotations for the forward rates imply the delivery of foreign exchange after a month, three months, or six months, at a price stated, say, on 5 March. Contracts for the forward rates are negotiated by exporters and importers of goods and services whose foreign exchange receipts/payments are in the future and who want to be sure of the domestic value of the foreign receipts.

Self-Assessment Questions

Define the following:

(a) exchange rate.
(b) spot exchange rate.
(c)) forward exchange rate.
(d) arbitrage.

13.2 THE DETERMINATION OF FOREIGN EXCHANGE RATES

The rate of exchange is generally defined as the domestic money price of foreign currency. Thus, it shows an equivalence between, say Malaysian ringgits and pounds sterling, e.g. MR 5.00 = £1.00. The exchange rates are quoted daily in the national and international newspapers. In the following sections we shall discuss the main factors that determine the rate of exchange between different currencies. We shall concentrate first on the determination of spot rates in foreign exchange markets which are free from government intervention. We also assume away all forms of restrictions on trade in the foreign exchange (FE) market. Note that, in practice, the government intervenes in the FE market from time to time to alter the exchange rates in ways which are likely to satisfy some domestic economic targets, e.g. lowering of inflation expectation and wage demands, reducing the pressure on export competitiveness, etc.

The Equilibrium Exchange Rate

In the absence of restrictions on private trading and government intervention in the FE market, the exchange rate will change according to the normal forces of demand for, and supply of, foreign exchange. In a way, the determination of the price of foreign exchange is like the determination of the price of a commodity in a competitive market. In the absence of liquidity problems and risk differences in different financial markets, the FE of any country is like a homogenous product. There are many buyers and sellers of this product. Thus, no single buyer or seller can influence the market price and hence, for any agent, its price is fixed.

The demand for foreign exchange is a *derived* demand because it is derived from the *debit* items of the BOP of any country. Thus, if Malaysian imports from the UK rise, the demand for foreign exchange will rise. Like any other commodities, the amount of foreign exchange demanded by Malaysia will vary negatively with its price, i.e. the higher the price of foreign exchange, the lower will be the demand, and the lower the price of foreign exchange, the higher will be the demand. If the exchange rate goes up (from any arbitrary level, say MR 5.00 = £1.00) the Malaysians will have to offer more ringgits to get the same amount of British pounds. Hence, as the exchange rate goes up, imports fall and the demand for foreign exchange in Malaysia falls. Using the same logic, it can be shown that if the exchange rate falls, imports will be cheaper and the demand for foreign exchange will rise.

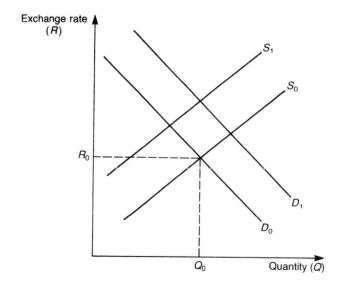

Figure 13.1

The demand-for-foreign-exchange curve is shown in Figure 13.1 by the downward-sloping demand schedule, D. It shows the different amount of pounds demanded at different rates of exchange against Malaysian ringgits. It is worth pointing out at this stage that factors like income, taste, prices, cost, interest rates, etc., can change the demand for imports and thereby the demand for foreign exchange regardless of the movements of exchange rates. If that happens, the whole demand for FE schedule will shift, e.g. if the Malaysians buy more British goods due to a rise in their income, the demand for FE schedule shifts to the right to D^1.

By referring to Figure 13. 1, check for yourself that the following factors account for a change in the demand for MR:

(1) A change in Malaysian exports;
(2) A desire by foreigners to make transfer payments in MR;
(3) The desire of foreigners to buy Malaysian financial assets;
(4) The desire by Malaysians to sell foreign assets and bring back funds to Malaysia;
(5) The desire by foreign banks and individuals to raise MR holdings.

Similarly, the supply of MR will be affected by the following factors:

(1) Imports by Malaysia;
(2) Malaysia making transfer payments to the foreign countries;
(3) Malaysian purchases of foreign assets;
(4) Selling by foreigners of financial assets held in Malaysia;
(5) Foreigners reducing their MR holdings.

In sum, the equilibrium exchange rate is the product of the demand for, and supply of, foreign exchange in a free foreign exchange market. The forces behind the demand curve for *FE* are the debit items in the BOP schedule and the forces behind the supply curve of FE are the credit items. (The BOP accounts are discussed more fully in Section 13.4 below.)

The Stability of the Equilibrium Exchange Rate

In economics, equilibrium means a situation of rest where demand is equal to supply. Equilibrium could be **stable, unstable** or **neutral**. A stable equilibrium is defined as a position when any deviation from the equilibrium will generate forces to bring the economy back to the point of equilibrium. An unstable equilibrium occurs when any deviation from the point of equilibrium takes the economy further away from the point of equilibrium. A neutral equilibrium arises when a departure from equilibrium does not generate any force to bring the market back or take it further away from the point of initial disturbance. Readers can easily check that when the upward-moving supply curve intersects the downward-sloping demand curve, the equilibrium is stable, with certain provisos. When the supply curve is also downward-sloping and intersects the downward-sloping demand curve from above, the equilibrium is unstable. For example, in Figure 13.2 points *C* and *A* are stable, whereas point *B* is unstable.

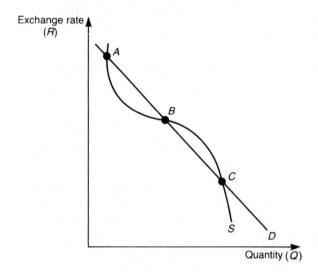

Figure 13.2

Algebraically, for stability in the FE market, the following condition must hold:

$$dQ^D{}_{MR}/dR < dQ^S{}_{MR}/dR \qquad (13.1)$$

i.e. as long as the appreciation of the exchange rate (*R*) results in a smaller fall in the quantity demanded than in the quantity supplied. It is only when the supply curve is negatively sloping (i.e. backward-bending) and flatter than the demand curve at the necessary point of equilibrium that the problem of unstable equilibrium emerges.

It is possible to restate the stability condition in terms of elasticities. Let the demand elasticity of the currency be defined as

$$k_{MR} \equiv -dQ^d{}_{MR}/dR \times R/Q^D{}_{MR}$$

Similarly, the supply elasticity is defined as

$$e_s \equiv dQ^S{}_{MR}/dR \times R/Q^S{}_{MR}$$

Expanding (13.1), we can write

220

$$-[dQ^D{}_{MR}/dR][R/Q^D{}_{MR}][Q^S{}_{MR}/R] < [dQ^S/dR][R/Q^S{}_{MR}][Q^S/R] \qquad (13.2)$$

Since in equilibrium $Q^D{}_{MR} = Q^S{}_{MR}$, we can write, after substituting for elasticities, the stability condition:

$$-k < e_s \qquad (13.3)$$

13.3 COVERED INTEREST ARBITRAGE (CIA)

The theory of covered interest arbitrage (or CIA) seeks to explain the movements of capital, particularly in the short run, among different countries. In a world without exchange risks, the CIA theory states that if the interest rates (r) in two countries or financial centres (A and B) are different (i.e. $r_A \neq r_B$), funds will flow to that centre where the returns from short-term investments are highest.

We will use the following notations to explain the principles of the CIA.

Let: r_A = three months' interest rate in A (say Malaysia)
  r_B = three months' interest rate in B (say UK)
  R_s = number of MR, needed to buy £1 in the spot market
  R_f = three months' forward rate for £1 sterling against MR
    (i.e. MR per £ three months hence)

The forward difference (d) is defined as:

$$d \equiv \frac{R_f - R_s}{R_s}$$

If $d > 0$, the pound sterling is at a **forward premium**.
If $d < 0$, the pound sterling is at a **forward discount**.

Suppose Uncle Homaid in Malaysia is given MR (a specific sum of money). If he invests in Malaysia, he gets r_A interest rate on MR sum of money. But if he buys £s in the spot market and invests in Britain, after three months he gets $(MR/R_S)(1+r_B)$. To avoid exchange risks (which may occur due to a £ depreciation), Uncle Homaid sells £s forward and after three months he gets $(MR/R_S)(1+r_B) R_f$. His initial capital was MR. The 'covered' rate of return, r_B^*, is therefore:

$$r_B^* = \frac{\left[\dfrac{MR(1+r_B)R_f}{R_s}\right] - MR}{MR}$$

$$= (1+r_B)\frac{R_f}{R_s} - 1$$

Where will Uncle Homaid place his money? The answer is where the total financial return will be highest. More importantly, because all rational international investors will tend to act in the same way as Uncle Homaid, any covered interest differential in favour of a particular currency will lead to heavy short-term capital flows into that currency, driving up R_S (and pushing down R_f, since the spot purchases of the currency will be covered by forward sales of the currency) until, in equilibrium:

$$r_A = r_B^*$$

$$\text{Since } r_A = (1+r_B)\frac{R_f}{R_s} - 1$$

$$\frac{1+r_A}{1+r_B} = \frac{R_f}{R_s}$$

For example, if $r_B^* > r_A$, hot money would tend to flow out of ringgits and into sterling, driving up R_S, while at the same time, investors would be making forward purchases of ringgits (thereby depressing R_f) to cover their extra holdings of sterling.

When $\dfrac{1+r_A}{1+r_B} = \dfrac{R_f}{R_s}$ covered interest parity (CIP) is said to hold.

It should be pointed out that the CIP may not always hold, for a number of reasons. First, it ignores the role of transaction costs completely. With positive transaction costs, CIA may not be profitable. Second, r_A and r_B cannot easily be uniquely determined, as investors face a range of interest rates. Third, the supply of arbitrage funds may not be completely elastic in real life. Finally, for political risks, foreign assets may not be perfect substitutes for domestic assets.

13.4 THE BALANCE OF PAYMENTS

The **balance of payments** (BOP) records all *economic* transactions between residents of two countries. Such transactions include exports and imports of goods and services, cash receipts and payments, gifts and unilateral flows, gold flows, loans, short- and long-run capital movements. The BOP thus registers the total international transactions of a nation.

A BOP account is a three-tier system for recording all economic transactions. Its compilation must satisfy some major rules: first, only economic transfers between foreign and domestic residents are to be taken into account; second, the *credit* items of the BOP should be distinguished very carefully from the *debit* items; third, the BOP is a *double-entry* book-keeping device, where every debit item generates a corresponding credit item so that the overall sum of the total assets and liabilities must be the same. In this sense, BOP always balances. Note carefully that when individuals represent their government in foreign countries, they are regarded as residents of their country.

All *debit* transfers imply payments by domestic residents to foreign residents. All *credit* transactions involve receipts by domestic residents from foreign residents.

We may now ask: if BOP always balances, why should people or businessmen worry about it? The answer lies in the understanding of the two types of trade balance: one is related to balance of trade (a narrow view), the other is related to the overall BOP which is always in balance. The latter occurs because whenever a balance of trade, defined as the *difference between total exports and imports of goods and services,* is in disequilibrium (i.e. in **surplus** or **deficit**), it is offset by **compensating capital flows**, both short and long term, in the capital account. Thus, in the first tier of the BOP account, the exports and import flows of goods and services are recorded. These are shown in the **current account**. In the second tier, we have short-and long-term capital flows.

If the capital flows are not enough to offset the trade (current account) disequilibrium, then we have gold and foreign exchange reserve flows in the third tier. Nowadays, gold flows are, however, very rare. Finally, if the total of all credit items is not equal to the total of all debit items, we have a way of adjusting it by a balancing item called 'errors and omissions'.

Table 13.1 shows the use of four major concepts: (1) the net goods and services balance; (2) the net current account balance [note that rows (a) + (b) = balance of trade (BOT)]; (3) the basic balance; (4) the official reserve transactions balance.

In Table 13.1 rows (a) plus (b) show that Malaysia has a net surplus (credit of $MR1250$ as it has spent less on foreign goods and services than it has earned by selling goods and services abroad during a certain period (usually a year). However, the surplus earned on trade in goods and services was partly offset by 'unilateral transfers' overseas (for example by residents sending money to children studying abroad). As a result, the **net current account balance** was only $MR500$. This latter sub-total reflects the extent to which Malaysia is 'paying its way' in the world. A deficit implies that the country is spending more than it earns, borrowing the difference from abroad. A surplus means that the country is earning more than it spends, allowing it to save by lending to other countries.

Table 13.1: A Hypothetical Balance of Payments Account for Malaysia (in million MR)

	Debits	Credits
(a) Goods (net) exports		1000
(b) Services (net) exports		250
Net Goods and Services Balance		1250
(c) Unilateral Transfers (net)	750	
Net Current Account Balance		500
(d) Direct Investment (net)	300	
(e) Portfolio investment (net)		200
Basic Balance		400
(f) Short term capital flows (net)	1200	
(g) Net errors or omissions	100	
Official Reserves Transaction Balance	900	
(h) Gold Export or Import (net)		100
(i) Change in foreign exchange (net)		600
(j) Change in liabilities to foreign banks (net)		200

Since we have a surplus of $MR500$, Malaysia is a net lender in the international market (according to *our* table).

The term 'basic balance' refers to the total of the current account balance and the net flow of long-term capital (i.e. direct and portfolio investment: remember that portfolio investment means purchase of domestic shares or equities issued by companies). Note that a basic balance deficit shows a weakening of the long-term BOP of a country ('a fundamental disequilibrium'). In our table, however, a surplus of MR400 reflects the country's underlying economic strength – overall, it is earning more than it spends by an amount which comfortably exceeds its net long-term capital outflows.

The **official reserves transaction balance** (ORTB) differentiates between transactions of monetary authorities and all other transactions that are placed above this balance. It shows the pressure of the exchange market on the currency of a country. The usual method of financing the reserve balance is to alter the liabilities to foreign central banks and the official reserve assets like gold and convertible currencies. The ORTB is very important in maintaining stable exchange rates, by supplying the compensatory financing needs to offset autonomous transfers, i.e. by offering necessary foreign exchange demanded and supplied by all agents. Thus, the amount of ORTB demonstrates the degree of intervention in the market.

In Table 13.1, since the ORTB displays a deficit of MR900, the monetary authorities in Malaysia are obliged to intervene in the FE market with compensatory financing to maintain stable exchange rates. Thus, the stability in MR against sterling is maintained by exporting MR100 of gold, using MR600 of her foreign exchange reserves, and borrowing MR200 from foreign central banks.

Our analysis clearly shows how the BOP has enormous practical use in an international monetary system which wishes to promote stable exchange rates. Needless to say, in a system of flexible exchange rates, governments do not intervene (unless it is what is called a 'dirty float' in which intervention is undertaken on an occasional basis) because changes in exchange rates bring about BOP equilibria. Note also that a BOP statement is a very valuable piece of information to assess the relative economic strengths of different economies and to measure changes in underlying economic positions over time. But simply because the balance of payments always balances, a country cannot continue to indulge in an excess of autonomous imports over exports (or exports over imports) indefinitely. Foreign exchange cannot be produced at home and in the long term it must be earned via exports of goods and services. That is why any adjustment to a chronic problem of deficit (generally suffered by less-developed countries) must imply restructuring of production, consumption, exports and imports. There are a large number of reasons to account for a BOP disequilibrium: they could be random or completely unexpected (e.g. due to flood or drought, which is unpredictable, and consequent supply failure); structural (e.g. composition of output in the economy brought about by changes in income distribution, taste or terms of trade, i.e. the ratio of export to import price); cyclical or speculative (e.g. due to sudden, sharp movements in short-term capital – usually known as 'hot money'). The BOP adjustment problems are then really related to the diagnosis of the correct sources of disequilibrium.

Table 13.2 Balance of Payments Summary Table

Debits

(a) Imports of goods and services bought from foreign residents.
(b) Purchases of Malaysian residents travelling abroad.
(c) Services supplied by foreign-owned capital in Malaysian production.
(d) Gifts to foreigners.
(e) Investment abroad by Malaysian residents.
(f) Imports of gold.

Credits

(g) Exports of goods and services.
(h) Purchases of foreigners travelling in Malaysia.
(i) Services offered by Malaysian-owned capital in foreign production.
(j) Gifts received from foreign residents.
(k) Investment in Malaysia by foreign residents
(l) Exports of gold.

BOP Accounting

$$CU + CA \equiv 0 \tag{1}$$

where CU = current account transactions
CA = capital account transactions

$$(X-M) + (STC+LTC+G) \equiv 0 \tag{2}$$

where X = exports
M = imports
STC = short-term capital flows
LTC = long-term capital flows
G = gold flows

Self-Assessment Question

Under what circumstances might a current account deficit improve, rather than reduce, the economic welfare of future generations?

13.5 BALANCE OF PAYMENTS ADJUSTMENT

A balance of payments disequilibrium can occur either due to a surplus or a deficit in the balance of trade (i.e. current) account. Countries who are lucky enough to experience BOP surplus do not worry too much about 'adjustment' policies (though they may have to if the value of their currencies rises continuously in the foreign exchange market!). It is only when countries face persistent BOP deficits that policy-makers, businessmen and economists are under pressure to 'adjust' the domestic cost-price structure in a way which will be in line with the international cost-price structure of export and import industries.

One of the major ways to reduce deficits is to reduce home demand for imports. This can be achieved by an increase of domestic taxes (i.e. direct and indirect). Income and import taxes may have to rise. If the country has a high marginal propensity to import (MPM, i.e. high extra spending on imports due to additional income or high dM/dY where M is import and Y is income), then such demand-management policies could reduce imports. Some developing countries impose a total ban on some imports (usually 'inessential' or 'luxury' goods). Such import controls clearly affect consumers' choice but they also reduce imports.

Other countries use tariffs to reduce deficits. Figure 13.3 illustrates this. On the vertical axis, price and tariff on the importable goods are measured, whereas the horizontal axis measures the quantity of goods demanded and supplied. D is the domestic demand curve and S is the domestic supply curve. At price OP for imported goods, the domestic demand is AB, the home supply is OA. Thus, the BOP deficit is AB. A tariff of PP_t raises domestic supply by AC (the 'infant industry' protection case), reduces the import demand by BD (the demand effect) and raises the government *revenue* by $EFHG$ [e.g. (tariff) x HG (imports)]. The BOP deficit is now only CD instead of AB. The demand effect (FHM)

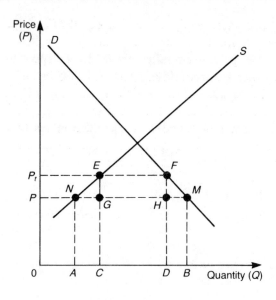

Figure 13.3

and the production effect (*ENG*) represent the net welfare costs to the economy of cutting imports.

Tariffs may confer other types of dynamic gains, e.g. learning by doing. Some economists, however, argue that a tariff is an inefficient method of protecting industries because such protection does not offer any incentive to business persons to cut costs, increase productivity and become more competitive. That is why some developing countries have simply developed 'high cost' and inefficient industries which have resulted in significant loss of welfare. Many now suggest that devaluation, i.e. changing the ratio of export to import price by reducing the value of domestic currency to foreign currency in the international market, is a more effective method of adjustment of BOP deficits.

This principle is known as a 'price switching' instrument. The argument is that to cure a BOP deficit, it is necessary to increase the price of imported goods so that imports will fall and reduce the price of export goods, e.g. rubber in Malaysia, so that exports will rise. Clearly, the success of such a policy will critically depend on the export and import elasticity of the demand for imports and exports. In the extreme case, e.g. if the country cannot do without imports (import elasticity 0) and foreigners would not increase the demand for home exports (export elasticity 0, i.e. near or equal to zero), then devaluation is unlikely to improve the BOP position.

The effect of 'price-switching' policy thus depends on the price sensitivity of the imports and exports. It has been proved that for a devaluation to reduce the BOP deficit, the *sum* of the export and import demand elasticities must be greater than one, i.e. $E_X + E_M > 1$. This is known as the **Marshall-Lerner condition**. Assume that trade is initially balanced and all relevant supply elasticities are assumed to be equal to infinity. We also assume that only exchange rates change, whereas other factors are held constant.

Since the BOP 'problem' is really about a shortage of foreign currency, it is necessary to measure exports and imports in units of foreign currency. Let

$$B = RX - M$$

where B = BOP measured in foreign currency

R = exchange rate (foreign currency units/domestic currency units)

X = exports measured in domestic currency

M = imports measured in foreign currency

For a devaluation to improve the BOP position, $dB/dR < 0$. Differentiating, we have

$$dB/dR = X + R\delta X/\delta R - \delta M/\delta R$$

$$= X \left[1 + \frac{R}{X} \cdot \frac{\delta X}{\delta R} - \frac{\delta M}{\delta R} \cdot \frac{R}{M} \cdot \frac{M}{RX} \right]$$

Recall that

$$-\frac{R}{X} \cdot \frac{\delta X}{\delta R} = E_X \text{ (i.e. price elasticity of export demand)}$$

$$\text{and } \frac{R}{M} \cdot \frac{\delta M}{\delta R} = E_M \text{ (i.e. price elasticity of import demand)}$$

Now assume $E_X > 0$ because exports respond positively to a favourable (i.e. cheaper) exchange rate and with a given foreign price of imports $E_X > 0$ if imports fall with a fall in the exchange rate, R. If trade is initially balanced, i.e. $M = RX$ (so $M/RX = 1$), we have

$$dB/dR = X(1 - E_X - E_M)$$

therefore, for $dB/dR < 0$ then $E_X + E_M > 1$.

The last equation shows that the BOP deficits will fall if the sum of the price elasticities of demand for imports and exports is greater than one. In simple terms, if exports (volume) rise proportionately with a fall in foreign export price ($E_X = 1$), the BOP deficit will remain the same. Therefore, any fall in imports because of a rise in the home price of imports after devaluation (i.e. $E_M > 0$) will be enough to improve the BOP.

There are obvious limitations to the 'price-switching' game. For one thing, it ignores the effects of income changes. For another, the impact of monetary changes has been completely ignored. A more realistic appraisal of BOP 'adjustment policies' should also include effects of income, money and other structural factors in the economy.

Sometimes a devaluation can *worsen* the trade balance at the outset before its eventual improvement. This is called the **J-curve effect** and is illustrated in Figure 13.4. Assume that the economy starts at time T_o, at which point a devaluation of the exchange rate takes place. While this devaluation might be expected to improve the BOT in the long term, the immediate effect is perverse and, in the period up to time T_1, the BOT actually worsens. Why should this happen? The deterioration reflects lags in adjustment by importers and exporters. The orders for the physical quantities of goods coming into, and going out of, a country have been placed weeks, or possibly months, before.

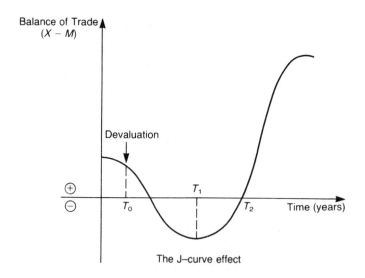

The J–curve effect

Figure 13.4

When the exchange rate is devalued, increasing the domestic currency price of imports and reducing the foreign currency price of exports, importers would like to import less and exporters to export more, but both parties are bound in the short term by contracts that have already been made. The result is that the domestic currency value of imports increases (by the same percentage as the devaluation), while the foreign currency value of exports correspondingly falls. Only later, as importers scale back their orders and exporters gear up for an expansion into more profitable overseas markets, do import and export quantities begin to respond to the earlier change in relative prices, so leading to the expected improvement in the BOT. The term 'the J-curve effect' derives from the path traced out by the BOT during this adjustment period.

Self-Assessment Question

Between 1985 and 1988, the US dollar depreciated sharply against the Japanese Yen, but America's current account deficit improved only slightly. Explain.

Further Reading

Krugman P. R. and Obstfeld, M. (1988) *International Economics: Theory and Policy*, Scott, Foresman and Co., Boston.

Thirlwall, A. P. (1986) *Balance of Payments and the United Kingdom Experience*, 3rd edition, Macmillan, London.

Kane, D. R. (1988) *Principles of International Finance*, Croom Helm, London.

Madura, J. (1989) *International Financial Management*, 2nd edition, West Publishing Co., New York.

14

Advanced Theories of Exchange Rate Determination

Chapter 14 completes our review of the international macroeconomy by considering some of the major theories of exchange rate determination. Just as there are several schools of thought with regard to the determination of output, prices and employment in the domestic macroeconomy, so there are a number of alternative approaches to the determination of the exchange rate.

14.1 POST-KEYNESIAN THEORIES OF EXCHANGE RATE DETERMINATION

This theory of exchange rate determination is an extension of the standard Keynesian model of an open economy. The Fleming-Mundell model, as it is often called, recognises the interdependence of the money market, the goods market and the balance of payments. None of these three can maintain a position of equilibrium unless it is simultaneously a position of equilibrium for the other two. Such a simultaneous equilibrium for all three is marked A in Figure 14.1.

In Figure 14.1 LM represents the money market equilibrium schedule. Each point on the LM curve is a combination of interest rates and levels of income such that the demand for real balances is equal to the supply. The money market is therefore in equilibrium only on the LM curve. The positive slope of the LM curve shows that an increase in the interest rate is accompanied by an increase in the level of income for the money market to be in equilibrium. This is because an increase in interest rates reduces the demand for real balances; to maintain the demand for real balances equal to the fixed supply, the level of income has to rise. In an open economy with international capital movement, the money supply is influenced by inflow or outflow of capital in response to foreign exchange movements.

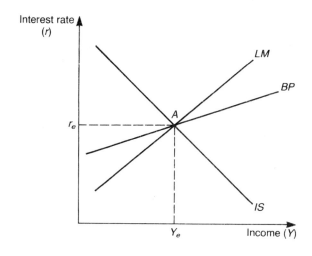

Figure 14.1

The *IS* curve is the goods market equilibrium schedule and shows combinations of interest rates and output such that planned spending equals planned income. At each point on the curve, planned injections equals planned withdrawals. The negative slope reflects the fact that an increase in aggregate demand is associated with a reduction in the interest rate. A lower interest rate increases investment spending, thereby increasing aggregate demand and thus the equilibrium level of income.

In the open economy case, withdrawals include imports which, like the other withdrawals of savings and taxes, are a function of income (i.e. $M = mY$, where m is the marginal propensity to import, which is in turn determined by the exchange rate). Similarly, injections also include exports, together with investment and government spending. Exports are determined by the exchange rate. Note that a change, say a devaluation, in the exchange rate has two effects on the *IS* curve. Firstly, it reduces the marginal propensity to import, making the *IS* curve flatter in the same way as a tax cut. Secondly, it increases exports, which shifts the *IS* to the right in the same way as an increase in government spending. In analytical terms, therefore, the extension of the *IS-LM* model to the open economy allows us to use the same tools already developed above.

In an open economy with international trade there is also a new balance of payments equilibrium schedule (*BP* in Figure 14.1). The schedule represents combinations of income and interest rates that keep the balance of payments in equilibrium. Assume that the balance of payments is initially in equilibrium, and assume that there is an increase in the level of income, resulting in a rise in imports. This will result in balance of payments deficit. To restore equilibrium to the balance of payments, the interest rate will have to rise to induce net capital inflow. Thus, increases in income must be accompanied by higher levels of interest rates for the balance of payments to remain in equilibrium. This gives the *BP* curve a positive slope. All points to the south-east and right of *BP* are points of balance of payments deficit. It is when all three curves, *IS*, *LM* and *BP*, intersect that there is simultaneous equilibrium in the goods market, the money market and the balance of payments.

The exchange rate is determined within this standard macroeconomic model. The exchange rate influences the price competitiveness of export and import substitutes. Now, assume that we start from a position of equilibrium in the goods market, the money market and the balance of payments (i.e. point *A* in Figure 14.1). If there is an increase in money supply, interest rates will have to fall. Aggregate demand then increases to raise the level of income. This will be accompanied by an increase in net imports leading to a balance of payments deficit. To restore equilibrium in the balance of payments, the exchange rate will have to depreciate in order to increase exports. The actual mechanism for restoring equilibrium in the balance of payments and in the other markets is different under fixed and floating exchange rate systems. Under a floating exchange rate system the exchange rate acts as the equilibrating mechanism to keep the demand for, and supply of, the country's currency in balance. Under a fixed exchange rate system, however, the authorities will have to buy or sell currency (according to whether there is a deficit or surplus) in order to maintain the parity of the currency. Therefore a balance of payments deficit, for example, will have to be met by selling foreign reserves, thus reducing the money supply (foreign reserves being a component of the money supply). Reduction in the money supply restores equilibrium to the money market, the goods market and the balance of payments.

The working of the system under the fixed and floating exchange rate systems is illustrated in Figure 14.2.

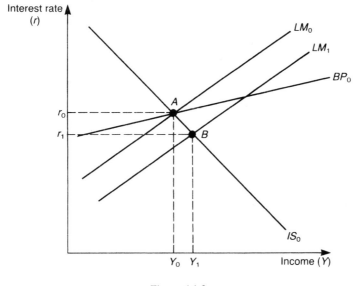

Figure 14.2

(a) In Figure 14.2 the initial position of general equilibrium is at A with interest rate of r_o and income of Y_0. An expansion of the money supply will shift the LM curve from LM_0 to LM_1. This results in equilibrium in the goods and money markets at B with lower interest rate, r_1, and higher income, Y_1. However, the balance of payments is in disequilibrium because higher imports and lower interest rates mean an increase in the outflow of capital. The outflow of capital will cause a fall in the money supply and the movement of the LM curve towards the left till it reaches its original position LM_0, where the balance of payments (as well as the money and goods markets) will be in equilibrium and the contraction of the money supply will cease. Interest rates and income will be back at their original positions. Therefore, the monetary expansion fails to have any permanent effect on either interest rates or income.

The authorities may continue to expand the money supply by domestic credit creation, thus preventing the *LM* curve from returning to LM_0. Such an action, however, cannot be continued indefinitely because the capital outflow will eventually exhaust the country's foreign exchange reserves. If the authorities institute exchange controls to restrict the outflow of capital, the balance of payments deficit will become chronic and the country will increasingly be unable to defend the fixed parity.

(b) Point *A* in Figure 14.3 again represents equilibrium in the goods market, the money market and the balance of payments, with income and interest rates of Y_0 and r_0 respectively. Again, an increase in money supply shifts the *LM* curve to LM_1, intersecting the *IS* curve at point *B*. The balance of payments is now in disequilibrium. But because the exchange rate is flexible, it will move (depreciate) to keep the balance of payments in equilibrium without any net movement of money. The *LM* curve, therefore, need not move back to LM_0. But at *B* the interest rate is lower and income higher than at the initial point, *A*. The lower interest rate will induce net outflow of capital while imports will increase as a result of the higher incomes. The exchange rate will depreciate to increase the price of imports and lower the price of exports. The

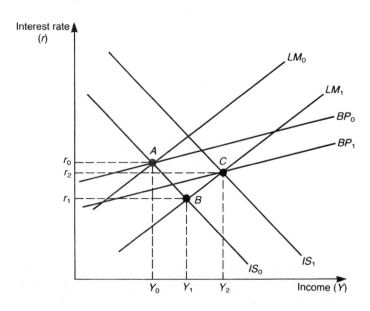

Figure 14.3

236

BP curve will then shift to BP_1 as exports rise and imports fall. This will also shift the *IS* curve to IS_1 because of the increase in aggregate demand. When all shifts have been accomplished, a new equilibrium is established at C, where interest rates and levels of income are higher than initially. But the external value of the currency (exchange rate) is lower than before.

Several criticisms have been made of this post-Keynesian model of exchange rate determination. First, it is alleged that the model ignores the fact that differences in international interest rates are sometimes due to exchange rate expectations, rather than differences in credit creation. Second, there is no recognition of the fact that currency depreciation may mean higher domestic prices and thereby a fall in the real value of money supply, which would then force the *LM* curve in Figure 14.3 to return to LM_0. Third, it fails to take into account the lags in the response of output and trade flows. It assumes that each and every country has the capacity to expand output in response to increase in money supply. Fourth, it assumes that output responds to interest rate changes. In many developing countries the real interest rates are negative and do not induce the same response in aggregate output and aggregate demand. Lastly, the role given to capital flows in the model may be appropriate only for short-run analysis. In the long run, capital flows may cease once stocks have been optimally allocated. In developing countries, capital flows may not perform the same role assigned to them because of the absence of suitable interest-yielding local assets which would induce capital inflow when required. The absence of capital and money markets also reduces the movement of capital, even if there are no exchange controls.

14.2 THE MONETARY APPROACH TO EXCHANGE RATE DETERMINATION

This approach has certain elements and assumptions. The first is that the balance of payments is a monetary phenomenon. There is a direct relationship between the domestic money supply and the balance of payments of an open economy. A balance of payments deficit, for example, will contract the monetary base and money supply. Attempts by the authorities to sterilise the changes in money supply are not feasible in a world of integrated financial markets and with a high volume of mobile international capital ready to take advantage of interest-rate differentials across international boundaries.

Secondly, the approach assumes that the demand for money is a stock demand, not a flow demand, and is a stable function of a small number of variables. The stability ensures that excess money supply, for example, is not absorbed in idle cash balances as in the Keynesian scheme, but reflected in the balance of payments. The demand for money model is usually set out as a function of the price level (P), the level of income (Y) and the rate of interest (r), i.e.

$$M = L(P,Y,r) \tag{14.1}$$

or in real terms

$$M/P = L(Y, r) \tag{14.2}$$

There is a similar demand for money function for the foreign country,

$$M^*/P^* = L(Y^*,r^*) \tag{14.3}$$

where * indicates the foreign country variable.

The approach thirdly assumes international commodity arbitrage, so that purchasing power parity (PPP) prevails among all national currencies. The PPP is represented as

$$P = EP^* \tag{14.4}$$

where E is the exchange rate. Equation (14.4) can be rewritten as

$$E = P/P^* \tag{14.5}$$

Substituting in (14.5) equations (14.2) and (14.3) gives

$$E = \frac{M.L(Y^*,r^*)}{M^*.L(Y,r)} \tag{14.6}$$

Equation 14.6 makes the exchange rate the relative price of the two national monies and is determined by the supply of, and demand for, those monies. This is the basic proposition of the monetary approach.

The fourth assumption is that national income is given at its full or natural level, so that increase in money supply *per se* cannot increase the national income.

Finally, the monetary approach assumes that interest rates are fixed by foreign rates and exchange rates expectations. Any difference between the domestic and the foreign interest rates is equal to the expected change in exchange rates. This is the interest rate parity condition, which is shown as

$$r - r^* = (E^c - E^s)/E^s$$

where $(r - r^*)$ is the interest differential, E^c is the expected future rate of exchange and E^s is the current spot rate. $(E^c - E^s)/E^s$ is then the expected depreciation of the domestic currency. If domestic interest rates increase by a certain percentage (from a condition of initial equilibrium) then the currency is expected to depreciate by a proportionate percentage.

With these elements of the monetary approach spelt out, it is easy to trace the effect on the balance of payments and exchange rate of a change in money supply.

Under a fixed exchange rate, the monetary approach provides a theory of balance payments determination. Assume that as domestic credit expansion results in excess money supply, individuals seek to adjust their portfolio by increasing the demand for foreign goods and assets. This has the tendency to depress the exchange rates. The authorities, wishing to maintain the fixed exchange rate, will have to sell foreign exchange. This contracts the monetary base and money supply until, eventually, equilibrium is restored in the money market.

Under a floating exchange rate, the monetary approach becomes a theory of exchange rate determination. The exchange rate is determined by the stock equilibrium conditions in the money market. An excess of money supply again puts the exchange rate under downward pressure, but, in the absence of official intervention, the exchange rate depreciates. Domestic prices will have to rise in line with PPP, leaving the real money supply unchanged. (Note that price elasticity of money demand is assumed to be unity.)

The monetary approach considers devaluation to correct balance of payments disequilibrium as effective only through its effect on the demand for, and supply of, money and work and only if they reduce the real value of nominal money balances through an increase in domestic price level.

Criticisms of the Monetary Approach

Like other economic models, the monetary approach has had a number of criticisms levelled against it. One criticism is the assumption of a stable demand-for-money function. It is argued that the demand for money may not be stable in all countries, and that not all the determinants of the function are appropriate in every country. For example, demand for money may not respond to interest rates in many developing countries. Here, the interest rates are institutionally fixed, real rates of interest are largely negative, or rural money markets play a significant role. In many developing countries, because demand for money has a strong liquid asset motive, the opportunity costs of holding money, as approximated by movements in the price level, are more important.

The link between the balance of payments and money supply in the monetary approach has been questioned on many grounds. First, it is argued that in the real world, especially in developing countries, the assumption of free trade and perfect capital mobility is not valid. Movement of capital in or out of the country may be restricted by government policy. Moreover, capital may not flow into a country in response to interest rate differentials. Capital mobility may be influenced by other factors including expectations which may, in turn, be affected by political and social considerations. At any rate, interest rates may be institutionally determined, which makes the assumption of international interest arbitrage invalid.

Second, the increase in the domestic money supply may not be completely reflected in a balance of payments deficit because of various lags in adjustment – even in the absence of government restrictions on international transactions. In such a situation, the increase in money supply may result in a rise in domestic prices and interest rates above their respective world levels before complete adjustment takes place.

Third, the approach pays inadequate attention to the possibility of sterilisation of external flows, either through open-market operations (at least in the short run) or through the government budget surplus or deficit. The inflow of money from a balance of payments surplus, for example, need not affect the money market equilibrium if accompanied by government budget surplus.

Finally, it has been argued that while it is valid to emphasise domestic credit restraint to cure balance of payments problems, the same result can be achieved by expenditure-switching policies that work through real flows and the government budget.

In spite of these criticisms, the monetary approach has shown some ability to explain the behaviour of the balance of payments. It focuses the attention of policy-makers on the need to co-ordinate monetary and exchange rate policies.

14.3 THE PORTFOLIO BALANCE APPROACH

This approach emphasises the need for equilibrium in a whole spectrum of assets which comprise an individual's wealth portfolio. Money itself is one of the assets, and the exchange rate, as the price that equilibrates the demand for, and supply of, money, is one of the prices that must adjust to ensure portfolio equilibrium. The market for each asset is viewed as an efficient speculative market. The foreign exchange market is dominated in the short run by speculation and international capital movements, rather than payments related to merchandise trade. The portfolio balance approach is therefore an extension of the monetary approach by contending that exchange rate movements are not the consequences solely of changes in money supply and demand. The exchange rate does influence the domestic currency value of foreign assets and thereby the value of the total wealth portfolio. Exchange rate changes can be caused by changes in the demand for, and supply of, foreign assets and domestic non-money assets.

As an extension of the monetary approach, the portfolio balance approach has suffered from some of the criticism of the former. In particular, there is the neglect of real and structural causes of balance of payment disequilibrium. Surely, the role of other non-money assets – both foreign and domestic – must be played down in many developing countries, and interest rates may not play the same role assigned to them in the absence of international interest rate parity.

14.4 THE RATIONAL EXPECTATIONS HYPOTHESIS OF EXCHANGE RATE DETERMINATION

This is also known under the name of the 'market efficiency' or 'speculative efficiency' hypothesis of the exchange rate, to show that it is a combination of all three hypotheses. The hypothesis often assumes rational expectations. Under floating exchange rates, with frequent daily movements of exchange rates, one would expect to find evidence of rational expectations. Rational expectations assumes that people know and act immediately on the systematic components of their economic environment, so that they need not make systematic mistakes.

If the foreign exchange market is efficient, in the sense that all available information is used rationally by risk-neutral agents in determining the spot and forward exchange rates, then there will be no expected rate of return to speculation, and the forward rate becomes an unbiased prediction of the future spot rate.

The origin of the hypothesis is the need to explain the large fluctuations that floating exchange rates have displayed in the aftermath of the generalised floating of 1973, and the poor performance of forward rates as predictors of future spot rates. In order to assess the desirability of government intervention in floating exchange rates or even decisions to peg the exchange rate, it is important to analyse the extent and causes of the volatility of exchange rates under a floating system and the degree of efficiency of foreign exchange markets.

The hypotheses is that forward prices in an efficient market (including that of the foreign exchange) are the best unbiased forecast of future spot prices. Any observed difference is due to transaction costs, information costs and risk aversion. In its basic form, market efficiency can be represented by the following equation:

$$S_{t+1} = E_t S_{t+1} + e_{t+1} \qquad (14.8)$$

where E_t is the expectation at time t, S is the spot rate, and e_{t+1} is a serially independent forecast error with mean zero and uncorrelated with any known variable. The speculative efficiency hypothesis makes the forward rate equal to the expected future spot rate,

$$F_t = E_t S_{t+1} \qquad (14.9)$$

where F_t is the forward rate at time t for transactions due in time $t + 1$, The equation assumes identical transaction costs in forward and spot markets and also risk-neutrality.

When equations (14.8) and (14.9) are combined, the result is:

$$S_{t+1} = F_t + e_{t+1} \qquad (14.10)$$

Various forms of this equation, or rather $S_{t+1} = a + bF_t + U_t$, have been tested by many economists.

The results of the tests have not always been encouraging. In general, the speculative hypothesis is rejected as the tests become more powerful. In developing countries the absence of forward markets and arbitrages means this model can hardly be applicable.

All theories of exchange rate determination surveyed here show the link between monetary policy and exchange rate policy. Unfortunately, the assumption of perfect capital mobility and interest rate arbitrage, with efficient money and capital markets or asset markets, does not fit the reality of less-developed countries.

14.5 EXCHANGE RATE DYNAMICS AND OVERSHOOTING

This model has been developed by Dornbusch. It incorporates many features of the monetary approach, especially the demand for money function. Besides, it assumes:

(a) Perfect capital mobility.
(b) Interest rate parity.
(c) Agents expect rationality in the foreign exchange market.
(d) Exchange rates and interest rates adjust to shocks more rapidly than do goods prices and wages.
(e) Output is fixed at the natural level.
(f) Money is neutral in the long run so that a $k\%$ increase in money stock will, in the long run, raise prices by $k\%$ and lead to a depreciation of currency by $k\%$.

Now let there be a rise in the money supply. As the *nominal* money demand function has current real income, prices and interest rates as arguments, equilibrium in the money market can be restored only by changes in prices and/or real income or via a decrease in interest rates. Note that real income stays at its natural level and *prices are expected to adjust sluggishly*. Hence, the money market attains equilibrium because of a fall in interest rates. However, this means a collapse of interest rate parity as the gap appears between the foreign and domestic interest rates. To close the gap, the exchange rate is likely to appreciate. If expectations are formed rationally, the exchange rate *must* appreciate.

The effect of a rise in money supply on exchange rate in the long run is depreciation of the currency. Indeed, rational agents will believe in such long-run depreciation.

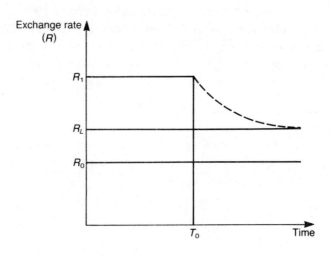

Figure 14.4

It may appear as a puzzle that the exchange rate can both appreciate and depreciate. But a little reflection will suggest that, at the outset, due to a rise in money supply, the exchange rate depreciates by more than is needed for long-run equilibrium, i.e. the rate *overshoots*. Figure 14.4 illustrates this. The initial equilibrium rate is R_0. A rise in the money supply at T_0 leads to a long-run equilibrium exchange rate (R) at R_L. But in the short run R falls sharply to R_1. The spot rate is now higher than R_L. Then the R appreciates until it reaches a new equilibrium. Exchange rate 'overshooting' is considered as a vital part of permanent monetary changes when short-run prices are sticky and capital is perfectly mobile.

14.6 THE IMPORTANCE OF EXCHANGE RATES FOR BUSINESS FIRMS

During the 1960s and 1970s world trade was gradually liberalised. Tariff barriers were reduced and quotas were removed. Firms now look to international markets rather than just confining their attention to domestic markets for finished products in manufacturing goods, for services and for raw materials and semi-manufactured products. The problem that firms face is that greater 'internationalisation' increases the risks that confront them. Changes in exchange rates will change production costs if imported raw materials are an important factor of production, and revenues will change if foreign markets are a significant source of orders. Variability in exchange rates will, therefore, make profits uncertain.

A firm in country X, which contracts to supply goods to country Y in six months' time, with the contract fixed in the currency of country Y, could make considerable gains or losses if the exchange rate changes during the period from signing the contract to payment on delivery. If it sets its price in its own currency and in the intervening period its currency appreciates, then it might price itself out of the market (i.e. follow-up orders will not be forthcoming). To understand the risks involved in the marketing and production side of an internationally oriented company requires an understanding of the movements in exchange rates and how such risks may be minimised by adopting appropriate strategies.

A firm operating in international markets will also hold its portfolio of assets in different currencies. As with any portfolio the firm will wish to maximise its return whilst minimising its exposure to risk. The returns will depend upon the relative interest rates in the different countries and also upon the exchange rates. Shareholders receive dividends in the domestic currency but in international firms returns are earned in overseas currencies. Thus shareholders will also be interested in exchange rate movements.

The forward exchange market might be used by firms to reduce exchange rate risk. The firm agrees a price today at which it will exchange foreign for domestic currency in six months' time.

How then do exchange rates impact upon pricing, sales and costs?

Many products (minerals and agricultural products) are traded on world-wide spot auction markets where prices are quoted in United States dollars. Any single firm is small relative to the size of the market: it is unable to influence price, hence it faces a horizontal demand curve.

Consider the case of an oil company operating in Britain. It extracts oil from the North Sea oil rigs which are within British territories and sells the oil on the international oil market. Suppose the average variable (and marginal) cost of extracting oil from a marginal oil field is £8.57 per barrel: if the pound sterling to US dollar exchange rate is 1.4$/£, then the cost of a barrel of oil is $12. If the world price of a barrel of oil of this quality is $15, then a profit of $3 per barrel is made. In sterling terms the oil companies receive 15/1.4, i.e. £10.7 per barrel; the profit is 3/1.4, i.e. $2.14. This is a profit margin over cost of 2.14/8.57, i.e. 25%. What happens if the exchange rate appreciates by 1.6? At $15 per barrel UK oil companies only receive 15/1.6, i.e. £9.375 per barrel. If their costs remain unchanged at £8.57, then profits fall to £0.8 per barrel, i.e. 9.3%.

Not all costs will remain constant in the above example. Oil companies import some equipment. A drilling component costing $50 000 will fall in sterling terms from £37 714 (=50 000/1.4) to £31 250 (=50 000/1.6), i.e. by 25%. These are minor improvements. On average, an appreciation in the exchange rate will adversely affect the profit margins of firms which act as price-takers on world markets.

Self-Assessment Questions

You are a manager of a copper mine selling on an international market. Your domestic currency appreciates in value. What will happen to:

(a) the domestic price of copper?
(b) the output of copper that is sold by your firm?
(c) employment in your firm?

In the above example the firm sold a product that was homogeneous. However, most manufactured products are specialised heterogeneous products with imperfect substitutes. Firms that produce these products face downward-sloping demand curves rather than the horizontal demand curves of the previous example. How should a firm with a downward-sloping demand curve react to changes in the exchange rate when setting its pricing strategy in overseas markets? If such a firm raises its price (because of exchange rate appreciation) above the world price it will not lose all of its market. It will lose some sales volume, but each unit sold earns more foreign exchange. This will depend upon the price elasticity of demand for the product.

Example. Suppose sterling against the US dollar appreciates by 14.3% from 1.4 to 1.6 and that a British exporter raises dollar prices from $15 to $16.5 (i.e. 10%) to avoid a squeeze on profit margins. At an exchange rate of 1.6 the sterling price is 10.31 (i.e. 16.5/1.6) and the fall in the sterling price is only 3.7% (i.e. 10.31/10.71). If the price elasticity of demand for the British product is -0.5, then the sales volume (i.e. quantity sold) only falls by:

price elasticity $=$ (% change in sales)/(% change in price)

i.e. % change in sales $=$ (% change in price) times (price elasticity)%

$$= 10 \times (-0.5)$$
$$= -5\%$$

Sterling revenue changes can be approximated by:

% change in revenue $=$ (% change in price) + (change in quantity)

$$= (-3.7) + (-5) = -8.7\%$$

This is less than the fall in sterling revenue of 12.5% (i.e. 9.37/10.71) when the firm is a price-taker. Thus, the more highly specialised the product, the greater is the buoyancy of world markets. Also, changes in domestic costs can be passed on in higher prices without a significant loss in market share.

Exchange Rates and Import Prices

The extent to which a change in exchange rates is transmitted to import prices (measured in domestic currency) is known as the **pass through effect**. In a period when the domestic currency is depreciating, the pass through effect has implications for domestic inflationary pressures as well as the degree of import substitution that is likely to take place. In periods of appreciation of the domestic currency, the pass through effect in part influences the extent to which domestic producers of imported competing goods experience increased competitive pressures. On the export side, the pass through effect refers to the extent to which an exchange rate change is transmitted to export prices (measured in foreign currencies). The prospects for export expansion depend upon (in part) the extent to which domestic exporters pass on an exchange rate depreciation in the form of lower foreign currency prices, while in periods of appreciation the pass through effect in part influences the degree to which the price competitiveness of exporters declines in overseas markets.

By what process are changes in the value of currency transmitted to the selling prices of imported goods in the domestic market? There are two stages of adjustment. First, in response to an exchange rate change overseas suppliers can elect either to maintain or change the foreign currency prices which they charge local importers. Second, importers, in turn, can choose to pass on all or part of these cost changes in the prices they charge local customers. What determines the size of the pass through effect – is it, for example, 100% or less?

Pass through is, firstly, likely to depend upon the relative elasticities of import supply and demand. The degree of pass through of an exchange rate change is likely to be higher the greater is the elasticity of import supply and the less elastic is import demand. In the case of a small open economy, where a country is assumed to face a perfectly elastic supply curve for imports, and to be a price-taker in world markets, then 'pass through' will be complete. Second, aspects of the macroeconomic environment may either reinforce or offset these demand and supply influences. If an exchange rate depreciation is accompanied by increasing domestic prices and real income, and hence increasing demand for imports, the degree of pass through would be expected to be relatively high irrespective of the elasticities of import supply and demand. Third, the size of the pass through effect in individual industries is expected to be influenced by the nature of the product being traded and structural features of foreign and domestic markets. These factors affect the shape and elasticity of the demand curve facing foreign suppliers and hence influence their pricing policies.

Pass through is expected to be complete where identical products are traded in an integrated world market (this applies to basic commodity-type items like copper or tea). In a market of this kind any pay differentials between countries should be arbitraged away so that the export price of overseas suppliers to the domestic market should be identical to their export price to world markets generally. If world prices are given in foreign currency terms, a change in the exchange rate is automatically reflected in a proportional change in the domestic currency price of imports.

Further Reading

Llewellyn, D. T. (1980) *International Financial Integration: The Limits of Sovereignty*, Macmillan, London.

Hallwood, P. and MacDonald, R. (1986) *International Money: Theory, Evidence and Institutions*, Basil Blackwell, Oxford.

Dornbusch, R. (1980) *Open Economy Macroeconomics*, Basic Books, New York.

Part VI

STRATEGIC PLANNING
AND THE
MACROECONOMIC
ENVIRONMENT

15

Cyclical indicators of the Macro-economy

This book is about the macroeconomic environment within which modern businesses operate. Only by understanding the way in which macroeconomic forces interact to determine output, unemployment, inflation, the exchange rate and rates of interest can companies make fully informed strategic decisions about their own optimal investment, production and stock levels. In an operational setting, this means that decision-makers must not only be able to quickly assess the implications of newly available information (for example about a change in the government's policy stance or a rise in energy prices) for their particular company, industry or market, but, insofar as it is feasible, also try to predict significant developments in the macroeconomic environment before they develop.

For example, consider the position of an automobile manufacturer producing primarily for export to the US market. How should the company respond to the news that the marginal propensity to save in the United States has slumped in the last quarter? The answer is far from straightforward. First the company will have to decide whether the change in savings behaviour is likely to be a purely transitory phenomenon or whether it will be more durable. In the latter case, the counterpart to the fall in savings will be an upturn in consumption and, as cars typically have an income elasticity of demand well in excess of unity, as US income grows, so the demand for imported automobiles will rise. On the other hand, unless monetary policy is simultaneously relaxed, the rise in income will also increase the demand for money, pushing up interest rates. Because most cars are either bought by consumers on credit, or by companies to add to their car fleets as part of their wider investment programmes, such purchases are normally highly sensitive to changes in interest rates. So the demand for cars may be choked off by the induced rise in interest rates, even though income in rising. Moreover, the increase in US income on the one hand, and interest rates on the other, will have opposite, but by no means equal, effects on the exchange rate which the automobile exporter will have to take into account. The worsening of the current account caused by the additional spending will put downward pressure on the US dollar, while the higher interest rates will attract capital inflows, tending to push up the exchange rate. Depending on which of the two effects is the more powerful, the competitive position of the exporting company may be either damaged or enhanced by the exchange rate changes the US tax cuts trigger. After considering all the forces at work, the company may conclude that, on balance, the demand for its products in the United States will grow in the future and it accordingly decides to accelerate investment and increase production.

Between receiving the news of the fall in US saving and reaping the benefits – in terms of higher export sales to the US – of the investment and production decisions it finally takes, the company will experience a significant and unavoidable time-lag. The sources of the delay are, analytically, very similar to the policy lags discussed in Chapter 9. The company first has to recognise the importance of the change in savings behaviour; it then has to process the information and form a judgement about the likely impact of these changes on the US car market and the exchange rate; and finally, it has to put into effect whatever response it decides is appropriate, accepting that it will take time to install new capacity, ship extra units to the US and gear up its distribution network to handling a higher throughput. The competitive advantage of being able to shortcircuit this protracted process, by correctly predicting the fall in the marginal propensity to save before it occurs and, by tailoring the company's responses so that the increase in supply is co-ordinated with the surge in demand, can hardly be overstated. Just as stabilisation policy is most successful when governments can correctly anticipate, and by their actions neutralise, fluctuations in private-sector spending, so companies can profit at the expense of their competitors by predicting and planning for changes in the macroeconomic environment.

Part VI explores the ways in which companies can reduce and, under certain circumstances, eliminate the lags between changes in key macroeconomic variables and changes in their own investment, output and employment. One approach is to rely on the use of 'cyclical indicators', which provide early warning about the behaviour of the economy. In many countries, monthly sales of new cars provide a crude, but regularly updated, guide to broader trends in consumer spending, giving companies information in advance of the national expenditure data which may take many months to collect and compile. House prices are typically the first to start rising during an inflationary boom, thereby signalling an upsurge of demand in the pipeline. The nature and role of cyclical indicators is discussed more fully in this chapter. The key feature of such indicators is, however, that they are macroeconomic variables which are influenced by current, ongoing changes in the economy. However much in advance a cyclical indicator warns of a change in, say, consumer spending, the indicator itself is being determined by forces that are already at work (e.g. a fall in interest rates and an increase in the money supply).

An alternative, and less mechanistic, technique is to use formal macroeconomic theory to forecast the behaviour of the economy. In the example above, basic theory suggests that savings behaviour is a function of, *inter alia*, inflation, unemployment, real interest rates and the degree of credit rationing in the financial markets. Inflation, in turn, is a function of the growth of aggregate demand, productivity and real wages; and so on. By statistically estimating the precise nature of the relationships between the key macroeconomic variables, a fully-specified model of the whole economy can be built up. Given a starting set of assumptions about those 'exogenous' variables for which no explanatory equation can be identified (e.g. the degree of credit rationing, the rate of income tax, etc), the forecast values for all the other 'endogenous' variables can be calculated by solving the system of simultaneous equations. For example, consider the simple system below:

(i) $\qquad A = 10 + 3B + 5K$

(ii) $\qquad B = 20 - A/2$

If the exogenous variable, K, is assumed to be equal to 2, then by solving the two simultaneous equations, it follows that A is 32 and B is 4; similarly, if K is assumed to be 4, then A, which is a positive function of K, will be higher at 36, while B, which is negatively related to A, will fall to 2. In much the same way, forecasts for output, inflation, real wages, consumption, etc can be generated by inserting baseline assumptions for a small number of exogenous variables into large-scale macroeconomic models of the economy. The use of model-based forecasting is examined further in Chapter 16.

15.1 TYPES OF CYCLICAL INDICATORS

Economic indicators are the descriptive and anticipatory data used as tools for the analysis of business conditions and forecasting. There are potentially as many subsets of indicators as there are different targets. (See Chapter 9 for a discussion of targets.) For example, some indicators relate to employment whilst others relate to output and prices. Indicators are used to monitor, signal and confirm cyclical changes, especially the turning points in the general economy. The series that serve this purpose are selected for being comprehensive and systematically related to business cycles and are known as 'cyclical indicators'. Business cycles are recurrent sequences of alternating phases of expansion and contraction. They are accounted for by a diverse set of economic processes. We have already looked at the business cycle and the factors that might generate it in Chapter 6.

Businessmen want to be able to predict the turning points of economic series. This aids them when making decisions. Managers, when making decisions such as investment decisions or strategic decisions, need to know whether or not the economy will be expanding or contracting over the next few years. The precise future state of the economy will influence their decisions because it will have an impact upon the flow of financial returns to their decisions. The timing of turning points in the economy influences the timing of decisions. Given our earlier analysis of the multiplier and of accelerator interaction, the timing of decisions based upon the expected time in which the turning point will incur will influence the timing of decisions about investment, which will, in turn, influence the timing of the turning point.

There are, however, a number of reasons why it is difficult to know if a turning point has, in fact, occurred in an economic time-series data set. Any data series contains trends as well as long swings in the data.

On top of these long-term changes there are short-run changes which might be systematic (i.e. based upon some reasoning about how the economy behaves) or random. If they are interpreted as long-run changes, then turning points could be illusory. Furthermore, data contain measurement errors which are subject to revisions. What might be seen as a turning point today need not be so tomorrow.

How do we find turning points? How do we predict them? One way is to look at the economic indicators that lead the rest (**leading indicators**). If these indicators turn, then there is a good chance that the rest of the economy will turn also. Leading indicators tend to reach their turning points before the corresponding business cycle turns. Many time-series reach their turning point after the peaks and troughs of the business cycle. They are referred to as **lagging indicators**. In general the leading series are flow and price variables. They show large cyclical rises and declines. Lagging indicators tend to be stocks.

Most indicators display, in addition to cyclical fluctuations, trends that cover decades and which reflect mainly economic growth and (for nominal variables) inflation. Indicators are, therefore, composites of trends and cyclical irregular movements. They can be divided into:

(1) Leading indicators: they turn before the aggregate economy does;
(2) Coincident indicators; they turn at about the same time as the economy does;
(3) Lagging indicators: they react slowly to changes. If a change is found in these indicators it is clear that a change has taken place elsewhere.

There is a large number of different economic series from which to choose the indicators. Many indicators are distilled into a smaller number of summary indicators. Each single indicator is given a weight on a scale of 0–100 depending upon:

(1) Statistical adequacy;
(2) Historical conformity to business cycles – does it track the cycle?
(3) Cyclical turning record: does it lead or lag?
(4) Promptness of publication: how long does it take to publish this indicator – if it is too long then it weakens its usefulness.

15.2 DEFINITIONS OF TERMINOLOGY

In analysing the cyclical behaviour of an individual economic variable, two particularly significant points may be identified in each cycle: a peak, when expansion changes to contraction, and a trough, when contraction changes to expansion. Peaks and troughs are collectively referred to as turning points or turns. Some variables are clearly negative variables, almost moving in an opposite sense to the general economy. For example, an economic peak would correspond to a trough in unemployment. To maintain consistency in analysing variables, such series are analysed in an inverted form, that is with peaks interpreted as troughs and vice versa.

When many series showing cyclical behaviour are considered together, it is often found that there are systematic timing relationships between their corresponding turning points. Those variables which regularly turn earliest are known as leading variables, those which turn latest as lagging variables.

There is usually a central group of variables, whose turning points are close together in time, and which may be regarded as, together, summarising movements in the economy as a whole. The group will typically include measures of such major economic factors as industrial production, retail sales and employment. Considering these variables together, it is possible to derive a set of turning points representing the cyclical movements of a hypothetical variable which may be thought of as 'aggregate economic activity'. The aggregate cycle is the reference cycle, and its turning points constitute the reference chronology. The identification of the reference cycle is usually one of the principal objectives of cyclical analysis.

Conformity

Given the reference cycle, other variables may be classified according to their usefulness as indicators of the cycle. The first requirement of an indicator is conformity to the cycle, in the sense that its turns may be matched with those of the reference cycle, with few missed or extra turns. When the turns have been matched with the reference cycle, it is possible to measure the lead or lag of the series at each turn. The median lead is used to determine the timing class of the series, that is, to label it a leading, coincident or lagging indicator (coincident should be interpreted as 'roughly coincident', and includes indicators with a median lead close to zero). Much interest naturally attaches to leading indicators, and the whole exercise is sometimes referred to as 'leading indicator analysis'. However, coincident and lagging indicators are useful as confirmation of an evolving cyclic pattern.

Months for Cyclical Dominance

One important factor in judging the usefulness of an indicator is the ease with which the cyclic pattern may be identified. Many series show a great deal of irregular period-to-period variation, which may be sufficient to obscure the cycle. Rules have been suggested for identifying turning-points in such series, but in difficult cases it may be necessary to use some form of smoothing. The commonest procedure is the MCD moving average (MCD is short for 'months for cyclical dominance'). Roughly speaking, MCD indicates the degree of irregularity of a series by showing the number of consecutive values which must be averaged to ensure that irregular variations have less influence on the result than the underlying cyclical movement. Smoothing must be used with care, since it is well known that calculation of moving averages may produce the appearance of cyclic behaviour in random series. Another problem is that a series may display sub-cycles or minor cyclical variations superimposed on the major cycles. Again, rules may be devised to eliminate sub-cycles from the analysis. However, in extreme cases these problems may lead to a series being regarded as unsuitable for use as an indicator.

The early development of cyclical analysis is associated with the National Bureau for Economic Research (NBER) in the USA, and particularly with the names of Burns and Mitchell.

Identification of Turning Points

Although examination of the shape of a curve will usually show quite clearly the general areas in which turning points lie, it is not always easy to assign them to precise months. However, for the purpose of cyclical analysis such an assignment is essential. The NBER has suggested guidelines dealing with such questions as extra cycles, step patterns, double or multiple peak situations, extreme values, minimum duration and amplitude of cycles. A computer program is available from NBER which will locate turning points automatically.

Identification of the Reference Cycle

The variables used to define the reference cycle are selected because of their relevance to aggregate economic activity, and then checked to ensure that they showed a reasonable conformity in their cyclical movements. The variables chosen are the three measures of gross domestic product at constant prices, industrial production and retail sales volume; account was also taken of notified employment vacancies, but making allowance for the fact that it seemed to lag the other variables. In some cases there might be room for disagreement over the precise location of turning points, but the margin of doubt should not be more than a month or two.

15.3 SELECTION OF INDICATORS

About 150 variables were chosen in Britain as potential indicators. The selected variables were all judged to have some economic relevance, and covered most economic sectors and processes. As far as possible they were taken from official published sources. Where necessary, series on difference bases were linked together to obtain a long run of data, and seasonal adjustment was carried out on those series which are published only in unadjusted form.

Each potential indicator was trend-eliminated and analysed as already described, and the list was progressively reduced to those which seemed most satisfactory as indicators. The following criteria were applied in selecting the shortlist:

(1) There should be clear-cut cyclical behaviour.
(2) Peaks and troughs should show conformity with the reference cycle.
(3) The emphasis should be on leading indicators, since these are generally of most interest.
(4) Chosen series should each have obvious economic significance.
(5) Together the series should cover a wide spread of economic processes and sectors.
(6) Monthly series should be preferred to quarterly ones.
(7) Smooth series should be preferred to irregular ones.
(8) Series with a long run of data should be preferred.
(9) Series without extreme values should be preferred.

Combination of Indicators

Having found groups of indicators with similar timing relationships to the reference cycle, it is of interest to see whether the indicators in a group can be combined into one synthetic indicator. Such a combination provides a convenient summary of the group, and it might be hoped that it is less affected by irregular variations than the individual indicators. Several kinds of combined indicators have been proposed in earlier work, particularly by the NBER. The two classes which we will look at here are **composite indices** and **diffusion indices**.

A composite index is formed by combining together in some way the actual values of the indicators at corresponding times. One cannot simply add together the values of the indicators, since they may be in different units of measurement; some form of standardisation to common units must be applied first. The usual procedure is to scale each indicator by dividing the values by a measure of the amplitude of the cyclical variations, and then add a constant so that the series takes the value 100 at a selected date. This process, which is known as **amplitude standardisation**, turns each indicator into a form of index number showing cyclical variations around 100 with a common amplitude. The indicators may then be combined using a simple average, or a weighted average may be used if it is possible to grade the series according to reliability. If some of the series are particularly irregular, it may be desirable to calculate an MCD moving average before combining them.

A diffusion index uses a scoring system based on the number of series which are increasing and decreasing at any given time. A simple diffusion index gives the number of series increasing minus the number of series decreasing, expressed as a percentage of the total number of series: a cumulated diffusion index is formed by adding together the values of a simple diffusion index from the start of the series. Either type of series may take positive and negative values, and will usually show cyclical variations about zero. Because it is a scoring system, a diffusion index does not require any standardisation of the indicator series and, in general, gives equal weight to all indicators. Again it may sometimes be desirable to use MCD-smoothed indicator series.

With any type of combined indicator, it is necessary to devise rules dealing with the situation where some indicators are not available for the entire span of the series. This arises particularly with the most recent values, since some series have longer reporting delays than others. The choice is either to use an incomplete set of indicators for the latest observations, or to have a combined indicator which is delayed by an amount equal to the longest reporting lag.

15.4 LEADING INDICATORS

It has already been pointed out that leading indicators decline before the general economy peaks and recover sooner at troughs. In the USA the Commerce Department's Bureau of Economic Analysis publishes 300 economic indicators each month in the *Business Conditions Digest*. Of these, 65 indicators are regarded as leading the economy through the business cycle. The most important leading indicators are added together into the 'leading indicator composite', which is made up of 12 leading indicators. These are (a) housing permits (b) liquid assets, (c) money supply, (d) stock market, (e) average work week, (f) sensitive prices, (g) business formation, (h) lay-off rate, (i) plant/equipment orders, (j) inventories, (k) vendor performance, (l) new consumer orders. Together these indicators, on average, lead the rest of the economy by about ten months. These 12 indicators do not peak and trough at the same time. Each has its own timing.

Information about the performance of the leading indicators changes over time. Indicators are therefore re-evaluated and updated every few years. One problem in recent years has been that during stagflations, when the economy experiences both a decline in output and a rise in the rate of inflation, those indicators which were expressed in nominal terms kept rising because of the rate of inflation. At the same time real indicators were falling because of the recession. The *net* effect was that the nominal indicators dominated and kept the composite index rising whilst the real economy had turned down. Thus, the usefulness of the leading indicator series is greatly reduced during periods of stagflation. This can, however, be remedied by only including real variables (all nominal indicators having been suitably deflated by a price index).

The timing relationships depend on the state of the economy. Just before and during recoveries, delivery periods get progressively longer and in booms the capacity to produce is strained. When the economy slows down and contraction develops, delivery times get progressively shorter. The change in manufacturing and trade inventories and the change in order books tends to turn before sales to which the desired level of stocks is adjusted (a type of accelerator relationship). The ratio of inventories to sales is a component of the lagging index.

Sensitive prices of industrial materials are related to new orders and inventory investment. The leading composite index in the USA now includes the rate of change in an index of these prices. This is, however, a very volatile series.

A nominal indicator is the rate of change of business and consumer credit outstanding. This leads because the new loans serve to finance investment in processes that are themselves leading (e.g. inventories, housing and consumer durables). Compared with credit flows, rates of growth in monetary aggregates (i.e. measures of the money supply) show lower cyclical conformity and more random variations. Historically they have long and very variable leads.

A stock market index, for example an index of the performance of the top 100 or 500 shares in a country, is also useful and is included in the leading composite. The stock market tracks or anticipates the movements in corporate earnings. Money wages are usually less than prices in recoveries and more than prices later in an expansion, whilst output per hour of labour fluctuates with the cycle and generally with leads. Labour costs per unit of output therefore also move with the cycle but with a lag – they are a component of the lagging index. If these tendencies in labour costs per unit of output are connected with cyclical changes in sales and the rates of utilisation of labour and capital, then profit margins and total profits will lead.

15.5 AN ASSESSMENT OF THE INDICATOR APPROACH

If there is cause and effect in the economic system then it follows that various economic processes will peak and trough at different times. When indicators were first used they were criticised on the grounds that they were not causal, i.e. there was no logical link between the variables used as indicators. Recently, as research has established causal links between variables in the economy, this criticism has subsided. Some leading indicators trigger off government policy responses. As the government observes that the economy is either overheating or moving into a recession, then governments will choose to activate policies (monetary or fiscal, etc). Governments tend to respond to leading indicators that have a long lead time. Other organisations in the economy, such as business firms, will then respond not only to the leading indicators' signals, but also to the reaction of government.

Policy leading indicators tend to lead by up to eighteen months and emanate from both monetary and fiscal policies. They are indicators of the money supply, taxes and interest rates. Other leading indicators that are affected by these are housing starts, liquid assets and new business formation.

Leading indicators with a medium length of lead (six to twelve months) are much more likely to correspond to the behaviour of factory operations than to government policy. These relate to orders, profits and employment. They confirm whether or not the longer lead policy indicators are working.

The shortest leads (one to six months) are highly influenced by inventories. Whilst inventories are sensitive leading indicators, they do pose problems. Inventory statistics are subject to large measurement errors and tend to be reported late. These problems cause inventories to lose their already short leads.

The indicator approach is usually contrasted with the econometric approach in analysing and forecasting the economy. The two approaches are, in practice, compatible. In econometrics timing differences are handled by means of regression lags. Housing starts are a leading indicator of furniture sales. It is several months before a new house is sufficiently completed to begin moving furniture into it. One of the important contributions of econometrics is that it can incorporate lead or lag relationships within the model through its principal technique, i.e. regression. However, the indicator approach is useful in that it offers a graphical representation of data. Examining economic time-series and observing the timing relationships between peaks and troughs suggests relationships that can be estimated statistically using more formal regression techniques. Many users of both the econometric and indicator approaches are required to justify their forecasts by both visual and verbal methods, so that the indicator approach provides a useful addition to econometrics.

One of the most serious criticisms of the indicator approach is that whilst the leading indicators have reasonably stable mean lead times, they suffer badly with respect to their standard deviations around their means. This defect forces those who use indicators to use large numbers of indicators, since one or even several indicators are simply not statistically reliable. It is, therefore, a mistake to concentrate on only a few indicators since they might be giving erroneous signals.

Recurrent fluctuations in the level and growth rate of the economy have been a feature of the Western industrialised nations for many years. These fluctuations have been termed 'business cycles'. A cycle in this sense consists of an expansion occurring at approximately the same time in many economic activities and sectors, followed by a contraction and revival leading on to the next expansion. The sequence of changes is recurrent but by no means regular, either in duration or amplitude of movement.

Cyclical Analysis

In seeking to analyse and interpret current and historical information about the economy, statisticians and economists have used several approaches. One is to construct econometric models, embodying hypotheses about the nature and direction of economic causality, and to use historical data to check the validity of the models and to estimate the magnitudes of the unknown coefficients. A model so constructed may be used to interpret the past and to predict the future. Another method, complementary to, rather than competitive with, model-building, is to use the set of techniques which have come to be known as 'cyclical analysis'. Broadly, these techniques involve studying a large number of series of economic data to see what regularities can be found in their cyclical behaviour, and using these regularities to obtain a description and, so far as possible, interpretation of cyclical movements in the whole economy.

Self-Assessment Questions

(a) Of what value are macroeconomic indicators to business executives who are making their business plans over the next three years?
(b) How might an examination of the United States of America's leading indicators be useful to business executives in Canada and Mexico?
(c) What macroeconomic indicators will be of value in the making of decisions in a manufacturing company?

Further Reading

Johnson, C. (1988) *Measuring the Economy: A Guide to Understanding Official Statistics*, Penguin, London.

Lomas, E. (1983) 'Cyclical Indicators: Some Developments and an Assessment of Performance', *Economic Trends*, November.

Central Statistical Office, *Economic Trends*, February, May, August and November issues, annually.

16

Forecasting the Macro-Economy

As we saw in Chapter 15, forecasting essentially involves the use of macroeconomic theory to calculate expected values for endogenous variables (i.e. those determined within the macroeconomic system), given starting assumptions for exogenous variables. In many countries, the government's department of finance and (sometimes) the central bank have forecasting units which use large, computerised models of the economy to predict future movements in the key macroeconomic variables. While the results are primarily intended for internal policy purposes (for example to inform the conduct of stabilisation policy or to support applications to overseas lending agencies like the International Monetary Fund), they may be published to assist strategic decision-making in the business community. In addition to official forecasts, universities, financial institutions and private companies often produce their own, independent forecasts, which are either provided free of charge or sold at commercial rates to outside users. With the advert of cheap, powerful computers, the number of private-sector forecasters has increased sharply in many countries.

In the United Kingdom, for example, there are presently 22 major forecasting organisations which regularly publish their results. The oldest is the British Treasury (the government's department of finance) which has developed a very large computer-based model, comprising approximately 700 equations and a total of 1,000 exogenous and endogenous variables. The London Business School model (160 equations and 400 variables) and the Liverpool University model (29 equations and 50 variables) are the best-known of a growing number of academic research models used to generate forecasts within British universities, while specialist forecasting companies like the National Institute of Economic and Social Research (NIESR), large commercial banks (e.g. Barclays Bank) and financial institutions in the 'City' of London (e.g. Goldman Sachs, Phillips and Drew) all prepare and disseminate regular forecasts. Unsurprisingly, the forecasts differ, partly because different groups select different starting assumptions for exogenous variables, and partly because the theoretical structure of the models differs.

Table 16.1 set out forecasts for the UK economy prepared at the beginning of 1991 for the year ahead by a government agency (the Treasury), a university (the London Business School), a specialist forecasting house (NIESR) and a City firm (Goldman Sachs). It shows considerable disagreement with regard to some variables – forecasts for investment growth range from a low of −6.3% (Goldman Sachs) to a high of −1.3% (London Business School) – and relative unanimity on others, notably inflation where estimates are clustered around 4.9–5.6%. (Because unemployment is such a politically sensitive issue in the UK, the Treasury does not formally release its unemployment forecasts.)

Table 16.1 Forecasts of the UK Macroeconomy for 1991 (% change p.a., unless stated)

	Treasury	London Business School	NIESR	Goldman Sachs
Consumption	0.5	2.4	2.0	1.0
Investment	−1.8	−1.3	−1.9	−6.3
Exports	2.5	3.0	6.3	1.5
Imports	1.3	1.8	5.9	−0.1
Real Income	0.5	1.4	0.8	−1.2
Inflation (4th Quarter)	5.5	5.6	4.9	5.0
Unemployment (4th Quarter)	n/a	1.87m	2.10m	2.54m

Source: Institute of Fiscal Studies.

16.1 WHY FORECASTS DIFFER

There are a number of reasons why forecasts differ. To illustrate the primary sources of disagreement between one set of forecasters and another, consider two very simple models of the economy, either of which could serve as the basis for a macroeconomic forecast of real income and prices. Model 1 below is a crude 'Keynesian' model, in which income is demand-determined and the price level is exogenously given. Model 2 is a 'monetarist' model, in which income settles at the natural rate in the long run and the price level adjusts to bring the demand for money into line with changes in the exogenous money supply. Both models have simple solutions, given by equations (16.7) and (16.8) for Model 1 and (16.13) and (16.14) for Model 2.

Model 1: A 'Keynesian' Model of the Macro-economy

$Y = C + I + G$	(16.1)	Y = real income, C = consumption, I = investment, G = government spending
$C = c_0 + bY$	(16.2)	c_0 = autonomous consumption, b = marginal propensity to consume
$I = I^*$	(16.3)	I^* = exogenous investment
$G = G^*$	(16.4)	G^* = exogenous government spending
$P = W$	(16.5)	P = price level, W = money wage level
$W = W^*$	(16.6)	W^* = exogenous money wage level
$Y = (c_0 + I^* + G^*)/(1 - b)$	(16.7)	
$P = W^*$	(16.8)	

Model 2: A 'Monetarist' Model of the Macro-economy

$M_d = kPY$	(16.9)	M_d = demand for money
$M_S = M_S^*$	(16.10)	M_S^* = exogenous money supply
$Y = Y_n + d(P^e - P)$	(16.11)	Y_n = natural level of income, P^e = expected price level
$P^e = P_{t-1}$	(16.12)	P_{t-1} = price level in previous time-period
$Y = Y_n + d(P_{t-1} - P)$	(16.13)	
$P = M_S^*/kY$	(16.14)	

Even using models with identical structures, forecasters may arrive at different results. For example, suppose two rival organisations both use Model 1. In utilising past data to statistically estimate the crucial relationship between consumption, C, and real income, Y (see Appendix to Chapter 16 below), each may have arrived at slightly different values for the behavioural parameters c_0 and b, which will clearly influence their forecasts of real income, all other things equal. Moreover, Model 1 calls for considerable judgement in selecting values for the exogenous variables, I^*, G^* and W^*, and each modeller may have a different view about the future course of investment, government spending and money wages. Differences between forecasts are, however, likely to be much greater when they are generated by models with different structures. A change in the money supply has no impact in the simple 'Keynesian' Model 1, whereas it has an equiproportionate effect on nominal income, PY, in the 'monetarist' Model 2. Conversely, an increase in government spending (unless financed by a monetary expansion) raises real income in Model 1 by a factor of $1/(1-b)$, but leaves both real income and prices unaltered in Model 2.

16.2 THE IMPORTANCE OF MODEL STRUCTURE IN FORECASTING

The nature of the underlying theoretical perspective therefore plays a central role in determining the forecasts that a model generates. Macroeconomic models are nothing more than mathematical representations of the theoretical frameworks which have been explored in the chapters above. The only difference is that the numerical sizes of the behavioural parameters (i.e. the marginal propensity to consume, etc) have been estimated (this process is sometimes termed 'calibrating' the model) using past data for the economy concerned (see Appendix to Chapter 16 below).

Consider the model below. (This section may be skipped by less mathematical readers, who should proceed directly to Section 16.3). It sets out the system of equations linking the goods and money markets which underpins the simple *IS-LM* model for a closed economy. The *IS* curve maps out combinations of real income, Y, and interest rates, r, which constitute equilibrium in the goods market, while the *LM* curve illustrates points of equilibrium in the money market. The equations of the two schedules are set out below:

IS curve: $Y = C + I + G$ (16.15)

$C = c_0 + b(1 - t)Y$ (16.16)

$I = d - er$ (16.17)

$G = G^*$ (16.18)

$$Y = \frac{(c_0 + d - er + G)}{(1 - b + bt)}$$ (16.19)

LM curve: $M_S/P = M_d/P$ (16.20)

$M_s = M_S^*$ (16.21)

$M_d/P = kY - mr$ (16.22)

$Y = M_S/Pk + mr/k$ (16.23)

$IS = LM$, where:

$$Y = \frac{mP(c_0 + d + G) - eM_S}{mP(1 - b + bt) + ekP}$$ (16.24)

In this model, an increase in government spending from G_1 to G_2 raises income by $m(G_2 - G_2)/[m(1 + b - bt) + ek]$. Diagrammatically, this is illustrated in Figure 16.1 by a shift in the *IS* schedule from IS_0 to IS_1, with simultaneous goods and money market equilibrium being re-established at Y_1. From the diagram, it is clear that the steeper the *LM* schedule (the slope of which is k/m), and the flatter the *IS* schedule (the slope of which is $(b - 1 - bt)/e$), the smaller the increase in real income which takes place.

The precise size of the income multiplier is therefore an empirical matter, which will vary from one country to the next and within a country from one time-period to the next, depending on the magnitude of the marginal propensity to consume (b), the marginal rate of tax (t), and the income-elasticity (k) and interest-elasticity (e) of the demand for money. By statistically estimating the size of these key parameters, the *IS-LM* model can be operationalised in the form of a

269

macroeconomic model, so that precise forecasts for real income can be generated from initial assumptions about the level of government spending.

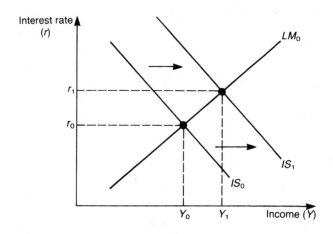

Figure 16.1

There are, of course, a number of ways in which this basic model might be extended. For example, suppose a wealth effect were to be incorporated into the behavioural equations for consumption and the demand for money as follows, where nominal wealth, F, is defined as the stock of outstanding government bonds, B (i.e. the summation of all previous budget deficits, abstracting from the issue of notes and coin):

IS curve: $Y = C + I + G$ (16.25)

$C = c_0 + b(1 - t)Y + cF/P$ (16.26)

$I = d - er$ (16.27)

$G = G^*$ (16.28)

$F = B$ (16.29)

$B = (G - T) + (G - T)_{t-1} + \ldots + (G - T)_{t-n}$
  $= (G - T) + B_{t-1}$ (16.30)

$$Y = \frac{P(c_0 + d - er) + (P + c)G + cB_{t-1}}{P(1 - b + bt) + ct} \qquad (16.31)$$

LM curve: $M_S/P = M_d/P$ (16.32)

$\qquad\qquad M_S = M_S^* \qquad\qquad\qquad\qquad (16.33)$

$\qquad\qquad M_d/P = kY - mr + nF/P \qquad (16.34)$

$$Y = \frac{M_S + Pmr - nB_{t-1} - nG}{kP - nt} \qquad (16.35)$$

$IS = LM$, where:

$$Y = \frac{mP(c_0 + d) + (mP + mc - en)G + (mc - en)B_{t-1} + eM_S}{mP(1 - b + bt) + mct + e(kP - nt)} \qquad (16.36)$$

An increase in government spending now has an ambiguous impact on real income, since the income multiplier is $(mP + mc - en)$/etc.). The larger the wealth effect on consumption (C), all other things equal, the larger the income multiplier, since consumption is boosted by the increase in the stock of government bonds which results from the deficit spending. But the larger the wealth effect on the demand for money, the lower the income multiplier, since the extra bonds increase the demand for money and force up interest rates, crowding out interest-sensitive investment. Figure 16.2 illustrates a situation in

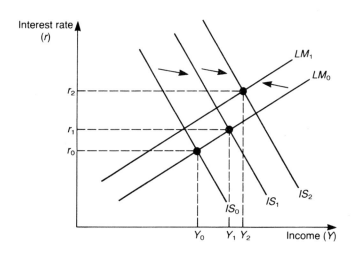

Figure 16.2

271

which the former effect dominates, but there is no *a priori* reason why this should be the case. Only by statistically estimating the relationship between consumption and wealth, and the demand for money and wealth (i.e. calculating the empirical values of c and n), can the precise impact of a change in government spending on income be predicted.

This example demonstrates the way that changing the structure of the model even slightly can give rise to very different forecasts of endogenous variables. However elaborate the statistical techniques employed to estimate the size of the various behavioural parameters, the basic theoretical perspective chosen is crucial, since it determines both the variables to be included in (and just as important, excluded from) the model and the basic form of the relationship between such variables. Models which assume market-clearing and rational expectations accordingly generate forecasts in which shocks are accommodated much more quickly and output diverges less from trend than more traditional models, built on theoretical foundations of adaptive expectations and sticky prices and wages.

16.3 FORECASTING RACES

Faced with a range of mutually inconsistent forecasts emanating from public-and private-sector organisations, one approach might be to ignore the reasons why the forecasts differ and give the greatest weight to that source which has been most accurate in the past. Most forecasters regularly assess the performance of their own models and 'forecasting races', in which the records of the main organisations are compared, are often conducted by independent researchers. There are, unfortunately, several difficulties with using this approach as a means of choosing between inconsistent forecasts. Since so many variables are being forecast, it is highly unlikely that one group will most accurately predict each and every variable. Rather, the balance of probabilities is that organisation A will have the best result for real income, B for unemployment and C for inflation. Moreover, the ranking of forecasters with regard to even a single variable may change from one year to the next. This is partly due to the element of random chance which bedevils the choice of values for exogenous variables: in one year, A may guess the (exogenously-determined) rate of growth of world trade more accurately than B, but then choose a less accurate figure the following year. But it also reflects the efforts of forecasters to

continually improve their models, so that a particularly poor performance by C in one year may inspire structural changes which
dramatically improve its ranking in future years.

It is also worth pointing out that forecasting races are further
complicated by the fact that different forecasters publish results for
different subsets of the total range of macroeconomic variables which
could, in principle, be predicted. For example, A may produce figures
for the visible trade balance, while B forecasts the current account
balance; B may cite unemployment forecasts in terms of adult
unemployment, while A uses a broader measure that includes jobless
school-leavers. As a result, it is not always possible to precisely map
each forecast from organisation A on to a rival forecast from B,
thereby allowing a full comparison to be made.

16.4 INTERPRETING FORECASTS

For the reasons outlined above, it is generally more appropriate to use
the range of forecasts available to get an overall impression of
forthcoming macroeconomic developments, rather than hoping a
forecasting race will throw up an unambiguous winner whose
forecasts can be uncritically accepted as 'correct'. One approach might
be to simply give each of the major forecasts an equal weight and
calculate a straightforward arithmetic mean forecast for each macroeconomic variable. Recasting the data presented in Table 16.1 above,
this would give a set of average forecasts which are set out in Table
16.2.

Table 16.2 Forecasts of the UK Macroeconomy for 1991
(% change p.a., unless stated)

	Mean	High	Low
Consumption	1.2	2.4	0.5
Investment	−3.7	−1.3	−6.3
Exports	2.7	6.3	1.5
Imports	1.4	5.9	−0.1
Real Income	0.3	1.4	−1.2
Inflation (4th Quarter)	5.2	5.6	4.9
Unemployment (4th Quarter)	2.08m	2.54m	1.87m

Source: Institute of Fiscal Studies.

Whether this is a sensible strategy depends on a number of factors. If all the forecasts are closely clustered around the mean, then the average forecast can be accepted with some confidence. If, on the other hand, one forecast is very different from the rest (so that it skews the mean away from the broad 'consensus' view), there might be a case for discounting it completely. Another possibility is that there is no majority view at all, with widespread disagreement amongst forecasters with regard to a particular variable. Under such circumstances, business planners might be advised to consider each prediction more closely in the light of the models within which they have been generated. For example, a model constructed around rational expectations will typically forecast lower output growth and more rapid inflation following, say, a rise in the money supply, than one built on adaptive expectations. It is not unreasonable in such a situation to assign the greatest weight to forecasts produced by models with the most subjectively convincing structural features.

Another consideration when interpreting conflicting forecasts is that the costs to the business of strategic responses based on under estimates and overestimates of future variables are unlikely to be symmetrical. For example, increasing investment in anticipation of a surge in consumer demand may prove highly damaging to the investing company's profitability and liquidity if the upturn in market conditions fails to materialise. For this reason, it may be useful to treat the highest or lowest forecasts of certain critical variables (e.g. interest rates, the exchange rate, consumption) as 'worst case scenarios' in deciding how to plan for the future.

16.5 THE LUCAS CRITIQUE

Some years ago, one of the best-known of the New Classical economists, Robert E. Lucas, made a powerful criticism of mainstream forecasting models which is worthy of note. He pointed out that the behavioural parameters (i.e. the numerical values for the marginal propensity to consume, etc) used in large-scale macroeconomic models have been estimated on the basis of *past* behaviour. For example, the consumption function ($C = c_0 + b(1 - t)Y$) is normally estimated by regressing past observations of consumer spending, C, on disposable income, $(1 - t)Y$, thereby obtaining values for c_0 and b (see Appendix to Chapter 16). Economic theory, however, suggests that consumer behaviour is also influenced by subjective expectations of the future, notably expectations about future levels of disposable income, unemployment and inflation. In a world of relative tranquillity, in which rates of income growth, unemployment and inflation are broadly stable, consumers' expectations will tend to be stable over time. As a result, macroeconomic modellers will be able to obtain stable estimates of the behavioural parameters, a and b, even though these are conditioned by consumers' views of the future.

Suppose the consumption function estimated has the form:

$$C = \$10bn + 0.8(1 - t)Y$$

This suggest that, on the basis of past behaviour, if the government were to introduce a cut in the marginal tax rate from 30% to 25%, then with real income initially at $300bn, consumption should rise in the first instance from $178bn to $190bn (over time, there will, of course, be additional multiplier effects at work). But suppose that, following the government's announcement, consumers judge that further tax cuts will be made in subsequent years, leading them to revise upwards their expectations of the future rate of growth of disposable income. Under such circumstances, households may decide that there is less need to save, with the result that their marginal propensity to consume increases from 0.8 to 0.9. Consumption accordingly jumps from $178bn to $203bn, rather than $190bn. Because the forecasters are unable to allow for the change in expectations induced by the tax-cutting policy, their models underestimate its likely effects.

In other words, because behavioural parameters estimated on the basis of past experience have a given set of subjective expectations embedded in their values, macroeconomic models are liable to perform badly under circumstances in which expectations are likely to change (e.g. when the government introduces a radical programme of tax cuts). Only by incorporating rational expectations into all the relevant behavioural equations, as the New Classical economists argue model-builders should (so that, in the example above, the marginal propensity to consume would become an endogenous variable, dependent on government policy), can this weakness be remedied.

Table 16.3 sets out the main forecasts of consumer spending for UK economy in the late 1980s. It is notable that all four of the major forecasting organisations significantly underestimated the out-turns for consumption. In 1987, the average underestimate was 1.5% compared with an out-turn of 5.4%, while in 1988 the average underestimate was 3.4% compared with an out-turn of 6.9%. One interpretation of these results is that a series of income-tax reductions by the British government over the period 1984–88 – during which time the marginal rate of income tax was reduced from 30% to 25% for lower income groups and from 60% to 40% for the higher income-earners – created an atmosphere in which these cuts were expected to continue into the future, so leading to an increase in the marginal propensity to consume which all the major forecasters failed to anticipate. The warning implicit in the Lucas critique is, therefore, that macroeconomic forecasts should be treated with special caution at times of unusual change.

Table 16.3 Main Forecasts of Real Consumer Spending in the UK

	Treasury	London Business School	National Institute	Goldman Sachs	Out-turn
1987	4.0%	3.9%	4.3%	3.3%	5.4%
1988	4.0%	3.3%	2.9%	3.8%	6.9%

Source: Institute of Fiscal Studies.

Self-Assessment Questions

Which of the following variables is likely to be the most difficult to forecast accurately:

(a) consumption?
(b) investment?
(c) government expenditure?
(d) exports?

Why?

Further Reading

Keating, G. (1985) *The Production and Use of Economic Forecasts*, Methuen, London.

Artis, M. J. (1982) 'Why do Forecasts Differ?', Paper Presented to the Panel of Economic Consultants No. 17, Bank of England, London.

Corker, R. J. (1983) 'Forecasting Uncertainty: How Accurate Can We Be?, *L.B.S. Economic Outlook*, Vol. 7, No. 5.

Timbrell, M. (1983) *Mathematics for Economists*, Basil Blackwell, Oxford.

APPENDIX: MULTIPLE REGRESSION ANALYSIS

This Appendix is intended only to provide a very simple overview of the process by which the equations which make up a full model of the economy are estimated. You are directed to the 'Guide to Further Reading' on pages 276–7 for a more detailed discussion of the statistical techniques involved.

To illustrate the basic procedure, consider the following highly simplified consumption function:

$$C = c_0 + bY$$

The parameter c_0 represents autonomous consumption and b represents the marginal propensity to consume. In terms of the conventional diagrammatical presentation of Figure 16.3. c_0 is the positive intercept value and b the slope of the consumption function.

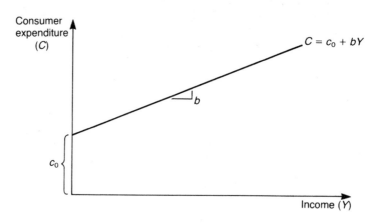

Figure 16.3

In order to translate this theoretical concept into a behavioural equation, which quantifies the precise relationship between consumption and income for a given economy, the modeller must first assemble the relevant data, an illustrative example of which is given in Table 16.4.

Table 16.4 Consumption and Real Income for Macroeconomia, 1980–90 ($bn)

Year	Consumption (Y variable)	Real Income (X variable)	XY	Y²	X²
1980	102	104	10 608	10 404	10 816
1981	107	112	11 984	11 449	12 544
1982	108	118	12 744	11 664	13 924
1983	112	127	14 224	12 544	16 129
1984	118	138	16 284	13 924	19 044
1985	127	154	19 558	16 129	23 716
1986	133	165	21 945	17 689	27 225
1987	139	172	23 908	19 321	29 584
1988	138	176	24 288	19 044	30 976
1989	141	185	26 085	19 881	34 225
1990	149	198	29 502	22 201	39 204
Total	1 374	1 649	211 050	174 250	257 387

By plotting consumption (on the vertical axis) against real income (on the horizontal axis), a scatter diagram can be obtained, such as Figure 16.4. The nature of the relationship between the two variables is quite clear from this Figure. Indeed, even with the naked eye, it would be relatively easy to draw in the consumption function which

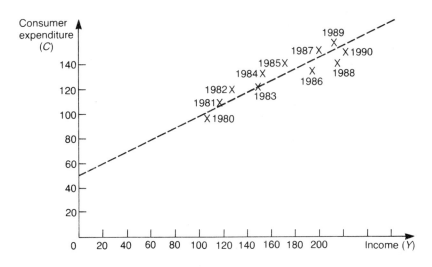

Figure 16.4

279

appears to underpin this relationship and, from this line, measure the positive intercept, c_0 and the slope, b. Conceptually, this is precisely the purpose of mathematical regression analysis, which allows macroeconomic modellers to formalise this procedure and calculate c_0 and b direct from the observations of the dependent variable (in this case, consumption) and independent variable(s) (here, real income).

The formulae for the calculation of c_0 and b are

$$c_0 = \frac{(EY)(EX^2) - (EX)(EXY)}{NEX^2 - (EX)^2}$$

$$b = \frac{NEXY - (EX)(EY)}{NEX^2 - (EX)^2}$$

where Y is the dependent variable (consumption), X is the independent variable (real income). E is 'the sum of' and N is the number of observations (11). Using the data in Table 16.4 to calculate c_0 and b, yields the following consumption function:

$$\text{Consumption} = 50.2275 + 0.4982(\text{Real Income})$$

There are various statistical tests which may be applied to the estimated relationship, to establish the 'goodness' of fit' of the relationship (i.e. the percentage of variations in consumption 'explained' by changes in real income). Normally, behavioural relationships are estimated using specially designed computer software packages, which not only perform the calculations, but also provide the user with the results of a battery of such 'diagnostic' tests, from which a judgement of the robustness of the relationship can be made.

The behavioural relationships in large-scale macroeconomic models are, of course, much more complicated than the simple consumption function employed above. Such equations normally embody more than two variables and are often non-linear in form, using logs for variables that grow over time. To capture the sluggish response of dependent variables to changes in the independent variables, the practice of regressing the current value of X against past values of itself and other variables is also common. The consumption function shown below is typical:

$$\log(C_t) = a + b.\log(C_{t-1}) + c.\log(C_{t-2}) + d.\log(DI_{t-1}) + e.\log(DI_{t-2})$$
$$+ f(STR_{t-1}) + g(STR_{t-2}) + h.\log(P_{t-1}/P_{t-2}^*)$$

where C_t is consumption in time-period t, etc. DI is disposable income, STR is short-term interest rates and P is the retail price index. Nevertheless, despite these added complexities, the basic mechanics of estimating the numerical values of the parameters a, b, c, etc is, in principle, the same.

Index

accelerator-multiplier interaction, 107–10
active balances, 18
actual output, business cycles, 104–5
AD curve, 78
see also aggregate demand
adaptive expectations
inflation, 114
Phillips Curve, 122–4
administrative lag, 153
aggregate demand, 39, 55
anticipated changes, 97–9
business cycles, 104–5
counter-inflation policies, 125
crowding out, 178
determination, 76–9
exchange-rate theories, 233–4, 237
fiscal policy, 158, 160
inflation, 113, 115–16
Keynesian model, 45–6
Keynesian theory, 134–5
New Classical theory, 97–8
policy instruments, 144–7
policy limitations, 207–12
aggregate demand and supply model
demand, 76–9
government instruments, 144–5
summary, 98–9
supply, 79–98
aggregate supply, 55, 79–80
actual versus potential, 79
classical theory, 80–3, 91–2
counter-inflation policies, 126
Keynesian theory, 83–92
labour supply, 79–80
New Classical theory, 92–8
policy instruments, 144–6
price fixing, 117–18
see also aggregate demand and supply model
amplitude standardisation, 259

Anderson, G. T., 59
Anderson, P. S., 131
Ando, A., 59
arbitrage
covered interest arbitrage, 221–2
definition, 216
exchange-rate theories, 238, 240, 243
Artis, M. J., 277
AS, see aggregate supply
assets
commercial banks, 197
exchange-rate theories, 237, 241, 245
flow-of-funds accounts, 11–12
foreign exchange, 219
monetary policy, 186, 188–9, 204
see also idle balances
automatic stabilisers, role, 164–6, 170–1
autonomous, definition, 43
autonomous consumption, 42–3
autonomous expenditure, 47, 63
change in, 52–4, 64

Backhouse, R., 206
Backus, D., 34
Bade, R. (Parkin), 131
balance of payments, 223–7
adjustment, 227–31
exchange-rate theories, 232, 234–41
government policy, 141
balance of trade, 223–4, 230
balanced budget multiplier, 160–3
Bank of England, 198, 200
banks
central, 190–1, 194–203
disintermediation, 205
foreign exchange markets, 215–16
government policy, 148
monetary control, 196–203
monetary policy, 152–3
money supply, 66, 190–3, 201
basic balance, 225

Begg, D. K. H., 212
Bhalla, S. S., 59–60
boom, business cycles, 104–5
BOP, *see* balance of payments
BOT, *see* balance of trade
Brainard, W. (Backus), 34
Bretton Woods system, 156
brokers, foreign exchange markets, 216
Brown, W. S., 99, 183
budget
  demand management, 167–71
  IS-LM model, 160–3
  monetary policy, 200–3
  national debt, 172–7
Buiter, W. H., 212
business cycles, 103–10
  accelerator-multiplier interaction,
    107–10
  IS-LM model, 105–7
  phases, 104–7
  unemployment, 134–5

capacity utilisation index, 28
capital
  aggregate supply, 79
  compensating flows, 223
  cyclical indicators, 252
  exchange-rate theories, 233, 236–8,
    240, 243
Carter, M., 212
central banks, and monetary policy,
    152–3
chain index, 26
classical theory
  aggregate supply, 80–3, 91–2
  flaws, 4–5
  perspective of, 3–4
  see also New Classical theory
coincident indicators, 255, 256–7
commercial bank model, 142
  see also banks
comparative advantage, 4
composite indices, 259
conformity indicators, 256–7
consumer price index, 25
consumption
  accelerator-multiplier interaction, 107
  categories, 18, 20
  counter-inflation policies, 125–6
  crowding out, 179–80
  cyclical indicators, 251, 253
  fiscal policy, 159, 161

forecasting, 266–8, 269–71
government spending effects, 45
IS line, 71
Keynesian model, 40, 41–3
Lucas critique, 274–6
luxury goods, 166
monetary policy, 186, 189, 205
multiple regression analysis, 278–81
convergent cycles, 108
Corker, R. J., 277
corporatism, 130–1
cost-push inflation, 118
cost-of-capital channel, 186–7, 204
costs, exchange-rate theories, 242, 245
counter-inflation policies, 125–7
covered interest arbitrage, 221–2
credit
  cyclical indicators, 252–3
  exchange-rate systems, 236–7
  restriction, 199
Cross, J., 7
crowding out, 162–3, 177–83
currency
  arbitrage, 216
  balance of payments, 223–31
  exchange-rate systems, 234, 243–5,
    247
  foreign exchange, 215–22
  interest rates, 205
  monetary control, 193–5, 196–203
  money supply process, 190–3
  national debt, 172–3
current account, balance of payments,
    223
cycles
  business, 263
  business/trade phases, 104–7
  convergent, 108
  explosive, 108–9
  macroeconomic indicators, 251–64
  reference cycle, 258
  unemployment, 134–5
cyclical budget deficit, 169
cyclical indicators, 251–64
  assessment, 261–3
  definitions, 256–8
  selection, 258–60
  types, 254–5

data analysis
  business cycles, 105–7
  cyclical indicators, 263

expenditure, 15–20
flow-of-funds accounts, 11–13
growth rate, 33–4
income, 17–20
national income accounting, 13–20
policy indicators, 149–51
unemployment stock, 30–1
Deaton, A., 60
debit transfers, balance of payments, 223
debt, developing countries, 156
decision-making
    data measurement, 8–9
    economic stability, 69–70
    government policy, 147–9, 152
    inflation, 112, 123–4
    IS-LM model, 72
    policy limitations, 207–12
deficit
    balance of payments, 224
    financing, 200
deindustrialisation, 125
demand management
    definition, 59
    limitations, 208–12
    monetary policy, 184, 188, 204
    policies, 125–6, 130–1, 135, 146–7
    see also aggregate demand and supply
        model
demand-pull inflation, 118
demand-for-money function, 239–40
demand-supply relationship, 39
depreciation, capital, 20
depression, business cycles, 104–5
devaluation adjustment, 228, 230–1
developing countries
    debt problems, 156
    exchange-rate theories, 239–40, 243
diffusion indices, 259
dirty float, 225
'discount window' lending, 197
disequilibrium
    aggregate supply, 92, 96–7
    balance of payments, 223, 227
    Keynesian theory, 5, 38
disintermediation, 205–6
dissaving, 42
Dornbusch, R., 131, 248

econometrics
    cyclical indicators, 262–3
    national income, 15–16, 47–9

economic growth
    environmental costs, 22
    limits, 51–2
    measurement, 31–4
elasticity, 229–30
employment
    classical theory, 81
    full employment
        equilibrium status, 58, 70–1
        government objective, 142
        inflation theories, 115–16, 118
        output, 113
        production function, 82–3
    inflation, 113, 115–16
    interdependence, 37–8
    IS-LM model, 70–1
    Keynesian theory, 85–9
    measurement, 28–31
    multiplier process, 52
    wage inflation, 123–4
    see also labour; unemployment
EMS, *see* European Monetary System
environment, costs of economic growth, 22
equilibrium, 55–9
    aggregate demand, 46
    aggregate supply model, 80–3
        Keynesian theory, 83–4, 92
        New Classical theory, 96–7
    autonomous spending, 56–7
    business cycles, 105–7
    classical theory, 5
    exchange-rate stability, 219–21
    exchange rate, 217–19
    interest rate, 62–3
    IS-LM model, 69–71
    Keynesian model, 39–46
    multiplier, 52–3
    national income determination, 47–9
    portfolio balance approach, 241
    unemployment cycles, 135
equivalence theorem, 180
error, aggregate supply model, 95–7
errors and omissions, 223
European Community, government
    constraints, 155
European Monetary System, 156
exchange rate
    cyclical indicators, 251
    determination, 217–21
        business significance, 244–8

dynamics and overshooting model,
  243–4
monetary approach, 237–40
portfolio balance approach, 241
post-Keynesian theories, 232–7
rational expectations hypothesis,
  241–3
Keynesian view, 83
exogenous money supply, 66
exogenous variables, 253–4
expectations
  aggregate supply, 93–7
  business cycles, 103, 104–5
  exchange-rate determination, 241–3
  inflation, 111–13, 120–5
  meaning, 93–5
  New Classical theory, 210–11
  nominal rates of return, 128–9
  theories, 208–9
expenditure, 20
  categories, 17
  crowding out, 178–83
  fiscal policy, 158, 162
  flow of income, 15–16
  government, 17, 19–20
  income interdependence, 17–18, 37–8
  interest-rate relationship, 61–5
  interest sensitivity, 73
  monetary policy, 200
  national debt control, 172–7
  national income determination, 47–9
  policy instruments, 144–6
  stabilisers, 164
  see also income-expenditure model
explosive cycle, 108–9
exports
  cyclical indicators, 252
  exchange rates, 233–7, 247
  foreign exchange markets, 215–16,
    223, 225–31

financial crowding out, 163
financial markets, 65–8
financial net worth, 11–12
fiscal drag stabilisers, 165
fiscal policy, 146, 150–1, 158–83
  automatic stabilisers, 164–6
  crowding out, 162–3, 177–83
  IS-LM model, 159–63
  monetary control, 199–202
  national debt, 172–7
  stance, measurement of, 167–71

Fischer, S. (Dornbusch), 131
Fisher effect, 176
fixed exchange-rate systems, 234–7, 239
fixed investment, 18
fix-price model, 116
Fleming-Mundell model, 232
flex-price model, 82, 83, 97
  inflation, 116, 131
floating exchange-rate systems, 234,
    239, 241–2
flow-of-funds accounts, 10–12
  assets and liabilities, 11–12
  stocks and flows, 12–13
flow of income
  diagram, 15–16
  government policy, 146
  withdrawals, 46
forecasts, 265–76
  differences, reasons why, 267–8
  government policy, 154–5
  interpretation, 273–4
  Keynesian model, 267
  Lucas critique, 274–6
  macroeconomic policy, 139
  model structures, 268–73
foreign exchange, 215–22
  balance of payments, 223–31
  covered interest arbitrage, 221–2
  market structure, 215–17
  monetary approach, 237–40
  see also exchange rate
forward discount, 221
forward market, 216, 245
forward premium, 221
free trade, exchange-rate theories,
    240
frictional unemployment, 132
Friedman, Milton, 5
  inflation explanation, 113, 120
  LM curve debate, 74
full employment, *see* employment

Gapinski, J. H., 75
GATT, *see* General Agreement on
    Tariffs and Trade
GDP, *see* Gross Domestic Product
General Agreement on Tariffs and Trade,
    156
GNP, *see* Gross National Product
gold flows, 223
goods market, exchange-rate theories,
    232–7

goods and services
    balance of payments, 223–4, 226
    exchange rates, 245
    foreign exchange, 215–16
    government spending, 159–61
    stabilisers, 164–6
    tax structures, 165–6
Gordon, R. J., 34, 99, 206
government
    budget constraint, 172–3
    counter-inflation policies, 125–7, 130
    disintermediation, 205–6
    exchange rates, 240, 242
    expenditure measurement, 17, 19–20
    fiscal policy, 158–83
    foreign exchange, 217
    inflation control, 123–4
    macroeconomic role, 6–7, 139–57
    monetary policy, 193–203
    money supply, 66, 190–1
    national debt, 172–7
    policy limitations, 207–12
    policy objectives, 140–4
government spending
    budget balances, 167–71
    crowding out, 162–3, 178–83
    expansionary effect, 160–1
    fiscal policy, 158–61
    forecasting, 270–2
    full-employment equilibrium, 58
    IS line effect, 71
    Keynesian model, 44–5
    'printing money', practice of, 201–2
Gowland, D. H., 183
Great Depression (1930s), 143
Greenaway, D., 156, 206
Greenhalgh, C. A., 136
Gross Domestic Product
    definition, 15
    per capita measure, 21–2
Gross National Product, 13–15
    counter-inflation policies, 126
    definition, 13
    economic growth, 22, 33–4
    formulae, 23–4
    inflation, impact of, 130
    quality of life measurement, 21–3

Hallwood, P., 248
high-cost industries, 228
Hillier, R., 183
Hoover, K. D., 7

hot money, 226
housing expenditure stabilisers, 164

idle money balances
    crowding out, 162–3, 180–2
    exchange-rate theories, 238
    monetary policy role, 185–6
IMF, *see* International Monetary Fund
imports
    counter-inflation policies, 125
    exchange rates, 233–7, 247–8
    inflation impact, 118, 127
income
    aggregate demand, 76–8
    aggregate supply, 79–80, 90
    counter-inflation policies, 126–7
    demand elasticity, 166
    demand sensitivity, 185–90
    expenditure relationship, 17–18
    flow diagram, 15–16
    GNP distribution, 22–3
    government objectives, 140–1, 145
    interest rate changes, 61–3, 68
    IS-LM model, 69–75
    money market, 65–6
    money supply, 67–8
    multiplier process, 49–55
    national, 47–9
    spending interdependence, 37–8
    taxation stabilisers, 165
    withdrawals and injections, 16–17
    see also income-expenditure model
income-expenditure model, 37–60
    complete model, 61–75
    IS-LM model, 69–75
indexation, inflation impact, 130
indicators, 149–51
    see also cyclical indicators
indices
    capacity utilisation, 28
    cyclical indicators, 255, 259–60
    employment ratio, 29
    prices, 24–6
individuals, financial net worth of, 11–12
inflation, 111–31
    adaptive expectations, 95
    alternative theories, 115–18
    business cycle phase, 105
    consumption effect, 42–3
    cost-push, 118
    cyclical indicators, 251, 253, 255

definition, 111
demand-pull, 118
disequilibrium effect, 38
economic growth, 130–1
government objectives, 141–4, 147–8
impact, 127–30
import prices, 247
measurement, 112
monetarist explanation, 113–15
national debt, 176–7
rate of, 111, 127
unemployment link, 118–25
information
effect on expectations, 103
job vacancies, 135
New Classical theory, 92–4, 96–7
injections
flow-of-income, 46
GNP component, 16–17
IS line function, 63
inside lags, 151–5
fiscal policy, 164, 170
interest rates
aggregate demand, 76–8
aggregate supply, 83
business cycles, 105
changes, effects of, 62–3
consumption effect, 43
counter-inflation policies, 125–6
covered interest arbitrage, 221
crowding out, 162
cyclical indicators, 251–3, 262
Dornbusch model, 243
exchange-rate theories, 232–40
full-employment equilibrium, 58
government policy, 146, 147–8
income-expenditure model, 61–5
investment, 44
IS-LM model, 69–75
monetary control, 194–6, 202–5
monetary policy, 185–90
money market, 65–6
money supply effects, 66–8
national debt, 175–6
portfolio balance effect, 181
supply-side identity, 203
intermediate policy targets, 149
International Monetary Fund, 156, 184, 265
inventories
economy indicators, 260–1, 262
equilibrium, 56–7

inventory investment, 18, 19
investment, 17, 39
business cycles, 105, 107–9
capital consumption, 20
categories, 18–19, 20
covered interest arbitrage, 221
counter-inflation policies, 125–6
crowding out, 179–80
cyclical indicators, 252
economic growth, 130
employment, 85
exchange-rate theories, 233
fiscal policy, 159
interest rates, 61
interest sensitivity, 186, 187–8
IS line, 63, 71
Keynesian model, 43–4
monetary control, 205
multiplier process, 51
spending components, 20
IS line
aggregate demand, 76–8
autonomous spending change, 64
meaning, 63
see also IS-LM model
IS-LM model, 69–75
aggregate supply, 76–8
business cycles, 105–7
economic stability, 69–70
employment, 70–1
exchange-rate determination, 232–7
fiscal policy, 159–63
forecasting, 268–72
monetary policy, 185–90
multiplier effect, 73–5
national debt, 176
price levels, 71–2

J-curve effect, 230–1
Johnson, C., 264

Kane, D. R., 231
Keating, G., 276
Keynes, J. M., 4–5, 38–9
Keynesian theory
accelerator-multiplier interaction, 107–10
aggregate demand, 45–6
aggregate supply, 83–92
consumption function, 41–3
crowding out, 181–2
demand management, 208–10

demand for money, 204
equilibrium, 38–9, 46
exchange-rate determination, 232–7
forecasting model, 267–8
government spending, 44–5
investment, 43–4
LM curve debate, 74
model assumptions, 39–41
monetary policy, 188–90
perspective of, 4–5
unemployment, 88–9, 133–5
Krugman, P. R., 231

labour
aggregate supply, 79–80, 82
classical theory, 81–2
Keynesian theory, 84–90
New Classical theory, 92–4
counter-inflation policies, 126
fixed nominal contracts, 127
geographical mobility, 135
price-fixing, 117
utilisation measurement, 28–31
wage rates, 123–4
see also employment; unemployment
lagging indicators, 255, 256–7
lags
automatic stabilisers, 164
balance of trade, 230
cyclical indicators, 262
exchange-rate theories, 237
inside, 151–4
outside, 147–8
Laidler, D. E. W., 131
Laspeyres indices, 26
Layard, P. R. G., 136
leading indicators, 255, 256–7, 260–1
leisure time, aggregate supply, 80
lending rate, banks, 195
Levacic, R., 7, 75, 110, 157
liabilities, flow-of-funds accounts, 11–12
Liverpool University, forecasting model,
265–6
Llewellyn, D. T., 248
LM line
aggregate demand, 76–8
meaning, 67–8
see also IS-*LM* model
loans
disintermediation, 205–6
interest-rate control, 194–6
monetary policy, 198–9

Lomas, E., 264
London Business School, forecasting
model, 265–6
long-run aggregate supply curve, 80,
93–4, 96–7
inflation, 113
LRAS, see long-run aggregate supply
Lucas, Robert E., 274–6
lump-sum taxation model, 45

MacDonald, R. (Hallwood), 248
McKenna, C. J., 136
macroeconomic policy, *see* policy
Maddock, R. (Carter), 212
Madura, J., 231
management, 28
marginal propensity to consume, 41–2
marginal propensity to import, 227
markets
aggregate supply
classical theory, 80–2
Keynesian theory, 90–1
New Classical theory, 96–7
foreign exchange, 215–17, 232–48
oligopolistic, 91
Marshall-Lerner condition, 229
Matthews, R. C. O., 110
MCD, *see* months for cyclical dominance
measurement
criteria, 8–9
economic growth, 31–4
fiscal policy, 167–71
flow-of-funds accounts, 10–13
GNP, 13–15, 23–5
inflation, 112
labour utilisation, 28–31
national income accounting, 13–20
output, 27–8
per capita GNP, 21–3
potential output, 31–4
price indices, 24–6
Miller, R. L., 206
minerals, exchange rates, 245–6
Minford, A. P. L., 136
models
AD and *AS*, 76–99
commercial bank, 192
complete income-expenditure, 61–75
fix-price, 116
Fleming-Mundell, 232
flex-price, 82, 83, 97, 116

forecasting, 265–72
income-expenditure, 37–59
inflation, 114
information availability, 92–4
IS-LM, 69–75
  aggregate supply, 76–8
  business cycles, 105–7
  exchange-rate determination, 232–7
  fiscal policy, 159–63
  monetary policy, 185–90
  Keynesian, 39–46
  multiple regression analysis, 278–81
  Phillips Curve, 122–3, 124–5
Modigliani, F. (Ando), 59
monetarism
  cost-of-capital channel, 204
  forecasting model, 267–8
  government policy, 148–9
  inflation explanation, 113–15
  LM curve debate, 74
  monetary policy, 184, 188, 210
  perspective of, 5
monetary policy, 146–7, 184–206
  basic principles, 193–6
  control, 193–203
  exchange-rate determination, 237–40
  IS-LM model, 185–90
  Keynesian view, 188–90
  monetary control, 199–202
  money supply process, 190–3
  problems, 204–6
money markets, 65–8
  LM line, 71
  money supply, 66–8, 113–15, 125–6
money supply, indicators, 260, 262
monopolies, markets structure, 90–1
months for cyclical dominance (MCD), 257, 259
MPM, *see* marginal propensity to import
multi-bank commercial system, 196–203
multiple regression analysis, 278–81
multiplier, 49–55
  autonomous spending change, 64
  balanced budget use, 160–3
  crowding out, 162, 178
  definition, 49–51
  IS-LM model, 73–5
  monetary control, 193–4
multiplier-accelerator
  cyclical indicators, 254
  interaction, 107–10

NAIRU, *see* non-accelerating rate of unemployment
National Bureau for Economic Research, 257, 259
national income
  business cycles, 108–10
  debt, fiscal policy, 172–7
  definition, 15
  determination, 47–9
  exchange-rate theories, 238
  flow-of-income diagram, 15–16
  measurement, 17
  money analysis, 67
national income accounting, 13–20
  GNP, 13–14
  government expenditure, 19–20
  income and expenditure, 17–19
  summary, 20
  withdrawals and injections, 16–17
National Institute of Economic and Social Research, 266
'natural' output equilibrium, 83
NBER, *see* National Bureau for Economic Research
net current account balance, 224
Net National Product, 20
  definition, 15
New Classical theory
  aggregate supply, 92–8
  inflation, 113–15
  Lucas critique, 274–6
  perspective of, 6
  stabilisation policy, 210–11
  unemployment, 133–5
  see also classical theory
Nickell, S. J., 60
NIESR, *see* National Institute of Economic and Social Research
NNP, *see* Net National Product
nominal GNP, real GNP relationship, 23–4
non-accelerating rate of unemployment, 134–5
  inflation, 119
non-residential investment, 18

Obstfeld, M. (Krugfeld), 231
official reserves transaction balance (ORTB), 224–5
oligopolies, markets structure, 90–1
open-market operations, banks, 197, 198

ORTB, *see* official reserves transaction
balance
output
    AD and *AS* model, 76–80
    aggregate supply, 55
    business cycles, 104–5
    cyclical indicators, 251
    economic growth measurement, 31–4
    full-employment level, 83
    measurement, 27–8
    money supply equation, 114
    outside lags, 147–8
    fiscal policy, 166
overshooting, exchange-rate model,
    243–4

Paasche indices, 26
Parkin, J. M., 131
Parkin, M., 131
pass-through effect, 247–8
personal disposable income, 20
personal savings, 20
Phillips Curve, 119–23
policies
    balance of payments, 227–31
    fiscal, 158–83
    macroeconomic, 139–57
        constraints, 155–6
        forecasting, 154–5
        formulating, 147
        instruments, 144–7, 149–51
        lag effects/indicators, 147–54
        limitations, 207–12
        objectives, 140–4
    monetary, 184–206
    prices and incomes, 126–7
portfolio balance, 181
    exchange-rate approach, 241
post-Keynesian exchange-rate theory,
    232–7
potential output
    aggregate supply, 79, 83
    business cycles, 104–5
    measurement, 31–4
PPP, *see* purchasing power parity
price deflator, calculation, 24–5
price indices, 24–6
price levels
    aggregate supply
        classical theory, 80–3, 91–2
        Keynesian theory, 83–92
        New Classical theory, 92–4

aggregate demand, 76–8
    counter-inflationary policies, 126–7
    economy indicators, 260
    exchange rates, significance of, 245,
        247–8
    fixing, 116–18
    flexibility, 91
    government objective, 141
    inflation, 111–31
    IS-LM model, 71–2
    Keynesian view, 39
    unemployment, 134
price-switching mechanism, 228–30
prices and incomes policies, 126–7
printing money, 201–2
private consumption, 17, 18
private investment, 18
production, and aggregate supply, 82–3,
    89, 92, 93
profits
    business cycles, 105
    economy indicators, 262
    investment source, 44
    market structures, 90–1
    price-fixing, 116
    unemployment theories, 133
public debt, 173
Pulsinelli, R. (Miller), 206
purchasing power parity, 238–9

quality of life, per capita comparison,
    21–2
quantitative controls, 199

rational expectations, 95–7
rational expectations, exchange-rate
    hypothesis, 241–3
rationing variable, 146
real budget deficit, 177
real GNP, 23–4, 25
real indicators, 260
real interest rates, 175–6
real money, 76, 185–90
real wages, *AS*, 79–80, 82
Rebmann, A. (Levacic), 7, 75, 110
recession
    business cycles, 105
    expenditure stabilisers, 164
    interdependence, 37–8
    Keynesian view, 38–9
    luxury goods, 166
    taxation stabilisers, 165

recognition lags, 152
reference cycle, identification, 258
replacement ratio, automatic stabilisers, 171
reserve balance, *see* official reserves transaction balance
reserve ratio, money supply process, 191–3
reserves
  bank, 196–7
  exchange-rate systems, 234–5
  monetary policy, 196–9
residential investment, 18
restrictive demand policies, 130
retail price index, 112
Ricardian equivalence theorem, 180
Ricardo, David, 3
Rowan, D. C., 110

sales, investment influence, 44
Samuelson, Paul, 107, 110
SAS line, *see* short-run aggregate supply curve
savings
  consumption, 41–3
  economy indicators, 251–3
  fiscal policy, 159
  IS line, 63, 71
search unemployment, 132, 135
seasonal unemployment, 132
securities
  crowding out, 162
  idle balances, 181–2
  monetary policy, 188–9, 200–1
  national debt, 172–3
seignorage, 200
Shaw, G. K., 156, 206, 212
Shone, R., 182
short-run aggregate supply curve, 80, 93–4, 97–8
  inflation, 113–14
  monetary policy, 208–11
slump, business cycles, 104–5
Smith, Adam, 3
Smith, G. (Backus), 34
spending
  autonomous changes, 64
  consumer, 41
  government, 44–5
  income, 37–8
  interest rates, 61
  multiplier process, 49–55

planned, 57–8
spot market, 216–17
spot rates, 238–9, 242
stabilisation policy, 146
  limitations, 208–11
stabilisers, automatic, 164–6, 170–1
stagflation, 5, 127, 130
statistics, limitations, 208
sticky prices, 96–7
stock market indices, 260, 261
stocks, 12–13
  definition, 12
  equilibrium, 56–7
  exchange-rate theories, 237, 239
  investment, 19
  policy indicators, 151
  price levels, 111
  unemployment category, 30
structural deficit, 168
structural unemployment, 132
subsidies, fiscal policy, 158
supply, *see* aggregate demand and supply
supply-side
  identity, 203
  policies, 135
surprise supply function, 210–11

tariffs
  balance of payments adjustment, 227–8
  exchange rates, 244
taxation
  budgets, 167–71
  counter-inflation policies, 125–7
  crowding out, 178–80
  cyclical indicators, 262
  fiscal policy, 158–63
  full-employment equilibrium, 58
  government policy options, 144–6, 155–6
  government spending, 45
  indirect, 166
  IS line, effect on, 71
  Lucas critique, 275–6
  monetary control process, 200–1
  national debt, 172–7
  real yields, 129–30
  stabilisers, 165–6
technology, effect on aggregate supply, 79
Thirlwall, A. P., 231
Thompson, J. L. (Vane), 157

Timbrell, M., 277
time-lags
  cyclical indicators, 252
  stabilisers, 166
  variables, 147–54
Tobin, J., 7, 34
trade cycles, *see* business cycles
trade unions, inflation, 124
training programmes, 135
transfer payments, 219
  fiscal policy, 158–9
  taxation stabilisers, 165
transmission mechanisms, *IS-LM*
    model, 185–90
Treasury (UK), 265–6
turning points, 257, 258

unanticipated changes, aggregate
    demand, 97–9
under-employment equilibrium, 57
unemployment, 132–6
  adaptive expectations, 95
  business cycles, 104–5
  costs, 135–6
  cyclical indicators, 251, 253
  expenditure stabilisers, 164
  government objectives, 141–4
  inflation effects, 118–25
  involuntary, 135–6
  Keynesian theory, 39, 83–4, 88–9
  measurement, 28–31
  natural rate, 142

theoretical perspectives, 133–5
  types, 132
  voluntary, 135–6
  see also employment; labour
unilateral transfers, 224

values
  GNP data, 13–15
  inventories data, 19
Vane, H. R., 157
variables, cyclical indicators, 253, 260
velocity of circulation, 113–14, 115

wages
  aggregate supply, 80
    classical theory, 82
    Keynesian theory, 89–90
    New Classical theory, 83–9
  counter-inflationary policies, 126–7
  inflexibility, 89–90
  money versus real, 122
  price-fixing element, 117–18
  unemployment, 133–5
Walras, Leon, 4
wealth
  consumption, 42–3
  Keynesian view, 39
withdrawals
  flow of income, from, 46
  GNP component, 16–17
  IS line, effect on, 63
World Bank, 156